E 745 . M3 G8

THE RIDDLE OF MACARTHUR

Books by John Gunther

THE RIDDLE

OF

MACARTHUR

Japan, Korea and the Far East

by JOHN GUNTHER

HARPER & ROW, PUBLISHERS

New York and Evanston

TO CASS CANFIELD

In Old Friendship, and for Services Rendered
of Heroic Form

CONTENTS

NOTE

THE AUTHOR wishes to express his deep indebtedness to Gardner Cowles, editor and publisher of *Look*. Mr. Cowles generously sent us to Japan and we proceeded along the rim of crackling Asia until we completed an arduous trip around the world. Also I want to thank Daniel D. Mich, who was executive editor of *Look* when we set out. Parts of the first three chapters and of Chapter Eleven appeared in *Look* in preliminary form.

We met hundreds of people en route who helped us in one way or other, of all camps and categories, from General MacArthur himself to Japanese communists fleeing his purge, from Prime Minister Nehru in New Delhi to G.I.'s polishing their bayonets in Okinawa, from expertly efficient and courteous men and women on the staff of Pan American World Airways to Chinese bankers in Hong Kong squinting at scenes of their former glories in Shanghai, from Japanese shopkeepers in Kyoto to British seafarers running Chiang Kai-shek's blockade, from Siamese princelings to Indo-Chinese refugees, from American diplomats working out a policy for Formosa to Indian villagers trying to work out a way to get enough to eat and clothe their miserable bones.

To one and all, let me say thanks.

Events are moving with extraordinary velocity these days, and the convulsion taking place in Asia makes it difficult, if not impossible, to keep this report up to date. Yet the essence of what I have written will, I hope, remain valid even if each new day brings fresh crises.

This, anyway, is the story as of the second week of December, 1950, as these pages go to press.

J. G.

FOREWORD

RECENT compelling events in Asia, the Korean war and Chinese intervention in the struggle not least among them, cast a spectacular new spotlight on MacArthur. Whatever may happen to the Supreme Commander in the future, he has set the pattern of much of American policy in the Far East. To tens of millions of Asiatics he is America, but most Americans do not understand him perfectly, nor does he altogether understand the contemporary United States. To weigh MacArthur against the background of his work in Japan, to say nothing of Korea, is not easy; his career demands the most careful scrutiny, from stem to stern, with all of the Far East taken into account.

The brutal incursion of North Koreans across the 38th parallel at dawn on June 25; the subsequent fighting with its sharp reverses, victories, and disappointments; behind this the extension of the cold war between Washington and Moscow; the startling entrance of communist China into the war and the military and political catastrophe that followed; the disruptive forces and counterforces at irrevocable play in Indochina, the Philippines, Malaya, Burma, Indonesia, Siam, and elsewhere; the position in these matters of the giant body of India under its high-minded and pacific leader, Mr. Nehru—all this is backdrop.

MacArthur, who is in his seventy-first year, must have been taken by surprise by the Korean outbreak. He had always kept somewhat aloof from Korean affairs, and he visited the country only once, staying only a single day, between 1945 and 1950.

Only a month before the war he told a correspondent of the New York *Times*, "I don't believe a [major] shooting war is imminent. . . . The Russian masses are probably just as opposed to a shooting war as the Anglo-Saxon masses. . . . The public realizes all too well in terms of the last war that there can be no real victor in a future war. . . . I think it is foolish to assume that the Russians wish to start an aggressive war now. The Russian is doing so well under the present no-shooting war that he would probably and logically wish to continue the existing successful system."

The Supreme Commander certainly did not want a war, and the Korean affair put his whole magnificent record in Japan in jeopardy. He announced on his birthday, January 26, 1950, "Modern war is so destructive that it must be outlawed completely. Civilization as we know it will be destroyed if world leaders fail in their responsibility to find a solution to the problems and permit a third world war."

But this book is not, except in passing, about China or Korea. It is about MacArthur's Japan. Additionally it contains material on the broad contours of American policy in Asia. Primarily, however, it must rest on what is happening in Japan. Of course, by reason of the events in Korea, China, and elsewhere, Japan has become much more important to the United States than it has ever been before. It is the indispensable pivot of our potential force in Asia. Overnight, from being the theater of an unprecedented peaceful evolution in social, political and economic reform, it has become the armed beachhead of American military strength in the Orient, as well as of political power. What will this mean to the future of Japan? What will it mean to us?

The MacArthur regime in Japan, no matter what eventual developments arise out of China or Korea, is worth sober study for its own sake. The United States never had the job of unilateral administration of a defeated world power before. But we have done a great deal more than a mere job of administration. The experiment is, in fact, unique not merely in our history, but in any history. What— to put it in the bare bones of a word or two—we have attempted to

xii

do in Japan is remake an entire nation, an entire civilization, in our own image. With no more than a handful of troops and civilian advisers, and without any use of force or threat of force whatsoever, MacArthur set out to create a new Japan.

The gist of the American experience in Japan is to prove to Asia that democracy is better than communism. Also it gives us a wonderfully useful store of information about the Oriental mind, as well as training in how to understand and deal with Orientals. Such knowledge is essential to American citizens if we are going to be able to meet the communist threat and solve intelligently the massive problems of the Far East pressing down on us. So a careful, unbiased description of the nature of the occupation and how it has worked out is of vital importance to us in broader spheres. Perhaps the United States is on the way to undertaking an altogether new responsibility in international affairs. If so, it is well to see how one of our early Caesars is performing.

MacArthur's own view, expressed in his familiar ornate prose, is that his five-year administration "is the greatest reformation of a people ever attempted." Japan, as he sees it, has become "a bastion to the democratic concept," and the experiment as a whole is "the greatest spiritual revolution the world has ever known." Let us explore these claims.

Many questions yearn for answer. What is the balance sheet of achievement? Has Japan really become democratized? What danger exists of a reversion to militarism or dictatorship? What do the Japanese think of their Emperor these days, and what do they think of us? Have we perhaps inadvertently opened the door to communism in the future by the very scope and vigor of our own reforms? Could the Japanese extreme right and extreme left ever combine? Was our dissolution of the great Japanese industrial combines (zaibatsu) genuine? What will happen if we are eventually forced to pull out? How many of the SCAP (Supreme Commander Allied Powers) reforms will stick? How much of the Japanese friendliness to the United States is falseface? Will the Japanese people be glad or sorry to see us go? What will be the results of the seeming debacle in Korea?

I arrived in Japan knowing very little about these matters; before I had been in Tokyo a week I became convinced that the MacArthur story is one of the worst-reported stories in history. By and large, the rank and file of Americans know extremely little about SCAP, its accomplishments and failures, its ambitions, objectives, and ideals. But before going into this we must come to grips with the person of Douglas MacArthur himself. A great deal of both truth and nonsense has been written about the Supreme Commander, and few people realize what an intricate character he is. I asked one illustrious Japanese what he thought of him. The answer was one of the few quick, sure answers I ever got from anybody in Japan. "Not a simple man!"

THE RIDDLE OF MACARTHUR

Chapter One

CAESAR OF THE PACIFIC

WHEN General MacArthur's plane first came into sight of Japan on August 30, 1945, the General was dozing quietly. The softly symmetrical white cone of Mt. Fujiyama became visible, and General Courtney Whitney, his chief political adviser, whispered to another general, "Wake the old man up." The other general was not rash enough to do so, and Whitney took the risk himself. He tapped MacArthur on the arm gently, then pointed to the sacred mountain outside the window. MacArthur woke up, murmured, "Well! Good old Fuji!" paid no more attention, and promptly fell asleep again.

The plane was the *Bataan*, the same private plane that took him to Korea five years later, and then—as now—it was unarmed. No other aircraft escorted it, and none of the passengers carried anything but side arms, even though few other Americans had arrived in Japan as yet, and nobody knew what they would find.

Nobody could guess what treachery there might or might not be. A fierce army of 2,500,000 Japanese, completely untouched by battle, still existed in the home islands. Fanatic militarists had just made a brief abortive revolt against the Emperor for surrendering. MacArthur's decision to accept the capitulation on the *Missouri* in Tokyo Bay before more than a handful of American air-borne troops arrived has been called the greatest gamble in modern history, in view of these and other circumstances.

Anybody who enjoys laughter at the discomfiture of experts has

1

only to glance back at some journalism of the period. Professors who studied Japan all their lives, military experts who knew every nook and cranny of the Japanese character, thought that MacArthur was taking a frightful risk. There were some—in those days—who in fact believed that the concept of any kind of occupation in Japan would turn out to be impossible. There would be guerrilla warfare for years within ten miles of Tokyo. No American administrator would be safe without permanent heavy guard. The Japanese would devote themselves to passive resistance mingled with the most savage type of organized brigandage. The country would blaze with a permanent flame of hatred for the conquering Americans. And so on.

The MacArthur party landed at a pockmarked airport called Atsugi, used by the Japanese as a Kamikaze strip until a few days before. The General put up for the night in the New Grand Hotel in Yokohama, the only one in operation. It was filthy, decrepit, and alive with small animal life. The Japanese staff, petrified at what was going on, managed to dig up a steak for dinner. General Whitney, sitting next to MacArthur, thought that the food might be poisoned; only by vigorously restraining himself did he resist the spontaneous impulse to snatch the meat away as MacArthur started to eat. MacArthur simply ate.

The Supreme Commander had ordered the Japanese to provide fifty motor cars for the trip into Tokyo the next day, to take care of other members of his staff who came in by air that night. It was a revelation to the Americans to discover that fifty automobiles that actually ran did not exist in the entire Tokyo-Yokohama area.

The party set out for the enemy capital, after signal and radio crews had gone ahead. MacArthur saw several of his officers carrying arms. "Put all guns away," he said.

A few weeks later the General returned to Atsugi to meet Mrs. MacArthur, who came with their son Arthur and his Chinese *amah* (nurse), Ah Chu. Mrs. MacArthur, who knows her husband well, was astonished to discover that there was no guard at all at the airport. The General, unarmed, with one aide, unarmed, constituted the entire reception committee. The group drove back to Tokyo through the broken streets, still packed with rubble, unlighted, and menacingly deserted. "Isn't it dangerous?" Mrs. MacArthur whispered. "Not at all," the General smiled.

These episodes, minor as they are, tell a good deal about MacArthur. They demonstrate his undoubted courage, his instinct for understanding Orientals, his simplicity in some respects, his fatalism, his fixed sense of objective, and something else that has led him into danger on occasion—a tendency to exaggerated optimism, based on his unalterable conviction that he is a man of destiny.

I heard someone who admires him greatly say, "In the abstract, would you say that it is wise to have a Supreme Commander who never had a single moment of pessimism in his entire life?" Of course great egoists are almost always optimists.

Cracking Down

Some people in Japan, even after the occupation had been going on for several months, did not fully realize that MacArthur was the boss; they thought that the American administration would, in time, go soft. MacArthur's gloves were so coated with kid that the Japanese were tempted to neglect what was underneath. On January 4, 1946, came the first "purge" order, and this was a stark awakening. Later we will treat of the celebrated purges in some detail; suffice it to say now that three or four members of the cabinet had to be dismissed, because they had been militarists, i.e., war criminals, before the war.

The prime minister at the time was the venerable Baron Kijuro Shidehara, a fine old liberal who had always stood out against the warmongers so far as any Japanese could dare to do. (Nowadays Baron Shidehara is plain "Mr." Shidehara, because titles have been abolished in Japan except for a few members of the royal family.) His foreign minister was Shigeru Yoshida, the prime minister today. Both, even though they had opposed the war, thought that MacArthur's purge went too far, and, full of Japanese pride and the in-

3

stinct to reach for every advantage, decided to risk a showdown with MacArthur and announce the resignation of the cabinet in protest.

In those days, before the new constitution was in force, a cabinet resigned in the conventional manner, by turning in its mandate to the Emperor. Shidehara, fearful of a personal encounter with Mac-Arthur, had a diplomatic "illness," and sent the wily Mr. Yoshida to represent him. The Supreme Commander received Yoshida at once, with General Whitney present. Yoshida thereupon proceeded to say that the cabinet would present its resignation to the Emperor the next day, and the Emperor would then presumably charge Baron Shidehara with forming a new government.

MacArthur, affixing Mr. Yoshida with his famous burning (but cold) stare, said the following: "Mr. Minister, I have the highest regard for Baron Shidehara, and I know of no one better qualified to carry out the terms of MY directive [about the purge], but if the Cabinet resigns en masse tomorrow it can only be interpreted by the Japanese people to mean that it is unable to implement my directives. Thereafter Baron Shidehara may be acceptable to the Emperor for reappointment as Prime Minister, but he will not be acceptable to ME." There followed, in the words of an official account, "a moment of profound silence." Mr. Yoshida said finally and falteringly that he would transmit this message to the Prime Minister; General Whitney accompanied him down the corridor to the elevator.

"You understand what the Supreme Commander said, did you not, Mr. Minister?" Whitney asked politely.

Yoshida replied, "Too well, too well!"

The cabinet did not resign. The purged ministers resigned, their places were taken by others acceptable to MacArthur, and the government continued to function without crisis or interruption, carrying out the Supreme Commander's further orders.

A somewhat subtle point arises here. It might be thought that the episode proves that as of that date the Japanese cabinet was totally subservient to MacArthur. Actually the General took the course he did partly because of his policy to let the Japanese themselves run

4

their own show and deal with their own problems in their own way so far as possible. MacArthur did not want to become subject to the charge that he had made the cabinet resign. He wanted it to continue in office, after it had purged itself.

But from that date to this, no Japanese prime minister or other high official has ever dared to take any major political step without carefully sounding out MacArthur's headquarters first.

Why Doesn't He Come Home?

MacArthur has not been in the continental United States since May, 1937, when he returned briefly to New York (in order to get married there) from the Philippines. Why has he never come back since? How shall one account for the fact that he has stayed out of his own country for almost fourteen years? How can one explain the fact that his son, now aged twelve, has never even seen the United States? Of course travel was difficult for MacArthur during the war; he was a busy theater commander, always short of men and supplies. But other American commanders returned to Washington, if only for consultation, during the war, and several returned a number of times. Since 1945 MacArthur can justly plead the fact that he has been too heavily submerged in duties in Japan, but even so his prolonged absence without even a brief holiday is remarkable.

I asked at least a dozen people in Tokyo and elsewhere, both friendly and unfriendly, how they explained this, and I got a wide variety of answers.

1. Duty. He has the feeling that there is a job to do in Tokyo, just as there was a job to be done in the Pacific during the war, and that it is not right for him to leave until it is completed.

2. His ego. He has an obsession that he is utterly indispensable and that the whole structure of SCAP might fall to pieces if he left even for a month or so. Contrariwise, he is afraid to go home, for fear that his absence might prove that he is *not* indispensable.

3. He identifies himself with the United States and fears that, if he should leave Japan, millions of Asiatics will interpret this as meaning that America is pulling out of Asia.

5

4. He waited too long. A triumphal return to the United States might be an anticlimax now.

5. Back in America (if he stayed) he would be no more than a retired general—and in Tokyo he is an emperor.

6. He takes the line that he has said everything he has to say in his public reports, and that for him to repeat these in person back home would be otiose.

7. He thinks that most efforts to get him back are politically flavored, and he doesn't want his name to be used for any partisan purposes.

MacArthur is said to be on record with the statement that he would go back if formally ordered to do so; on the other hand several high officials in Washington have tried to get him to return, totally without success. I asked one friend what would happen if Mr. Truman himself asked him to come home. Answer: "Probably he'd argue."

Some Tokyo observers believe that he has so convinced himself of his "divine" mission in Japan that he will stay there till he dies. (Even so, this would not seem to preclude a short vacation home some day.) Others believe that he wants to come home now and that it is an acute personal sacrifice for him to have to stay on in Tokyo, but that events in China and Korea make him remain. The General himself makes mild jokes about the issue on occasion. He hates to fly, and he once told an executive of Northwest Airlines that he would be delighted to go to Washington if someone would develop an airplane that would get him there in twelve hours.

If the General ever does leave Japan, those indisputably in a position to know say that he will do two things he has never done before: (a) address a joint session of the Diet; (b) call on the Emperor.

He Almost Never Leaves Tokyo

MacArthur practically never leaves Tokyo, which is another odd and suggestive point. Between September, 1945 and the outbreak of the Korean war in June, 1950, he left Tokyo or its environs exactly

6

twice. He went to Manila for the celebration of the Filipino Independence Day on July 4, 1946, and to Seoul for the proclamation of the Korean Republic in August, 1948. When he journeyed to Manila, he planned to proceed to Baguio and spend a lazy week there; but abruptly after the ceremonies he changed his mind and decided to fly back to Japan at once. Similarly on his first trips to Korea in 1950 he invariably contrived to return to Tokyo by nightfall of the day he left.

What is more, in Tokyo itself, he almost never varies from a fixed routine. Twice a day he drives the short distance from the American Embassy, where he lives, to the Dai-Ichi Building, where he works, and back. Occasionally of course there are visiting dignitaries to meet or see off at Haneda Airport, military functions to attend, and the like. But by and large the mile and a quarter between the Embassy and the Dai-Ichi constitutes the entire physical experience of his life in Tokyo. This—and only this—is the sum total of his arc.

Something even more extraordinary is that he meets very few Japanese. He never, under any circumstances, sees *any* Japanese socially, and his professional acquaintance is limited to a handful. He will receive the Emperor, the prime minister, the foreign minister, the heads of both houses of parliament, and the chief justice of the supreme court, on official business. *No*body else. Thus, astonishing as the fact may seem, MacArthur in his five years in Tokyo has never talked at length to more than, let us say, a dozen or so Japanese officials. He carries this policy of exclusion to the most extreme lengths. For instance, Mrs. MacArthur has never met either Emperor or Empress, and he himself has never met the Empress.

For that matter he sees comparatively few Americans. In the early days of the Korean fighting his trips to the front did a great deal to lift up morale, if only because so few G.I.'s had ever seen him before. He seldom reviewed troops in Tokyo; he almost never paid visits of inspection to military posts. One of the chief show places of contemporary Japan is the naval base at Yokosuka, where Admiral Benton W. Decker did magnificent work for several years; it is only

7

thirty-eight miles from Tokyo, but never once did MacArthur visit it.

Why does the Supreme Commander keep himself so rigidly aloof? One reason is that, over seventy, he wants to conserve his energy; he hopes to live a long, long time, and sets his pace accordingly. Another, more important, is that he feels he understands Oriental "psychology," and that the Japanese will respect him more if he is seldom seen. MacArthur has almost become a Japanese himself, particularly in the matter of self-discipline. By being unapproachable, almost invisible, he elevates his own prestige. And, of course, his ego plays a role. God does not choose often to expose himself.

MacArthur's habits of seclusion put, it goes without saying, an onerous burden on his subordinates, since he is dependent on them for the quality of the information he receives. Seeing little himself, he has to rely on the eyes (and ears) of others. Are they good enough? This is a hotly disputed topic in Tokyo.

If only in the realms of pleasure and the delights of the picturesque the General pays a considerable price for his austerity. He has not had much fun in Japan, a country in which a great deal of fun is available. MacArthur has never (during this tour of duty at least) squatted on a *tatami* mat to have a ceremonial Japanese dinner. He has never seen at first hand the way the Japanese make stairs steep in order to save space, the exquisiteness of Japanese gardens where perspectives of the broadest scope are imprisoned in a tiny area, or the way a Japanese servant cooks water for a bath. He has never met Mr. Yamashita, the bearded dignitary who superintends the bizarre spectacle of cormorant fishing at Gifu, or seen the tissue-paper messages tied to the trees outside the Kiyumizo Temple in Kyoto. He has never bought a ten-cent fountain pen on the Ginza, or gazed at the autumnal landscape through the bland windows of mountain villas near Nikko. He has never listened to a geisha play the samisen, walked through the dark aisles of the cryptomerias in the deer park at Nara, or eaten raw fish with chopsticks.

But do not think that MacArthur does not know a great deal about the Japanese. He does. Many Americans in Japan, as we shall

8

see, are lamentably, almost grotesquely, deficient in knowledge and understanding of the people they rule; some of his chief subordinates have scarcely ever met any Japanese at all. But there is little lacking in the Supreme Commander's own basic grasp and intuition.

The fact that MacArthur keeps himself so glassily isolated gives rise to one of the more elementary paradoxes of contemporary Japan. It is that he imposes democracy—like a dictator.

MacArthur and Roosevelt

The General's antipathy to the New Deal is well known, and it is generally assumed that he heartily disliked Mr. Roosevelt. In actual fact this was not the case. He disapproved of much that FDR did, and, during the war, like most theater commanders, he felt that he was being starved while other fronts were favored; also MacArthur would probably have adopted a different strategy for the war as a whole. But his personal regard for Roosevelt was always high, and the two men were good friends for many years.

MacArthur, though this is not well known, owes a great deal of his career to Roosevelt:

1. When he became President in 1933 FDR kept him on as Chief of Staff, though it was unprecedented for a Chief of Staff to serve an extra year.

2. Roosevelt encouraged MacArthur to accept the offer from the Philippine government whereby he was enabled to go to Manila in 1936.

3. Above all, well before Pearl Harbor (on July 26, 1941, to be precise), FDR drew MacArthur back into active service, and appointed him Commanding General, United States Army Forces in the Far East.

4. It was FDR who ordered MacArthur out of Bataan in 1942, and so, indirectly at least, made possible the long march back.

5. Roosevelt took MacArthur's side in the Honolulu conference held in the summer of 1944, when it was decided (over spirited Navy

9

objections) to push for reconquest of the Philippines rather than attempt to land on the coast of China and elsewhere.

To hear MacArthur reminisce about Roosevelt is a fascinating experience, as I am lucky enough to know. The Hawaii conference just mentioned has been neglected in Roosevelt literature and I asked MacArthur if he could throw some light on it. He talked for forty minutes without a stop. As he describes the occasion a great array of admirals—Leahy, King, Nimitz, Halsey—were on one side: he himself was alone on the other. Roosevelt listened to the Navy, and appeared to be committed to its point of view. Then MacArthur put forward his case, and did so with such pertinacity and fervor that FDR began to swing over. Before a final decision was made Admiral King returned to Washington, thinking that *his* policy had been accepted. Roosevelt then called MacArthur in, and told him that he, MacArthur, was the winner after all, and that the Philippines would be the next great target. MacArthur, as he relates this anecdote, does so with the most vivid relish, suggesting rather than overtly stating the weight of forces set against him, and how subtly he managed to overcome them. Roosevelt's last words were, "Well, Douglas, you win! But I am going to have a hell of a time over this with that old bear, Ernie King!"

MacArthur had planned to leave Honolulu the next day, because he had a new amphibious operation to superintend thousands of miles away. FDR turned to him, "Douglas, would you mind staying with me one more day?" Of course MacArthur consented, and the two men spent most of the next twenty-four hours together. Most of FDR's talk was about the past, and his mood was poignant. They took a drive out of the city and saw hundreds of tanks ready for dispatch to the Pacific front; Roosevelt asked MacArthur if he remembered the day in 1933 when they had asked Congress for just twenty tanks for the defense of Hawaii, and Congress had refused. And here were tanks massed wheel to wheel as far as the eye could reach!

MacArthur asked Roosevelt only one political question. This was shortly before the 1944 election (in which MacArthur himself had been spoken of as a potential candidate) and the General inquired politely, "Mr. President, do you think you are going to have a hard time against Dewey in November?" Roosevelt grinned and replied, "I'll beat that son of a blank in Albany if it's the last thing I ever do!"

MacArthur was convinced during this meeting that FDR was dying. Only his spirit, his inner fire, his reservoir of soul, kept him alive even then, the General thinks. When he returned to his headquarters in Australia he told his wife, "Jean, the President will be dead within six months." He was only two months wrong.

Roosevelt and MacArthur met for the first time in World War I, when FDR was assistant secretary of the Navy and MacArthur was a major on the general staff. They were on first-name terms, and FDR had high regard for him as a soldier. They kept in touch intermittently in the ensuing years, but because MacArthur was away in the Philippines most of the time they did not meet between 1936 and 1944.

A good many analogies exist between FDR and MacArthur. Roosevelt was wellborn, devoted to the American tradition, and a gentleman to his finger tips; so is MacArthur. Both were, in a sense, mama's boys; the mother of each lived to a great age, doting on her son. Roosevelt's character was full of dash—even bravado—and he loved to talk; ditto MacArthur. FDR was more of a "fixer" perhaps; MacArthur has a simpler force. Roosevelt was a more subtle person, with far deeper sensitiveness to the major pressures of his time, and a much more profound sympathy for the underpossessed; MacArthur is a stronger personality in some ways, more forthright and histrionic, more apocalyptic, and also a good deal fancier and showier. Politically FDR was of course much further to the left than MacArthur. He was a broader person, with more social vision. Yet it would be unwise to think of MacArthur as a reactionary, and—strange as it may seem—there are strong traces of the New Deal in SCAP.

A Word in Estimate

MacArthur has several times been compared to Caesar, and there are several analogies worth making, even if they are a bit farfetched —prolonged absences from his native country; subordinates not in his own class; strong will, imperiousness, narcissism; an acute interest in history; great military skill and valor; patriotism complicated by merciless ambition; the ability to make use of conquered peoples; administrative capacity; desire to leave behind him a structure of law; and a taste for benevolent autocracy.

Several other proconsuls whom MacArthur calls to mind, if the necessary allowances are made, may be mentioned. One is Marshal Lyautey, the great French soldier-administrator who created modern Morocco. Lyautey, before his prodigious accomplishments in North Africa (where he is still regarded as a demigod), also had much to do with the development of Indochina and Madagascar. He was both a pacifier and a colonizer. Like MacArthur he ruled in part by making full use of the native populations; like MacArthur, too, he was used as a catspaw by reactionaries at home.

Another is, of all men, Don Juan of Austria, the illegitimate son of Charles V of Spain and half brother of Philip II. Philip, to get rid of Don Juan at home, and after he had destroyed the Turks at the brilliant battle of Lepanto, sent him to the Netherlands. Here Don Juan, largely ignoring instructions from Madrid, set out to make his own policy, which was to push the war against the heretic British to the ultimate degree. Philip thought that Don Juan was intemperate; Don Juan thought that he, Don Juan, was inspired. He refused to subordinate his own policy to that of the home government, and simply could not understand that Philip should have contrary views. Exposed in his outpost, he behaved as if he were an archangel; he thought that the people at home were pussyfooters. Philip in Madrid looked at his wars globally; Don Juan simply looked across the channel. History is full of proconsuls who—perhaps because they are away from home too long—turn sour.

MacArthur, even though he may be as vain as the Earl of Essex (another proconsul—in Ireland), has great virtues. Mainly they are virtues of a somewhat antique type, more notable in classic ages than our own—strict honorableness, belief in the right, moral courage, and dedication to an ideal. But he has plenty of defects, and is fiercely hated as well as loved. Nobody in American public life is so controversial. One reason is, I think, something that MacArthur cannot help—that he comes of a military family. This may be a strange thing to say, and certainly there have been plenty of military heroes in American history; yet we do not have many generals who seem, both in background and career, to personify so rigidly, so flamboyantly, the ideas of military caste. This is still a civilian country. Another reason is MacArthur's theatricality: what can only be called his hamminess. If you pin down people who dislike him, it is this theatricality that they dislike most.

Still another, since the disaster implicit in Chinese intervention in Korea, is that MacArthur is too "dangerous." Many Americans felt in the grim days of early December, 1950, that his strutting and bombast, his imperiousness and dislike of adjusting himself to external advice—together with shockingly gross blunders by his subordinates in the realm of information—might get us deeper into war. This is largely unfair. MacArthur's patriotism is indisputable, and his military acumen rich; above all he did *not* want to get us embroiled in a full-scale China war. And he was in an extraordinarily difficult position, since he could not bomb the enemy above the Manchurian frontier. Even so, the way he was caught by surprise and the consequent retreat of his stupefied armies can hardly be excused.

What does MacArthur believe in most? The defense of the United States. Is he a truly great man? At least he performed the extraordinary feat of conquering an enemy, occupying its territory, and making its people *like* it.

Once he told an American interviewer, "Only God or the Government of the United States can keep me from the fulfillment of my mission." So we must investigate carefully what he thinks his mission is.

Chapter Two

WHAT MACARTHUR IS, AND HOW HE GOT THERE

FIRST let us put straight certain technical and terminological matters. General MacArthur wears, as the saying goes, several hats. He is:

1. Supreme Commander for (not "of") the Allied Powers, or SCAP. In this role he has become curiously depersonalized, since he is an institution as well as a man. In Tokyo you hear the word SCAP forty or fifty times a day, and occasionally somebody will say "the Scap," meaning MacArthur himself, but generally the term has come to mean headquarters. People, referring to a SCAP program or directive, say that "it" did something, not "he."

2. Commander in Chief, Far East (CINCFE). As such MacArthur is commander of all United States Army, Navy and Air forces in the area of the Far East Command. His authority in this capacity goes far beyond Japan itself; even before the Korean war it embraced Okinawa and the Ryukyu Islands, the Philippines, the Marianas, and other island groups including Guam.

3. Commanding General, United States Army, Far East. This is overlapped by the above, and MacArthur does not maintain a separate headquarters as army commander. As SCAP and CINCFE, however, though there is considerable merging in actual operation, he is two completely distinct and separate entities.

To whom is MacArthur responsible in his United States Army

14

function? It is often assumed that he has no boss at all, but this is not correct. Like any American general in the field he has at least four superiors: General Collins (Chief of Staff), General Bradley (Joint Chiefs), Mr. Marshall (Secretary of Defense), and Mr. Truman, the President of the United States. A five-star general can, of course, pretty well make his own rules, and nobody has ever excelled MacArthur in his capacity to tear the guts out of a directive, but by and large he is scrupulously careful to maintain the military proprieties. There may be occasions when he communicates secretly with the President, over anybody's head; nobody would know except a few signal officers and technicians. Mostly, however, he proceeds "by the book." After all, as I heard it said, "He himself helped write the book."

One striking—indeed unprecedented—point is that MacArthur has no deputy either as SCAP or CINCFE. His chain of command includes, of course, a chief of staff, and the Eighth Army, his chief unit, has a splendid commanding officer—General Walton Walker. But neither is *his* deputy. There is no second man in the MacArthur organization, and never has been.

4. Since July 8, 1950, MacArthur has been United Nations commander in the Korean fighting, under the blue and white United Nations flag.

5. MacArthur is not head of state (the Emperor is) but he assumes several of the functions of a head of state. The government of Japan has, for instance, no relations whatsoever with the outside world except through SCAP. A foreign diplomat assigned to Tokyo is accredited, not to the Emperor, but to SCAP, and it is MacArthur, not the Emperor, who receives ambassadors, heads of missions, and the like. He is a kind of baby sitter for the entire nation.

In blunt fact MacArthur's authority is so great and his powers so sweeping that he is the actual *ruler* of Japan. The manner of rule is often indirect, and a semitransparent façade is carefully maintained behind which Japanese authority is exerted in many fields, but MacArthur is in fact the allpowerful boss of 83,000,000 Japanese,

15

and will remain so until a peace treaty is signed. Occasionally he has been overruled by Washington, but not often. Ex-Secretary of War Kenneth Royall, by appealing to Mr. Truman, twice at least compelled MacArthur to withdraw or modify a directive. And we know that Mr. Truman not only overruled but rebuked him about Formosa. But in relation to Japan itself MacArthur is seldom touched. The language of the document appointing him Supreme Commander leaves no doubt as to his powers; he is the *sole* executive authority for the allies concerned. "You will exercise your authority as you deem proper to carry out your mission," he was informed on September 6, 1945. "Our relations with Japan do not rest on a contractual basis, but on an unconditional surrender. Since your authority is *supreme*, you will not entertain any question on the part of the Japanese as to its scope."

Operating through the channels of the Japanese government itself, MacArthur by a single word can outlaw from public life any Japanese; he can disband any Japanese political party, order new elections, dissolve parliament, set aside the government, and rule by direct military order if necessary. Constitutional authorities differ on the question whether or not he could actually fire the Emperor.

Powers of this formidable nature are unique in American history, and it is a tribute to MacArthur that he has used them with such moderation. The British have been accustomed to producing viceroys for generations, and men like Clive, Curzon, Warren Hastings, and Cecil Rhodes are known to every schoolboy, but no American has ever held quite the job MacArthur holds. Not the least amazing fact is that he reached this unprecedented power through a series of circumstances partly haphazard and fortuitous.

*

The occupation of Japan has always differed radically from those of the allies elsewhere (Germany, Austria, Korea) for several reasons. These played greatly to MacArthur's advantage. First, Japan was not invaded and hence—though the Japanese suffered immense

and acute punishment from aerial bombardment—the country had not been crippled by military operations on the ground. Second, the Japanese government never ceased to exist. There has always been a prime minister, a cabinet, and a continuous process of government. Third and most important, the country was never divided into sectors or zones, like Germany and Austria, and the Russians never had troops in Japan. In consequence MacArthur had a freer hand than his colleagues elsewhere, and something reasonably intact to build on. One result is that SCAP has never had to impose *direct* military government.

As SCAP, MacArthur is an international official; the occupation is an allied occupation. In theory at least he is responsible (in his SCAP capacity) to thirteen different nations, including Russia. But the United States is the only substantial occupying *force*. It is quite true that the British Commonwealth had for a time a strong contingent of troops, and some Australians are still present, but there have never been any Russian, Chinese, French, or other *armies* in Japan. If any such had arrived in the early days they would have been under MacArthur's orders as Supreme Commander, and rather than accept this the Russians (and the Chinese also) preferred not to send any troops at all. Similarly, on the civilian side, the whole working force of SCAP is American. The occupation is "allied," but Americans constitute the only personnel. (For a time a few Englishmen and one notable Canadian held positions in SCAP, but no longer.) The thirteen nations whom MacArthur "represents" meet in Washington on the Far Eastern Commission, shortly to be described. But in Tokyo the whole performance is American.

The successive steps out of which this curious—and lucky—situation arose were the following. On July 26, 1945 came the Potsdam Proclamation, which outlined the terms whereon the Allies would accept Japanese surrender; all subsequent history of Japan rests on this document. The Russians were not at war with Japan as of this date, and hence could not sign the actual document, though they adhered to it later. On August 6 we dropped the first atomic bomb

on Hiroshima, and, knowing that this would be the *coup de grâce*, Russia slid precipitously into the Far Eastern theater by declaring war on Japan on August 8. Japan surrendered on the fourteenth after a vain attempt to bargain, and the actual instrument of surrender was signed on the *Missouri* on September 2. MacArthur signed this document, not as representative of the United States (the signatory for the United States was Admiral Nimitz), but as Supreme Commander on behalf of *all* the allies.

MacArthur had been appointed Supreme Commander, "for the purposes of receiving the surrender and putting it into effect," a few days before. He was at that time nothing more than a theater commander—Commander-in-Chief, U.S. Army Forces in the Pacific, with headquarters at Manila. Things happened in a violent rush in those days. There was no time for prolonged discussion or elaboration. To set up a mechanism for peace meant prodigious toil concurrently in any number of fields. So far as this writer can discover Mr. Truman consulted nobody outside his own immediate staff on the MacArthur appointment. Of course he was the obvious man for the job, though the Navy wanted Admiral Nimitz. The other interested countries, including Russia, were simply notified that the appointment had been made, and Russia did not protest or complain. So, in a flash, MacArthur became what he has been ever since, Supreme Commander for the Allied Powers, *including* the U.S.S.R.

On August 25, in order to get some sort of regime of control fixed in advance, the United States organized a group called the Far Eastern Advisory Commission, to sit in Washington. The Russians, perhaps realizing that they had made a blunder in accepting MacArthur, refused to sit on it, and it never came to life. This *was* a blunder, because it gave us a complete free hand; we had the ball now, and hugged it. On August 29 Washington issued a major document which constituted the first policy directive to MacArthur, called "United States Initial Post-Surrender Policy for Japan." The Russians never saw this till it was published, nor did the other allies, but it is under its principles that MacArthur entered Japan and is still its boss.

18

Of course this procedure, somewhat hurried and arbitrary, had to be regularized. So, in December, 1945, Secretary of State Byrnes went to Moscow for a tripartite conference of foreign ministers. (The U.S.A., Great Britain, and the Soviet Union were represented; China and France were excluded.) Here the mechanism which still operates the occupation was set up. First, a Far Eastern Commission was established in Washington, with eleven members; later when Burma and Pakistan became nations the eleven became thirteen. This FEC (not to be confused with the FEC which means Far East Command—unfortunately the initials are identical) has the power to "review" any decision made by SCAP. It meets in the old Japanese Embassy in Washington, and several of its members are distinguished men. The Russians attended its meetings regularly until early in 1950. But Byrnes was prescient enough at Moscow to retain important provisos by which the United States far outweighs the Soviet Union on the FEC. For one thing the United States, alone among the member nations, has the right to give SCAP what are called "interim directives." So far as I know the FEC has never dared to overrule MacArthur on anything. But it has on several occasions issued directives on matters of grave importance, which he has faithfully executed. One was the celebrated order of December, 1948, the "Economic Stabilization Directive," which completely reversed SCAP's economic policy.

When MacArthur gets an instruction from the FEC the procedure is somewhat as follows. First, agreement is reached by the powers concerned. Second, the State Department drafts the document. Third, this must be approved by the Joint Chiefs of Staff. Finally, the Pentagon sends it on to Tokyo.

MacArthur's language to his FEC superiors in Washington has been known to be short on occasion; a classic instance came on March 29, 1946. He had assisted the Japanese to write a new draft constitution which he was putting to the people in the first general election held since the occupation. The FEC thought that he was being somewhat hasty, that it was imprudent to throw the issue of the constitution into party politics, and that reactionary parties in

Japan might derive advantage from the situation. With extreme diffidence and politeness, and addressing the General in the third person, the FEC outlined its point of view and asked two questions:

1. Does the Supreme Commander share the apprehensions expressed above?

MacArthur's answer was a single word, *No.*

2. If so, would the Supreme Commander consider it possible . . . to require . . . a postponement of the Japanese elections?

Again MacArthur's answer was just one word, *No.*

Another body aside from the FEC was set up by the Moscow Conference; this, known as the Allied Council, meets in Tokyo. It has four members: the United States, the Soviet Union, China, and one representing jointly the United Kingdom, Australia, New Zealand, and India. Its function, as originally designed, was to consult and advise with SCAP on the spot, in reference to decisions made by the FEC; MacArthur was supposed to call it into consultation on any important matter. Of course he has never done so. He addressed the first meeting as the American member, saying in effect that he was happy to have the Council's advice, but would retain his power as *sole* executive, and has never attended a session since.

When the great directive of August 29, 1945, was drawn up in Washington MacArthur was intimately consulted. Emissaries even flew out to Manila bearing drafts for his scrutiny before Mr. Truman signed it. But in the negotiations preceding the Moscow meeting and the formation of the FEC and Allied Council MacArthur was not consulted at all. He informed Secretary Byrnes some six weeks before the Moscow meeting that the proposed plan for administering Japan through a four-nation Council was, in his opinion, "not acceptable." Thereafter Mr. Byrnes ceased all communication with him, and his spokesman announced tartly later, "General MacArthur never received any information from the Moscow Conference during the meeting and did not even know that Japan was being discussed until he saw it announced in the daily press." This cannot be strictly true; everybody knew that the main purpose of the Moscow Conference was to discuss Japan. MacArthur's comments were so sharp that serious observers discussed in such newspapers as the New York *Times* whether or not he would resign as Supreme Commander. But he did not resign. He concealed his bitterness and anger, and said simply, "I am here to serve and not to hinder or obstruct the American government. It is my full purpose to see the whole matter through." Of course MacArthur did not want the Russians to be allowed inside his administration in any way and he had been alarmed that the Americans in Moscow might give too much away.

The Russians, on their side, used the Council as a sounding board for a time, but have boycotted it for the past six months.

My wife and I attended one meeting—the 115th—of this shadow Council. The proceedings lasted exactly one minute. Mr. Sebald, the American member, called the meeting to order, and noted the absence of the Soviet member. The minutes of the previous meeting were approved, and since there were no procedural matters on the agenda the meeting was adjourned. The official report notes soberly that the session opened at 10:03 A.M. and closed at 10:04.

Some of the British do not like these methods, even though their net effect, by strangling the Council, is to strangle the Russians too. A former British member of the Council has written that MacArthur "treated the Council with frivolous derision,"* and I heard one important Englishman say, "MacArthur cannot stand to take advice. It is his greatest defect that he has to do everything alone."

When the General seriously opens up against the Russians, his polemics are furious, and he blares like forty trumpets. Some people think that his language, no matter how worthy the cause, is too violent to be dignified. He is not a very subtle performer with words. But they are words that the Russians understand. Recently the Soviet Union protested at SCAP's purge of the Japanese communist leaders, by means of a letter to the Council. MacArthur's reply

* Cf. *The United States and Japan,* by Edwin O. Reischauer (Harvard University Press), p. 48.

began, "I have received your note, and have carefully considered its context in vain search of some semblance of merit and validity. Rarely indeed have I perused such a conglomeration of misstatement, misrepresentation, and prevarication of fact."

On another occasion, when the Russians made objection to the American occupation of Okinawa, MacArthur concluded his reply, "I cannot accept the integrity of intent of your letter. It can only be regarded as a . . . provocative impertinence." Other letters use words like "callous," "hypocritical," "gruesome," and "blatant." Sometimes, however, the Supreme Commander uses a lighter touch with the Russians. For some years he had close contact with General Kuzma Derevyanko, the chief Soviet representative in Japan, and the two men, both hearty souls, probably have a sneaking personal regard for each other. Derevyanko returned to Moscow on leave some time ago. When he got back to Tokyo MacArthur clapped him warmly on the back and exclaimed, "Well, well, I never thought I'd see you again! I was sure that once Stalin got you back to Moscow he'd chop your head off."

Introduction to SCAP

MacArthur himself once referred to the Japan of the occupation as a concentration camp. This was in a 6,000-word letter he angrily wrote to the editors of *Fortune* in May, 1949. (The Supreme Commander and his close associates often write lengthy letters of rebuttal if something displeases them in an American magazine of consequence.) Specifically he was referring to the fact, little known but true, that no single person, American, Japanese, or foreign, may either enter or leave Japan without SCAP permission. The General wrote:

No stated time limit had been fixed for the Occupation. There was no definite indication as to whether it might be two years or twenty years before the participating Powers would agree that the terms of the Potsdam Declaration had been met and that the Occupation should end. Nor was there any commitment as to how long the American taxpayer, who was to bear the burden of the expense, would continue to give his sanction thereto. Japan thereafter became in effect a large concentration camp, as it still is, with the forces of Occupation becoming the gaolers of 81,000,000 persons, with no one permitted to enter or leave without specific Allied authority.

Then, however, he proceeded to what is the real issue, what SCAP has done with its opportunities, how it has fulfilled its prodigious mandate with imagination, tact, and decency. This indeed is the chief point to make about MacArthur in this field. His military record until the catastrophe in Korea was striking enough to give him a place among the greatest of American soldiers, and no one can doubt that he is a good administrator. But what really counts about the General is his idealism. The job SCAP has done in Japan proves this, even if the job is not complete, and MacArthur the Reformer should rank high in history even if MacArthur the Hero has to be forgotten.

Aspects of the MacArthur Character

Against this backdrop we proceed to explore some of the Supreme Commander's personal qualities, his root sources of power and attributes. His dominating characteristic, next to courage, is probably ego. Out of this ego, which is measureless, come some of his most useful characteristics, like confidence, magnetism, and the capacity to inspire utter devotion in his followers. Out of it, too, come some negative traits like his touchiness and sensitiveness to criticism, which is accentuated by the extreme touchiness of his staff. Also he has a conspicuous tendency to reward loyalty too much for its own sake—to count too much on old comrades in arms who have grown with him during the years. There should be newer blood around MacArthur. But he will not tolerate anybody near him being too big. I even heard it said, "None of MacArthur's men can *risk* being first-rate."

There is such a thing as a man being so vain that he is not vain. To pretend to have no vanity is the greatest of all vanities. MacArthur's ego is, in a way, of this special type. Everybody knows about the tilt of his gilt-edged cap, the carefully pressed uniforms and shining boots, the open-throated profile flung at cameras. The General has terrific style. If, in the abstract, you set out to draw a picture of the quintessentially ideal commander, the perfect type of composite soldier-hero, it might turn out to be astonishingly like MacArthur. Even the fact that he unostentatiously wears *no* decorations whatever is part of his ostentation. But his peacockry is more than merely a surface matter. Once he said to an interviewer (perhaps with tongue in cheek) that his major advisors were—Washington and Lincoln!

An eminent officer of World War I, General Enoch Crowder, once told a high official of the State Department, "I thought that Arthur MacArthur [the General's father] was the most flamboyantly egotistic man I had ever seen—until I met his son."

Just before the Korean war MacArthur had plenty of things on his mind but he found time to send a visitor to Tokyo, with the request that it be returned, a postcard he had just had from India. He thought the visitor might be amused by this example of his fan mail, and moreover he wanted to keep it. The address on the postcard was:

To His Most Gracious Majesty
The Old Friend
The Most Honorable
General MacArthur, Sahib, Bahadur,
Military Governor and Crowned King of Japan

Perhaps it is his sense of duty that makes MacArthur egotistic. He can be—and often is—relaxed, gay, and even shy. He carries the plumage of a flamingo, but his voice can be modest too. By no means is he always stern, pontifical, defiant. He is, in fact, almost as notable a winner-over of the reluctant as Roosevelt; persuasiveness is one of his paramount qualities. Consider what a tremendous impression he is apt to make on a casual visitor; then estimate how magnetic he must be to people close by. Still, few people outside his immediate entourage really *like* him. They may respect him, admire him, emulate him, or even worship him (as many Japanese and

Filipinos undoubtedly do) but it is hard to imagine him as a universal mass leader, at least so far as the rank and file of the American public are concerned. MacArthur is a Caesar, and not, let us say, a man overwhelmingly beloved like Gandhi.

But by his own men, the rockfast inner circle, he is adulated. Tokyo is full of retired oldsters who practically stand on street corners to tell you with pride how intimate they are with him even if they haven't laid eyes on him for a year. I have heard him seriously compared to Alexander the Great by a member of his staff, to Alexander's disadvantage. Another officer told me with absolute seriousness that he considered MacArthur to be the greatest man who ever lived.

His entourage, probably without his direct knowledge, goes to interesting lengths to perform various subtle—and sometimes not so subtle—maneuvers for augmentation of his prestige. After the communist attack on Korea, the word was quietly passed around that it was solely MacArthur's vigorous intervention in Washington which led Mr. Truman to announce that the United States would give military assistance to the South Korean government. A few days later, the "line" switched, and primary credit was passed on to Mr. Johnson, who was then Secretary of Defense. The reason was that the military news was bad and MacArthur's men did not want the Supreme Commander to be held responsible in case the Korean adventure continued to go wrong.

Another MacArthur trait is his signal tendency to overoptimism and wishful thinking, a characteristic which has led him to errors of judgment and blunders on occasion. For instance he did genuinely think in the late 1930's that the Philippines, given time, could successfully defend themselves against Japan. And—to come up to date—he most distinctly did *not* anticipate major Chinese intervention in Korea in 1950, though he had sounded noisy warnings about how dangerous the situation was. He is, most people in Tokyo believe, far from realistic about the future course of Japanese affairs. MacArthur wants desperately to believe that the democrati-

25

zation of Japan will progress and stick, if only because this would be his own supreme accomplishment. But how much of the SCAP reformation *will* endure no man can know.

MacArthur's positive qualities and merits are, of course, many. For one thing, he is packed with brains. For another, let nobody underestimate his sheer, immense force of character. An American officer who was a cadet when he was superintendent of West Point was asked his opinion of the General. Reply: "He's the only man in the world who could walk into a room full of drunks and all would be stone sober within five minutes."

His memory is photographic, and he is blessed with one of the most useful advantages that mortal man can possess—he reads very quickly. He has a profound knowledge of military history, and loves to quote from old historians. The story has been told that he got the idea for the Inchon landing by rereading accounts of Wolfe's campaign against Quebec in 1759. Apparently he never forgets *any-thing*. It is only a minor sidelight, but it certainly impressed me that in Tokyo in 1950 he recalled vividly and accurately some details of a conversation I had with him in Manila in 1938. Once he was discussing proposals to modify the original plans for the American invasion of Honshu, the main island of Japan. On his own authority MacArthur was working over the directives that had been sent him from Washington, and he wanted to land in a different place, north of Tokyo. Someone pointed out that the surf along that particular stretch of beach was apt to be nasty. "Certainly," the General said. "I remember seeing it when I came out to Japan with my father in 1905."

Dennis McEvoy, the representative in Tokyo of the *Reader's Digest*, presented his wife to the Supreme Commander some time ago. MacArthur began to reminisce about a prize fight he had seen in company with her grandfather, M. H. De Young, in San Francisco *forty-seven* years before. The General remembered who had won the fight, who had fought in the semifinals, and what other guests were in the party.

He has a pleasant and ready wit. At lunch in Tokyo, when he happened to be talking about the Prince of Wales, I asked him if he had seen an article in *Life* wherein the Duke of Windsor describes a golf match he had played with Emperor Hirohito in the 1920's. Both these regal figures were crown princes then. It became clear to the Prince of Wales that Hirohito had never had a golf club in his hand before, and so the Prince politely pretended that he too could not hit the ball. MacArthur laughed and then seized the point at once. "How pleasant that two men destined to be heads of state should be gentlemen with each other!"

His tact is marked. For instance, when he receives the Emperor today, only one interpreter is present, and it is always an interpreter whom the Emperor brings, not MacArthur's. Though nicely sensitive to the personality of visitors, he never agrees just for the sake of amiability, as Roosevelt did. He loves to talk, loves an audience, and loves applause.

That he talks a great deal—and eloquently—is famous. I have seldom met anybody who gives such a sense of the richness and flexibility of the English language; he draws out of it—like Winston Churchill—as out of some inexhaustible reservoir. His manner of delivery is somewhat jerky; his choice of words, again as with Mr. Churchill, is often archaic. Of course, like many great talkers, he never stops; he is an old-fashioned monologist par excellence. Sometimes he is so bewitched by his own eloquence that he forgets what he has just said. Recently he received a group of American friends at a lunch that lasted from two to five, and he hardly stopped talking once. At one point he told an anecdote about La Rochefoucauld. Twenty minutes later he told the identical anecdote, having already forgotten that he had just told it.

General Eisenhower called on him in Tokyo during the period when both men were being conspicuously mentioned for the Presidency. Eisenhower was before the war a junior member of MacArthur's staff in Manila. The two generals respect one another heartily. In Tokyo, however, members of the MacArthur entourage are blindly, savagely jealous of Eisenhower and his political prestige and popularity. Eisenhower could not get a word in for three quarters of an hour, while MacArthur reminisced about old times. Then Eisenhower interrupted to say, with emphasis and much elaboration, that he did not think that any military man should be President of the United States. His sincerity was manifest. But MacArthur cocked a wary eye at him and said, "That's the way to play it, Ike."

It is astonishing that anybody who talks as well as MacArthur should write so badly. Perhaps the Supreme Commander is not responsible for some of his more reedy speeches and the rodomontade he customarily employs. It is not merely that his style is pompous. It is worse than that. Once he replied to a congratulatory telegram from an admiral with the words, "May God protect and preserve them [the admiral's sailors] is my prayer from Tokyo as the world keeps turning over and over and over."

One of MacArthur's secrets is his sense of balance, as in all just men. He is a man of no softness whatever, but he likes to see both sides. The leader of a Japanese delegation that visited the United States recently was much struck when the General told him, "Look for the bad things too."

He has, like all competent executives, a capacity to seize things quickly and apparently by intuition. One of his close associates told me, "He only gets what *we* give him—how then does he always know so much more than we do? He is never wrong. If a junior officer is about to be invalided home, he knows about it before we tell him. How does he *know*?"

He throws himself into whatever task he has with complete absorption, he has inflexible belief in his own destiny, and he has the compulsive ego of the truly dedicated.

Finally, one of MacArthur's dominant qualities is the master quality of courage. His physical courage is legendary; it is quite safe to say that no general officer in modern history, let alone a theater commander, ever took such risks. Time and again, in both world wars, he has exposed himself to brutal fire in a manner reckless—but casual—almost beyond belief. He never wears a steel helmet, and seldom carries arms. He stalks a battlefront like a man hardly human, not only arrogantly but lazily. The attitude is Napoleonic; the bullet that will strike him has not yet been cast. He was called "Dugout Doug" by disgruntled sailors, marines, and G.I.'s in the Pacific; the accusation that he ever hid from anything is just plain silly. Japan is a country notorious (until recently at least) for its addiction to political assassination; but MacArthur never takes any but the most primitive precautions. He enters and leaves the Dai-Ichi four times a day, every day of the year, and invariably a crowd of from fifty to a hundred Japanese assembles by the doorway to watch him. Traffic is not permitted on the streets while he moves, and an elevator is held for him within the building, but the crowd itself is not watched, and MacArthur is never (nowadays) accompanied by a guard of any kind. Any crank could throw a bomb or grenade. He pays no attention.

A distinguished American admiral and specialist in the newly developed art of amphibious warfare was sent to MacArthur's headquarters in 1943. The General greeted him with considerable coldness, cast indirect aspersions on his ability, and then flatly warned him—without quite going so far as to insinuate that he was a "spy" —that he must not communicate directly in any way with his bosses in Washington, King and Leahy. "If you do," MacArthur intoned, "ECHOES WILL BE HEARD!" The admiral considered himself insulted, and was bitterly resentful, as indeed he had claim to be; he knew that MacArthur had a perfect right to demand loyalty, but not to forbid him proper contact with his own superiors.

For some months their relations were of the stoniest, though the admiral, a good soul, dutifully proceeded with his job. Then came an important landing, and the admiral accompanied MacArthur onto the beach immediately behind the first assault wave. MacArthur was so impeccably uniformed, so polished, creased, and immaculate, that the admiral became doubly furious—especially when, under hot fire, he summoned photographers to come up and take their pictures. A shell exploded a few yards from the group. The admiral—and the photographers—instantly fell flat on their faces. A few seconds later, he peeked up. There was MacArthur, in the midst of smoke from the shell, standing straight as a staff, his chin high, his arms calmly akimbo. The admiral slowly crawled to his feet, and wondered in trepidation how MacArthur would greet him. There was a pause, and then came the Supreme Commander's voice, "Damned glad, admiral, that *some*body on my staff has sense enough to lie flat!" From that moment to this, the admiral has adored him.

MacArthur's courage is, of course, a prime factor in his control of Japan. In most Oriental countries, the man who shows no fear is master.

Chapter Three

THE LIFE AND THE LEGENDS

ONE REASON why so many people dislike MacArthur is simple enough —they are jealous of his superiorities, which are, indeed, extreme. He was first in his class at West Point; his performance there was the most brilliant in many years, and in some details has never been surpassed. His over-all scholastic record for four years was 98.14 per cent, and in several courses he was the only cadet ever to have entered the Academy who made perfect marks—a flat 100 per cent.

He was the youngest division commander in France in World War I, the youngest superintendent West Point ever had, the youngest active major general in the Army, the youngest Chief of Staff, and the youngest man ever to become a full general. He is the only soldier in American history whose father was also Chief of Staff, and the first full general ever to win the Congressional Medal of Honor—his father won it too. He is the first American ever to become a field marshal in another nation's army, and the first American commander to fly the flag of the United Nations.

Biography in Brief

Douglas MacArthur was born at Little Rock, Arkansas, on January 26, 1880, the third son of Lieutenant General Arthur MacArthur, who was on post there at the time, and a lady of good

31

family from Virginia whose maiden name was Mary Hardy. Originally the father came from Wisconsin, and the present MacArthur still considers Milwaukee his home town. His paternal grandfather, a thistly character (the family is of Scotch origin), was a lieutenant governor of Wisconsin, and had considerable local fame. Young Douglas lived in Army posts most of his youth, and it is a matter of family record that, as a child, he heard the drum beats of hostile Indians. Camp life, army life, dominated all his early years, and it never occurred to him to be anything but a soldier when he grew up.

Lt. Gen. Arthur MacArthur had an exceptionally vigorous military career; there are pertinent similarities between father and son. The elder MacArthur enlisted for service in the Civil War at sixteen, and while still a youth won his Congressional Medal (for reckless gallantry under fire) at the Battle of Missionary Ridge. Also, like his son, MacArthur was severely wounded in several engagements, largely because he exposed himself with little regard for safety. MacArthurs are an impetuous breed. Again like his son, the elder MacArthur had a great deal to do with the Philippines. It was he, in fact, who cleaned up the last Filipino resistance after the Spanish-American War, and became the first American military governor of the islands. His policy there was, like that of his son forty years later in Japan, marked both by a stern sense of justice and magnanimity. It is a matter of great pride to the present MacArthur that it was his father who first introduced habeas corpus in the Philippines, just as he himself first brought this most cardinal and efficacious of democratic instruments to Japan.

"Whenever I perform a mission and think I have done it well, I feel that I can stand up squarely to my dad and say, 'Governor, how about it?'" MacArthur told a friend in Tokyo not long ago.

The father's career and character put a mark on MacArthur that nothing has ever effaced, but he was the child of his mother too. He adored her; she adored him. She deliberately brought him up to think that he was a child of destiny, and her influence was illimit-

32

able; much of his ambition comes from her, his personal force, and his faith in the future. When he was a cadet at West Point, she lived nearby, so that she could always be close to him; similarly Sara Delano Roosevelt took a house in Boston when FDR went to Harvard. Mrs. MacArthur coached her remarkable son, gave him love and confidence, and taught him to venerate his father. She outlived her husband by many years (again the analogy to Sara Roosevelt is close) and focused the entire weight of her life on her son's well-being. She died in Manila in 1935, aged eighty-two.

The manner of the father's death in 1912 has become a minor legend. Drama hangs copiously on the MacArthurs. The old general, living in Milwaukee in the evening of his life, said that he had only one regret, that he could not die at the head of his troops. His regiment was about to hold its fiftieth reunion, and its veteran members felt neglected, particularly when the governor of Wisconsin and the mayor of Milwaukee said that they were too busy to attend the ceremony. Somebody thought that the venerable General MacArthur, even though he was bedridden, might put in a brief appearance. He did so, though this meant defiance of his doctors. He rose to speak, and said that, considering the state of his health, this would be the last time he would ever be able to greet his comrades. On finishing his speech, he fell dead. So his last wish, that he might die with his own regiment, was remarkably fulfilled. His old aide, seeing the general collapse, rushed across the stage, seized the regimental banner, and flung it over the prostrate body. "A prayer!" he shouted. The veterans rose, knelt, and prayed. Two days later, overcome by the emotion and exhaustion of this experience, the aide fell dead too.

*

Young MacArthur had a lively time at West Point. I have heard one of his classmates say that "he was arrogant from the age of eight." He played baseball (and was a better fielder than hitter) and managed the football team. Though he must have spent most hours at hard study—consider his unprecedented marks—he was by no means a grind. He was head of the student body, class salutatorian, and the cadet voted the most likely to succeed. He was graduated, at the top of his class, on June 11, 1903, and because of his record automatically went into the Engineers.

His first post was, of all places, Leyte in the Philippines, where he was to land at the head of a conquering armada forty-one years later. Here, in fact, one of his jobs was to construct barracks which were still in use when he returned. He came back to the United States presently and went out to the Orient again as an aide to his father, who was Theodore Roosevelt's observer at the Russo-Japanese War then being fought. Thus MacArthur saw Japan for the first time in 1905; the man who was his interpreter still lives in Tokyo. His official biography, as prepared by SCAP, says that "while on this detail MacArthur was given a confidential mission which took him to several Oriental countries." Presumably he scouted around North China and Manchuria.

MacArthur became a first lieutenant quickly enough but he did not rise to be a captain till 1911. For a time he was an aide to President Theodore Roosevelt. In 1913 he was assigned to duty with the Chief of Engineers, and took part the next year in the expedition to Vera Cruz. In disguise he penetrated the Mexican lines. He became a major in 1915, worked as superintendent of the old State Department Building, and finally became a member of the general staff— one of his jobs was censorship—in September, 1917, six months after the United States entered World War I.

After that he rose like a rocket. It was he who conceived the idea for the famous Rainbow (42nd) Division of National Guard troops. The story goes like this, and perhaps it has overtones of the apocryphal. An acrid dispute split the general staff as to whether or not National Guard units should be sent overseas, and MacArthur, still very definitely a junior officer, was the chief backer of the idea that they should. After an angry session one of his outraged superiors said, "I can see, major, that you are not interested in pursuing your military career much further." MacArthur, despite this rebuke, kept hammering away at the proposal, and finally he was called in to see Newton Baker, the Secretary of War. Baker said, "On this issue every officer opposes you. What are the reasons for your stand?" MacArthur explained his position with vivid and persistent eloquence, and a day or two later the Secretary took him in to see President Wilson. "I want Major MacArthur to put a case to you, Mr. President," said Baker. MacArthur then sketched in detail his dream of a division containing men from every state in the union, from the Atlantic to the Pacific, like a giant rainbow. "Rainbow!" exclaimed the President, delighted. Wilson, so the story goes, then promoted him on the spot to colonel, and gave him the mission of helping to organize the division. To two Democratic presidents, the Republican MacArthur owes a lot.

MacArthur came with the Rainbow to France in October, 1917, and won practically every medal that the Army could bestow. His bravery was brilliant. He fought in the Champagne-Marne area, and took part in the Aisne-Marne offensive. He was wounded twice, gassed once. One legend is that the first wound came because of an error in the high command; his troops were bombarded by their own artillery. MacArthur rose to the rank of brigadier general and, at last, became commander of the division he helped create. One of his officers for a time, though he never met him, was a Missourian named Harry Truman. He fought at St. Mihiel, Wouvre, and Sedan. Then, after the armistice, he got his first taste of military occupation and the administration of a defeated enemy by serving briefly at Bonn, now the capital of western Germany.

Back home, he worked in the office of the Chief of Staff, and then for three years (1919-22) was superintendent of West Point. Twice he returned to the Philippines for brief tours (1923 and 1928), and in the United States he successively commanded the IV, III, and IX Corps Areas, until he was appointed Chief of Staff in November, 1930. In this post he won both loyal friends and unrelenting enemies. He pressed for bigger Army appropriations, gave heed to

35

the problems of a unified command, and preached for mechanization, mobility, and the vital importance of air and armored warfare. Normally his term would have expired in 1934, but Roosevelt kept him on till October, 1935.

Lewis Douglas, FDR's first director of the budget (who many years later became American Ambassador to London), had the job of paring down government expenditures 25 per cent. MacArthur came to a budget hearing, to resist cuts in the Army appropriation, and spoke for an hour strenuously. Then Mr. Douglas quietly asked him, "General, do you expect a serious epidemic of dysentery in the U. S. Army?" MacArthur, taken aback, said, "No." Mr. Douglas then inquired why his budget for toilet paper—among other things —was so extraordinarily high; he had gone through all the Army figures, and thought that they were padded. MacArthur was so furious that he stopped his testimony forthwith and bluntly left the room. A year or so later Douglas ran into him, and apologized for the way he had put the question. Then MacArthur handsomely apologized too.

Meantime, under Hoover, MacArthur had been the focus of a bitter controversy because he evicted the bonus marchers from Anacostia Flats in Washington, D.C. Photographs showing him in suavely shined boots and brilliant, glittering uniform as he directed this unfortunate business did not do him much good. But he himself was not responsible for the eviction; the order came to him from higher up, through Secretary of War Hurley, and he had no choice but to obey. There has never been an instance in MacArthur's history of specific refusal to obey an order. But it has taken him a long time to live down what seemed an outrageously harsh and flowery display of force against a hungry, miserable group of fellow citizens.

In May, 1934, the General brought a libel suit for $1,750,000 against Drew Pearson and Robert S. Allen of the *Washington Merry-Go-Round* (also against William Randolph Hearst's Washington *Times*, which printed the column). He made seven specific

36

complaints, on each of which he wanted $250,000. One was that Pearson and Allen said that he "swaggered" as Chief of Staff and "chafed because he wasn't being promoted fast enough"; Mac-Arthur claimed that such language made him "a ridiculous military character . . . guilty of conduct unbecoming an officer." Another was that they said he had proposed to friends in Congress a new law requiring a nineteen-gun salute for the Chief of Staff; MacArthur claimed that this showed him to be "lacking in military modesty." Another had to do with a new decoration the General was alleged to have planned for members of his staff, and still another took up his eviction of the bonus army, which was described as "unwarranted, unnecessary, arbitrary, harsh, and brutal." Finally, Pearson-Allen said that MacArthur was the real boss of the War Department, and intrigued against the civilian Secretary. The General asserted that this laid him open to charges of being "guilty of disloyalty and mutinous conduct, one of the most serious offenses in the Articles of War," as well as being "dictatorial, insubordinate, and disrespectful toward his superior officer."

For several reasons the suit never reached trial. Pearson and Allen stated later, without being contradicted, "No money was paid by us to General MacArthur for costs or otherwise. No apologies or retractions were given or asked for."

MacArthur didn't know quite where to turn when he finished his tour as Chief of Staff in 1935. He had reached the top; he was only fifty-five, ambitious, and in perfect health. The political atmosphere in Washington was not congenial. So when his old friend Manuel Quezon, President of the Philippines, suggested that he go out to Manila as military adviser to the Commonwealth, with the unprecedented rank of Field Marshal, he accepted. He retired from the United States Army in 1937, and devoted himself exclusively to the Philippines (his fourth term of service there) for the next four years. He liked the life of Manila, and worked at his job—the organization of Philippine defenses on a longrange basis—with zeal and acumen. He hoped, if the Japanese gave him time, to train 40,000

37

men annually for ten years, build up a small fleet of patrol torpedo boats, and create a seasoned air force. His basic tenet was to equip the islands so that an attack would cost an enemy more than the value received, he told me in Manila once. He was convinced that there were only two beaches in the archipelago where an enemy could land, and (again if he had time) that the invaders could be held. Like practically everybody else, he underestimated the Japanese.

*

It is hardly necessary to recapitulate here the story of MacArthur in World War II. By the summer of 1941 practically everybody knew that war was coming—sometime. Mr. Roosevelt recalled him to active status as a major general on July 26, 1941, and promoted him to lieutenant general the next day, in command of all U. S. Army Forces in the Far East; the Philippine army became part of the American command. MacArthur was severely embarrassed by the destruction of his planes on Clark Field on Pearl Harbor day. The Japanese caught him in exactly the same naked and exposed state as they caught the Americans in Hawaii, though he had ample warning since the Pearl Harbor attack had come ten hours before. Today the inclination of his staff is to blame a subordinate officer for this botch and blunder. Beyond this was the general atmosphere of those days, the feeling that the Japanese simply would not dare to attack with such wide and synchronized effect, and that they did not have the capability of doing so. MacArthur himself thought that war was inevitable, but he did not expect it till the spring of 1942, and he felt that the Japanese would probably by-pass the Philippines in favor of softer spots to the south.

One may bring this story up to the present again by mentioning that MacArthur has several times made serious blunders in judgment, based on faulty information. The attack on South Korea on June 25 apparently took him by complete surprise, and he thought that the Korean war was won after the landing at Inchon on September 15. He told Mr. Truman at their meeting on Wake Island a month later that the danger of Chinese intervention had passed, but the Chinese drastically fooled him. Then (though he tried to wriggle out of this by saying that the remark had only been "jocular") he predicted flatly that the American troops would be home by Christmas—only three or four days before they were caught by surprise and hammered back in a disaster that, at the moment of writing, is unpredictable as to its ramifications. MacArthur, having scouted the ground personally for what was to have been his final advance, crashed into a colossal trap—moreover a trap about which he was fully aware.

Yet he has been generally regarded as the very symbol and incarnation of military omniscience. Few people dared to criticize him when he lost his planes on the Philippines; it was almost as if a conspiracy of silence existed to protect him, and most people are loath to criticize him now.

Mr. Roosevelt was, as everybody knows, violently attacked because American officers at Pearl Harbor were caught unaware and unprepared. Those who like to calumniate FDR usually take earnest care to ignore the fact that MacArthur in the Philippines likewise lost most of his planes *on the ground*. Most Roosevelt haters are MacArthur lovers (and vice versa), which perhaps serves to explain their easy exculpation of MacArthur, while FDR is still venomously maligned.

MacArthur thought—another error—that Manila could be held for a long period, because Corregidor was "the strongest single fortified point in the world." He did not think that the Japanese, or anybody, were capable of the type of attack they launched. He was wrong.

The President ordered MacArthur from Corregidor to Australia in February, 1942, when it became clear that the American fight was hopeless. Mr. Stimson's memoirs describe pungently how the American authorities in Washington took a leaf from Churchill's book, and, in their instructions to MacArthur, followed the orders Churchill had given to the British commander in chief at Dunkirk. Nothing can be stupider than the charge still sometimes leveled

39

that MacArthur "deserted" his army at Bataan to get out to Australia. He did not. He was ordered out. The first order came on February 22, and MacArthur frightened Washington—people feared that, despite orders, he might refuse to go—by asking for a delay. This was granted, and he did not arrive in Australia till March 17. It can still, in fact, be argued that he left Bataan against his will. He did finally accept Washington's instructions for two reasons: (1) he was obeying an explicit Presidential order, (2) considerations of revenge. He knew that, if he arrived in Australia safely, he could devote the rest of his life to fierce persistent warfare against the Japanese. Hence the message that reverberated around the world when he reached Australian soil, "I came through and I will return!"

One close member of his staff told me that the hardest decision of his life was to pick and choose the handful who accompanied him. Incidentally the adventure is never described as an "escape" in MacArthur circles, but as "the successful execution of an order" or even as merely "a transfer of headquarters." A considerable mass of official documents and secret papers had to be brought out, and this cut down the number of people who could be carried. Also some junior officers who worked secretly on codes *had* to be taken. Four PT boats were available to the party on the first lap to Mindoro, and then two—just two—B-17's for the eleven-hour flight to Darwin. MacArthur took his wife, his son, their Chinese *amah* (that his family always accompanied him aroused, in its day, much mordant comment from officers less favored), and seventeen associates—out of hundreds whom he might have chosen, but whom he had to leave behind. Among those who went with him were three men who, to this moment, have scarcely ever left his side: Major General Charles A. Willoughby, Major General W. F. Marquat, and Colonel Sidney L. Huff. Huff, a former naval officer, played a substantial role in getting the PT boats assigned to Manila in the first place, against stiff opposition by naval officers more conventionally minded, who did not see what use they could be.

40

The official description of the journey, released on March 24, 1942, is a truly purple example of Army prose. It begins:

Manila had just been bathed in the warm sunlight of one of the sunsets for which it is famous. The sun slipped into the Chinese Sea out past Corregidor. In the deepening shadows of approaching night dark forms moved slowly from several directions . . . toward the mine fields.

Suddenly the silence of the newborn night was destroyed as the roar of powerful motors burst upon the drowsy bay. General MacArthur and his small party, in compliance with a Presidential order, had started upon their hazardous journey through Japanese lines to report to his new command in Australia.

There follows a long, resonant parenthesis discussing Mac-Arthur's record as Chief of Staff, how "his was a voice in the wilderness" pleading for more modern defense techniques, and how when he set out on his work in the Philippines "the world laughed." The story of the PT boats is ornately recounted, with mention of Mac-Arthur's personal intervention to Admiral Leahy to get them approved. Then:

Memories of frontier days, when beleaguered garrisons sent the youngest and most hardy through enemy lines . . . come to mind. Stories of men who made mad dashes . . . and brought up the cavalry have been the subject of novels, radio, drama, and movies. . . .

But this was different. This was not a young and husky scout who was ordered to come through. This was a 62-year-old man, a commanding general, a veteran of many wars. This was a man who had retired several years ago and who had been called back in a great emergency. This was a man who had been called up to fight his way through with his wife and child.

The decision [to proceed] was universally opposed as too desperate, except by . . . the general himself. The general said, "We will go with the fall of the moon; we will go during the Ides of March."

The PT boats roared on . . . The General was unable to stand on his feet because of the heavy seas. Mrs. MacArthur was the splendid soldier that she is . . . The General did not escape from Bataan. He came through to a greater task.

MacArthur at once set up headquarters as commander of the Southwest Pacific. To avenge Bataan became an obsession. He

41

did not have much to work with. But at once he made a characteristic decision: to defend Australia, however meager his strength, by at once *attacking* the Japanese in New Guinea, instead of waiting for them to come down. Subsequent details need not detain us long—the bad feeling that developed between MacArthur and men in his command, the strategy of island hopping, jurisdictional quarrels with Washington and eventual division of authority with Admiral Nimitz, the harsh jungle campaigns in miserable forgotten islands, and repeated charges that MacArthur was "sold short" in Australia as he had been in the Philippines. (But if Roosevelt had not ordered him out of the Philippines, he would have spent the war as a Japanese prisoner.) Two main points are worth making. MacArthur took more territory, with less loss of life, than any military commander since Darius the Great—true, most of the territory was water. Second, his forces made eighty-seven different major amphibious landings and were never once pushed off any island or atoll they landed on.

Members of the MacArthur entourage had, in those days as today, an absolute and exclusive fixity of mind about their own theater. Robert E. Sherwood went out to Manila (after MacArthur had retaken the Philippines) as an emissary of FDR's. He happened to be in the Manila map room when a report came that the Americans in Germany had performed the spectacular feat of crossing the Remagen bridge on the Rhine, thus making our victory in Europe certain. Sherwood asked General Willoughby, MacArthur's chief intelligence officer, if the Remagen news were true. Willoughby's answer, shrugging it off, was "We don't give a blank blank out here for anything that happens in Europe." Sherwood was profoundly shocked by this. It seemed to him almost inconceivable that any American officer could be so indifferent to the fate of other Americans in the same war.

Subsequently Sherwood had a long conference with MacArthur. This experience gave a different taste. MacArthur impressed him enormously, because he had already worked out to the uttermost detail the administration of Japan when it should be conquered.

His conception was so brilliant, broad, and daring that Sherwood left him, thinking that, no matter what happened in the military sphere, the General should certainly be given the chance to put his vast plans for Japan (which at that time seemed wildly chimerical) into full effect.

MacArthur's imperiousness mounted as his campaigns progressed. One curious item, forgotten nowadays, is that he never permitted the Office of Strategic Services to operate in his theater. Despite all efforts, General "Wild Bill" Donovan was never once able to get an OSS officer into MacArthur's vast domain. Mr. Churchill's latest volume casts oblique light on the General's behavior in another field. He records that MacArthur, going over everybody's head, asked for the diversion of British forces to Australia, the use of a British aircraft carrier, and large augmentation of shipping on the U. S.–Australia run. Apparently Washington had never heard of these requests, much less approved them, and they were promptly canceled. "Nothing evil happened," is Churchill's laconic conclusion.

Another row—on a smaller scale—came with the Office of War Information. The shrewd idea was thought up of dropping on Japanese-held areas millions of messages on the theme of "I will return." The OWI wanted to change the slogan to "We shall return"; MacArthur fought for months to keep it "I will return." Many vituperative exchanges occurred (a member of OWI told me that "MacArthur acted like a bull-headed baby") and in the end he won.

I have heard several explanations why so many officers, particularly of the Navy, disliked the General so vehemently, despite his record; even today, naval officers on duty in Japan may find themselves in difficulty with their old superiors in Washington if they are too overtly "MacArthur men." One is the charge, totally baseless, that he used naval craft like sitting ducks, to take most of the punishment. Another is that he sought to grab all the limelight for himself. For instance furious resentment was provoked when the Navy was not allowed to take part in the victory broadcasts after the landing at Leyte. His communiqués, which were often on the boastful side, talked of "my" Navy and "my" Air Force. Also many Navy officers disliked some of MacArthur's best air generals, like George Kenney, to whom he himself was devoted. The General would occasionally be blamed for what the Air Force did. Probably many Navy officers thought that the Marines were unjustifiably exposed to casualties—for instance on Iwo Jima—in order to get an easy airstrip for Air Force bombers en route home from Tokyo. A great many G.I.'s hated MacArthur's guts; this was probably for some such illogical reason as that he was seldom seen, and looked so blindingly spick-and-span when he was. Also they resented the misleading optimism of his communiqués after they themselves had been through savage fighting, and his prancing. Finally, MacArthur was such a dominant figure that he was blamed if anything at all went wrong, even if it was far from his own province.

MacArthur landed at Leyte on October 20, 1944, and at Lingayen on January 9, 1945. He took Manila on February 3, and by early July the reconquest of the Philippines was complete. The Japanese lost more than 400,000 men; the victory, on anybody's terms, was one of the most brilliantly comprehensive in military annals. MacArthur was a veritable knight in armor during this campaign. During one period his own headquarters were some miles ahead of his own army commanders. With the campaign over, his eyes turned north—to the homeland of the enemy, Japan.

MacArthur: Personal

MacArthur's first wife, whom he married in 1922 when he was 42, was Louise Cromwell Brooks, the stepdaughter of the Philadelphia millionaire Edward T. Stotesbury and sister of the James Cromwell who married Doris Duke. Her first husband was Walter Brooks, Jr., from whom she had been divorced a few years before. MacArthur met her when he was superintendent at West Point. His family, though comfortably fixed, was an Army family and not rich; now he was hurled upward into multimillionaire society. He did not like it

44

much. MacArthur is not gregarious; he is austere; he does not care for upper-bracket excesses and trivialities. Nor did Mrs. MacArthur enjoy life in the Philippines, which she apparently thought was the equivalent of transalpine Gaul. She divorced him in Reno in 1929; thereafter she married, first, Lionel Atwill, the well-known actor, and second, Alf Heiberg of Washington, D. C. MacArthur does not mention her in his biography in *Who's Who.*

People sometimes ask about the relationship of Douglas Mac-Arthur, II, who is the husband of Vice-President Barkley's daughter. He is the son of the General's older brother, Arthur, who died some years ago, and who was a captain in the Navy.

The first Mrs. MacArthur sometimes tells friends stories about the General, which are apt to stress his vanity and dignity. Once at a dinner party she reminisced about their early married days, when she belonged to a cycle club. MacArthur, it appeared, would not ride with her; someone asked her why not. She replied, "Heavens! Can you imagine Douglas on a bicycle!"

In 1935 Mrs. Arthur MacArthur, the General's aged mother, journeyed out to Manila to see her son, and on shipboard met a youthful, charming southern lady named Jean Marie Faircloth, of Murfreesboro, Tennessee. Miss Faircloth, born to wealth, was taking a cruise around the world. MacArthur's mother, a southerner herself, liked her, thought that she would be an ideal wife for her son, and asked her to stop off in Manila. The General and Miss Faircloth fell in love, and were married in New York (at the City Hall) on April 30, 1937. The MacArthurs returned to Manila, and neither has touched the American mainland since. Mrs. MacArthur is nineteen years younger than her husband. They have one son, Arthur, born in Manila, who is twelve.

Mrs. MacArthur is animated, dark, neat, pretty, and alert. She misses nothing. She is vitally important to her husband's life; he is crazy about her, and she worships him. She calls him not "Douglas" nor by any nickname, but "General," but this is not an example of stuffiness or awe of her husband; rather it represents a type of

45

traditional southern courtesy. Nevertheless it is something of a shock to hear her address him as "General" across an informal luncheon table. Mrs. MacArthur takes a good deal of the load off the Supreme Commander's shoulders. She represents him at multitudinous social functions (to which he never goes at all), pays his respects to various dignitaries, and, when he entertains at the Embassy, is a perceptive hostess. As a rule she awaits her luncheon guests in the large Embassy drawing room, alone or with Colonel Huff, and talks to them with cheerful high spirits till—sometimes half an hour later—the Supreme Commander enters. As he comes in the door, which is a tidy distance away, she utters a mild exclamation like, "Why, there is the General!"—almost as if he were an unexpected visitor. He advances rapidly, grasps her, says "Jeanie . . . Darling!" and kisses her warmly, in front of the guests, as if they had not seen one another for weeks, though they have in all probability not been separated for more than two or three hours. During lunch she carefully assists in giving the guests voice, in case they are too timid to talk or in the event that the General's eloquence is in full majestic flow, by interrupting gently and saying, "But, General, Mr. X wants to ask you about This-or-That." Previously, before he has entered, she has found out tactfully what subjects the guest is most eager to discuss.

Mrs. MacArthur maintains her role without the slightest pretension. At parties she does nothing to differentiate herself from other officers' wives, though, of course, people new to Tokyo feel a certain thrill when she enters and the assemblage whispers, "Mrs. MacArthur 'has arrived." She stands in line to cash a check at the bank like anybody else, shops at the PX, asks no special privileges, and is universally admired.

In her husband's actual work she takes little part, except that, for a period, she read and clipped the American magazines for him. If she has ever felt that his strange working hours make it difficult to maintain an easy household routine, she has never given a sign of it. In plain fact, she probably sees more of him than do most wives of husbands who work a conventional nine-to-five day.

Their boy, Arthur, is a handsome, alert, somewhat delicate child who is the utter apple of his father's eye. This young American, now approaching thirteen, has (a) never seen his own homeland, (b) never gone to school. The main reason is his father's insatiably protective love—he does not want to be separated from him even briefly, and hates to submit him to the hurly-burly of such schools as Tokyo can provide. Some years ago Arthur broke his arm skating. "The General," I heard it put, "went crazy." The fracture was simple, with no complications of any kind; yet the youngster was hospitalized for days, and the Supreme Commander demanded that dozens of X-rays be taken—one or two would have been enough. Of course the hospital was turned upside down, because MacArthur interrupted his own routine to visit him every day. The child has not been permitted to go skating since.

Arthur, so I heard it said, is deliberately kept *from* being a genius. Whenever he shows a special aptitude for something this is discouraged, so that he will grow up as a strictly normal youngster. The chief thing to report about him scholastically, at the moment, is that he is a bit slow with his spelling. For a time, growing up in Brisbane, he spoke with an Australian accent; now it has a British tinge. Arthur has few playmates; it happens that not many parents in the General's periphery have children of his age. He has three dogs, of whom he is very fond: Yuki, a white Japanese animal born of a dog that once belonged to General Joseph Swing; a black cocker, Blackie, trained by a German breeder who has lived in Tokyo for years; and Brownie, a Sheba terrier.

Once General Whitney got an urgent call from MacArthur early in the morning; he found him in his son's bedroom, wearing an old West Point blanket as a bathrobe, and playing with Arthur and all three dogs. The General sees the boy the first thing every morning, and instantly on his return to the Embassy at night. Members of the entourage think that on Saturdays they may have a good chance of getting away from the office early, say by 8:30 P.M. instead of the usual 9 or 9:30, because on that evening father and son customarily see a movie together, and the General is prompt in arriving home.

For some years the person closest to Arthur, next to his parents, was the Chinese nurse, Ah Chu (pronounced Ah Ju). She is a remarkably attractive old character, who cannot read or write.

After the family settled in Tokyo Mrs. MacArthur found Arthur a tutor in the person of Mrs. Phyllis Gibbons, known universally as "Gibby." Mrs. Gibbons was a schoolteacher in the Philippines, of British nationality, who got caught by the Japanese there and who spent three years to a day, from December 28, 1941, to December 28, 1944, in an internment camp in Baguio, and was later moved to prison in Manila. ("The Nips didn't treat me *too* badly," she told me charitably.) Before this she taught in various schools in China; she has not been back to England for seventeen years, and has never been in the United States. Mrs. MacArthur did not meet her in the Philippines before the war; she heard of her by chance later. "Gibby," a tall lady of great distinction, is as close to the MacArthurs as anybody, and no one is more highly valued. She is the queen of the MacArthur "court," and a delightful person. The boy, too, is devoted to her, and she adores him. ("He's a nice youngster. Such a lot of nonsense has been written about him. He's *very* nice. I'm teaching him American geography now out of your *Inside U.S.A.*") Many people in Tokyo, anxious for the MacArthur favor, treat the boy as if he were a veritable crown prince. But there is no nonsense like that with "Gibby." Her whole effort is to make him as normal and unspoiled as possible.

Some day, of course, young Arthur will have to go away to school. He will necessarily have to have competition and external disciplines, no matter how efficient Mrs. Gibbons' regime is.

*

I have described above the general processes of a MacArthur lunch. My wife and I had the good fortune to attend one, and we were the only guests. What struck me first was that the General

48

was not so tall as I had remembered him, or as his photographs seem to show. He is extraordinarily handsome—beyond doubt one of the best-looking men of our time; handsome not merely from the point of view of conventional good looks, but with a magnetism, a vitality, that come from within. Also he looks amazingly young. His hands—sensitive, slim hands, those of an artist or a surgeon—look somewhat frail, and they tremble slightly, but the appearance as a whole (I am not exaggerating) is that of a man of fifty, not seventy, moreover, a man of fifty in the very best physical condition and at the top of his form.

I asked Lt. Col. C. C. Canada, his personal physician, if MacArthur was a good patient. Answer: "I don't know. He's never sick." And in plain fact he has not lost a day on account of illness for almost thirty years.

This is the more remarkable in that he works so hard. But he has established a peculiar routine, which gives him plenty of time to relax. He gets up rather late, has a leisurely breakfast, does some (but not much) paper work, and sets out for the Dai-Ichi at about 11 in the morning, sometimes later. He works till 1:45 or 2, and then returns to the Embassy for lunch. After lunch, every day of the year, if possible, he takes a nap, a good nap, for an hour or so, as Winston Churchill does. Then he returns to the Dai-Ichi at about 5 or 5:30, and works till evening—9 or later. Dinner is when he gets home, invariably with Mrs. MacArthur alone. There are no social distractions of any kind. The General *never* pays calls, goes to parties, sees any outsiders socially, or entertains except at lunch. He usually sees a movie at the Embassy in the evening, or part of one, and is in bed by midnight.

MacArthur himself attributes his superb physical condition to three things. First, the daily nap. Second, his abstemiousness. He eats very little, and has not had a drink (except rarely on ceremonial occasions) since he was called back to active service in 1941. He smokes in moderation; his corncob pipes are well known. Third, he has the wonderful advantage—like Roosevelt—of being able to fall

49

asleep almost instantly. He never worries about a problem once the day's work is done.

He takes no exercise whatever, which some people think is odd. But, talking to people in his office, he paces a great deal; his friends say, in fact, that he covers three or four miles a day pacing, though this can hardly be true.

A distinguished American artist who painted his portrait recently said, "Of course MacArthur has never known what to do with his hands. It is impossible to paint his hands because they are never still. That is why he usually stands with his hands behind his back, or otherwise contrives to hide them."

His routine may seem comparatively easy, but on the other hand he never has a day off. I mean this literally. He works Sundays. He works Easter. He works New Year's Day. He works Christmas. There has not been a single day away from work since he took over in Japan, and certainly none since the Korean war. This is hard on his staff. In fact it is murderous. His leading officers have to keep *his* hours, in addition to doing the work of their own sections, which may mean that, year in and year out, they are on duty from eight in the morning till nine or even later at night, with never one day off—not even July fourth. I heard on one occasion an American officer superior in rank to MacArthur say that he thought this was too much to ask of anybody. Nobody on MacArthur's immediate staff can possibly have any social life, because the General is apt to demand their presence at any time, and of course they cannot accept normal luncheon or dinner engagements because his own eating hours are so late. When they want to get home to their wives at 6 P.M., after a long hard day, MacArthur pops into the office and work starts all over again. One of his men told me he got so sick of apologizing for not being able to come to parties at the last moment that he has simply given up ever accepting any engagements at all. Someone once brought up to MacArthur himself the fact that he worked his men too hard, that he was "killing" them. The Supreme Commander snapped in reply, "What better fate for a man than to die in performance of his duty?"

Not everybody knows that MacArthur likes to start work late in the morning. When Louis Johnson visited Tokyo before the Korean war he telegraphed from Guam suggesting that they meet for their first conference at 8:45 A.M. the next day. "Nobody had ever told me," complained Mr. Johnson later, "that MacArthur didn't get up that early." But the General was on hand at the moment designated.

To return to our lunch. Actual quotations from the General's talk are, of course, not permissible, though there is no harm in giving a rough impression of what he said. What struck me most was his lightness, humor, and give-and-take. The *mystique* of the great commander so surrounds MacArthur that one is apt to forget how human he is. I expected him to be oracular, volcanic, and unceasing. He was all that, but something else too; he laughed a good deal, enjoyed jokes, told some pretty good ones, permitted interruptions, and listened well. This is not to say that his talk was fluff. It was not. He talked of the differences between Japan and Germany, of the impossibility of cutting Japan adrift, of the way the situation of Japan has changed because the situation of the allies has changed, of the face of a girl he remembered in Yokohama fifty years ago, of the "thought police" in former days and how they even terrorized children, of a prostitute who won a recent election because all her clients (some 50,000 in all!) voted for her, of the divorce rate in Japan and how its rise worried him for a time though he did not object on moral grounds, of the way the Japanese had believed that the Americans would come as pillagers with fire and sword, of Eisenhower and the denazification program in Germany, of Vincent Sheean, of the Japanese war trials and how below a certain level a war "criminal" was just a patriot, of the Kabuki theater, of the sad state of American journalism, of the decency of blood and breeding in the Japanese royal family, and of how the Japanese, humiliated and humble, having lost faith and face by the terrible sting of their defeat, will never, *never*, NEVER revert to a life deprived of freedom, because they have now tasted that most immeasurably precious of all human attributes, the right of the free man to stay free.

51

MacArthur ate almost nothing, but drank several cups of coffee with heaping spoonfuls of sugar. Part of the time he looked directly at us or his wife; part of the time he talked with his face gazing steadily, fixedly, out of the window to his right. What was he looking for, looking at?

How the Supreme Commander Works

The route from the Embassy to the Dai-Ichi takes five and a half minutes. A signal is given by a Japanese police officer after MacArthur's car, a black Cadillac bought in Manila before the war, leaves the Embassy grounds, and is passed on visually by one Japanese policeman to another, about thirty in all, as the car proceeds. All traffic is, as I have already mentioned, stopped. This does not cause so much dislocation as one might think, although the route traverses the heart of Tokyo. The route never varies. MacArthur's car observes the speed limit carefully, and obeys the traffic lights, which are turned to green manually as the car approaches. Only once was it stopped. That was when it happened to run into a crowd turning out to greet a visiting American baseball team; the Japanese are rabid baseball fans, and the throng in the streets disorganized all normal (even MacArthur) traffic.

The Dai-Ichi Building—literally "Dai-Ichi" means "Number One" or "First"—is a handsome structure facing the imperial moat, which once housed a leading Japanese insurance company. One curious item is that each floor has a contraption to be used as a fire escape—a kind of concealed tube, or chute; I do not think that any but a very small American could ever squeeze into it, since it was made to fit Japanese. MacArthur's office is on the sixth floor. It is not particularly big or pretentious. What need has he for a sumptuous office? All Japan is his office.

As a rule General Whitney, who has the office next door, is the first person he sees. And Whitney will already have telephoned him at the Embassy with a quick résumé of the morning's news. Whitney is supposed to be the only person who can knock on the Supreme Commander's door and enter without previous arrangement.

MacArthur almost never uses the telephone once he is in his office—indeed there is no telephone on his desk or even in his own room—has no secretary, and seldom dictates anything. He does his correspondence by scribbling in longhand, often on the back of the letter he is answering. He had about 300 cables from all over the world on his seventieth birthday; he wrote an individual acknowledgment of each. Or he simply orders one of his aides to prepare a communication. He writes his own speeches, laboriously and in longhand, after a staff member prepares a draft. He makes, as a rule, three important declarations of policy a year: on New Year's Day, the anniversary of the new constitution (May 3), and the anniversary of Japan's surrender. He seldom speaks in public, and hates to speak ad lib.

When he issues a statement Japanese newspapers are obliged to print it in full, without cuts. One odd point is that, reproducing anything from MacArthur, the Japanese (and local English) papers always print his name twice, once to represent his actual signature, once to confirm that the name was typed on the original document. "Douglas MacArthur" (signature) is printed in blackface, "DOUGLAS MACARTHUR" (nonsignature) in caps.

He reads all his own mail. This he insists upon. To preserve the spirit of his instructions, and at the same time save him effort, his aides slit open *half* the edge of each envelope addressed to him. He then rips it open, and proceeds to read. No letter addressed to him personally may be physically opened by anybody else. The General is from this point of view extremely accessible. All anybody needs do to gain his attention is to write a letter.

He is also reasonably accessible for meetings in the flesh to (a) important callers, (b) his own highest officers. But even important members of SCAP are held at a remote distance; for instance MacArthur never even met the official largely responsible for the purge of the *zaibatsu*. Generally his advisers will keep an outsider hanging

53

around for three or four days, so that he will have gathered something of the atmosphere of Japan and so not bother the General with naïve questions. A brief dossier on each visitor is prepared before the audience. His list of callers is never printed, and guests at the Embassy for lunch are never announced in the press. If a Japanese sees the Supreme Commander, it will be the Japanese who lets the news out. Cases have been known when a Japanese, a bit too forward, has announced in advance that he was to be received; if such premature publication results in embarrassment to anybody, the interview is likely to be cancelled.

MacArthur hates to receive women in his office, and only rarely does so. An essential part of his atmosphere is crisp aloofness.

He reads a great deal—newspapers, reports, documents, and the like. The New York *Times* is neatly marked for him when it arrives by air mail. His office even takes out, and dutifully pays for, subscriptions to the local Associated Press, United Press, and International News Service cable file, so that he can read everything, domestic or foreign, that the American news agencies put out. He listens to the radio occasionally, and sometimes will embarrass a member of his staff by telephoning from the Embassy at midnight and asking his interpretation of something he has just heard on the news.

His relations with his immediate staff are close, but formal; he will open a meeting by saying, "Gentlemen, sit down." He calls most of his advisers by their first names, but they do not reciprocate. He is always "Sir" or "General." (Plenty of people still call him "Douglas," friends from old days in Washington or Manila, but mostly these are civilians.) Generally his officers refer to him, when he is not present, as "Mac," "Old Mac," "The Old Man," or "the C. in C.;" some people call him "Bunny." In written memoranda he is almost invariably addressed as the Supreme Commander. Staff meetings are not held on regular schedule; he will simply ask to see officers, when the occasion warrants. He *can* be overruled, but it does not happen often, if only because few survive long who disagree with him. But he will listen carefully to any argument. Once or twice he has been known to say, "I think this decision is wrong, but we will go ahead with it, because I do not wish to go against my staff." His approach during a discussion is that of a judge; he probes with questions, provokes varying answers, never says No without reason, and despises those who agree with him too easily.

MacArthur's chief defect as administrator is that he tries to do too much himself. Like most clever people he is inclined to be distrustful. He wants to keep everything close in his own hands, and he passionately loves detail. He himself makes the decision even on such a matter as, say, whether or not a visitor will be housed at the Hotel Imperial, or, if not, where.

On MacArthur's wall hangs a large framed document, a lengthy quotation from Livy entitled *A Roman General's Opinion of 'Military Critics,'* which embodies the views of a certain Lucius Aemilius Paulus who fought the Macedonians in 168 B.C.

In every circle, and, truly, at every table, there are people who lead armies into Macedonia; who know where the camp ought to be placed; what posts ought to be occupied by troops; when and through what pass that territory should be entered; where magazines should be formed; how provisions should be conveyed by land and sea; and when it is proper to engage the enemy, when to lie quiet. And they not only determine what is best to be done, but if any thing is done in any other manner than what they have pointed out, they arraign the consul, as if he were on trial before them. These are great impediments to those who have the management of affairs . . . I am not one of those who think that commanders ought at no time to receive advice; on the contrary, I should deem that man more proud than wise, who regulated every proceeding by the standard of his own single judgment. What then is my opinion? That commanders should be counselled, chiefly by persons of known talent; by those who have made the art of war their particular study, and whose knowledge is derived from experience; from those who are present at the scene of action, who see the country, who see the enemy; who see the advantages that occasions offer, and who, like people embarked in the same ship, are sharers of the danger. If, therefore, any one thinks himself qualified to give advice respecting the war which I am to conduct, which may prove advantageous to the public, let him not refuse his assistance to the state, but let him come with me into Macedonia. He shall be furnished with a ship, a horse, a tent; even his travelling charges shall be defrayed. But if he thinks this too much trouble, and prefers the repose of a city life to the toils of war, let him not, on land, assume the office of a pilot. The city, in itself, furnishes abundance of topics for conversation; let it confine its passion for talking within its own precincts, and rest assured that we shall pay no attention to any councils but such as shall be framed within our camp.

This remarkable—but antique—memorial tells much about the Supreme Commander, and it is interesting that it should have such an honored place in his office, if only for the reason that many people think that his chief defect is that, for all his wisdom and benevolence, he does not understand the storms and stresses of the *modern* world.

Chapter Four

MORE ABOUT MACARTHUR
THE MAN

MACARTHUR'S qualities are so indisputably great in his own field that it comes as something of a shock to explore the record and find that in others he can be narrow, gullible, and curiously naïve. He is, we have noted, a *dedicated* person—dedicated to his own concept of duty, to the fulfillment of his mission, and to the defense of the United States—and he treads on unsure ground when he steps off the path of what he really knows. Consider his adventures in two unhappy realms—politics and the world of news.

He has, in effect, run for the Presidency twice. Shortly after his arrival in Australia in 1942 the first MacArthur boom got under way, stimulated in large part by the extreme right wing of the Republican party, and supported by many of the most obstinate, vengeful isolationists. When two separate commands were established in the Pacific his adherents were prompt to say that the Roosevelt administration was cutting down his authority in order to make him less imposing as a Presidential possibility. At about the same time a joint Army-Navy board passed a ruling (which still holds good) that no member of the armed forces, while on active duty, could campaign for political office. An officer might accept nomination for office provided it was tendered "without direct or indirect activity or solicitation on his part," but only at the cost of sacrificing his commission. The law stated that "any officer elected or appointed to a civil office thereby ceases to be an officer of the army."

On October 29, 1942, MacArthur issued a statement putting himself out of the race: "I have no political ambitions whatsoever. Any suggestion to the contrary must be regarded as merely amiable gestures of good will . . . I started as a soldier and I shall finish as one. If I survive the campaign, I shall return to that retirement from which this great struggle called me."

But as 1944 came closer the MacArthur movement, even though the General himself had cast it down, took on new life. Senator Vandenberg came out for him. He made a handsome showing in the Illinois primaries despite the fact that he never lifted a finger himself. But he was abruptly eliminated as a national candidate largely because of a *faux pas* by one of his most vociferous supporters, a freshman member of the House of Representatives named A. L. Miller. Little was known of Miller at the time, except that he came from Nebraska, was a doctor of medicine, and violently hated the New Deal.

Dr. Miller wrote MacArthur two letters, to which the General replied. Miller then proceeded to publish these without his knowledge or consent, though one at least of the replies was marked "Personal." Some excerpts from Miller's first letter, of date September 18, 1943, are the following:

There is a tremendous ground swell in this country against the New Deal. They have crucified themselves on the cross of too many unnecessary rules and regulations. . . .

You should . . . permit the people of the country to draft you . . . I am convinced that you will carry every state in the Union and this includes the Solid South.

Let your friends in this country nail to the cross the many vicious underhanded moves which will be started to smear and destroy you as a citizen and commander in the Pacific.

Undoubtedly this letter will be read and perhaps censored. The New Deal, including President Roosevelt, is scared to death of the movement in the country for you. Roosevelt will probably not even be a candidate if you be nominated.

I am certain that unless this New Deal can be stopped this time our American way of life is forever doomed.

MacArthur answered on October 2:

I thank you so sincerely for your fine letter . . . I do not anticipate in any way your flattering predictions, but I do *unreservedly agree with the complete wisdom and statesmanship* of your comments.

I knew your state well in the days of used-to-be. . . . Those days seem singularly carefree and happy compared to *the sinister drama of our present chaos and confusion.*

Then Miller wrote some months later:

I again want to tell you there is a tremendous revolution on in this country. It is more than a political revolution. It is a mass movement by the citizens who are displeased . . .

If this system of left wingers and New Dealism is continued another four years, I am certain that this Monarchy which is being established in America will destroy the rights of the common people.

There is no movement which attracts so much attention and so little criticism as the one that is labelled MacArthur for Commander in Chief and President of a free America. . . . It is going to take an individual who is fearless and willing to make political sacrifices to cut out the underbrush and help destroy this monstrosity . . . which is engulfing the nation and destroying free enterprise and every right of the individual.

MacArthur wrote back on February 11, 1944:

I appreciate very much your scholarly [*sic!*] letter of Jan. 27. Your description of conditions in the United States is a sobering one indeed and is calculated to arouse the thoughtful consideration of every true patriot.

We must not inadvertently slip into the same condition internally as the one which we fight externally. Like Abraham Lincoln, I am a firm believer in the people, and, if given the truth, they can be depended upon to meet any national crises. The great point is to bring before them the real facts.

These letters, when published, created a turbulent, brief storm. MacArthur had to defend himself on charges that his language to Miller was pretty childish, that if he thought that Miller's views were "statesmanlike" and "scholarly" he had no right to run for President, and that his implied criticism of his commander in chief was unwise. Almost everywhere it was felt that, at best, he had shown himself to be politically immature, and at worst had made a disastrous blunder. MacArthur, nettled, explained that his letters "were neither politically inspired nor intended to convey blanket approval of the Congressman's views." In other words, the General crawled. Then, "I entirely repudiate the sinister interpretation that they [the letters] were intended as a criticism of any political philosophy or of any personages in high office." But could not the General read?

It did not improve MacArthur's chances with many that the Hearst press started booming him with boresome violence at just about this time, and that the Chicago *Tribune* printed a new photograph of him with the inscription, "To Colonel McCormick, with the admiration and deep regard of his old comrade-in-arms, Douglas MacArthur."

Supporters of MacArthur at this time fell into several categories. (1) He was the symbol of everything the New Deal was not: America was Janus-headed at that time, and people who hated Roosevelt naturally fell into the camp directly opposite. FDR personified one conception of America, MacArthur the other. (2) Isolationists who loathed the European war supported the General vigorously, because they sympathized with the war against Japan. A bill actually reached Congress in 1944 proposing that MacArthur should receive, by force of law, *any*thing he asked for. The Japanese war was a much "simpler" war; we had been grossly attacked; there was no confusing nonsense about coalitions; the Yellow Peril was still a peril. (3) Ultrareactionaries liked MacArthur as a kind of potential *Führer* or Man on Horseback. They attacked FDR for being a dictator, but they wanted a dictator in the person of MacArthur—someone who would make "order," reduce taxes, sweep out the left, crack down on labor, make America "strong," and ensure profits for big business.

But there were not nearly enough people who felt this way to give MacArthur any serious chance. The upshot was that he formally declared on April 30, 1944, "I request that no action be taken that would link my name in any way with the nomination. I do not covet it, nor would I accept it." The MacArthur organizations disbanded and the boom collapsed, with minor squeaks. He got exactly one vote at the convention; this single vote kept the nomination of Mr. Dewey from being unanimous.

*

1948 was quite another story. MacArthur wanted the nomination, thought that he had a good chance for it, and permitted his candidacy to be openly presented. The "MacArthur for President" clubs got started again and proliferated, and a fantastic lot of toadstool reactionaries jumped on his bandwagon. MacArthur ended what dubiety there had been about his own attitude by issuing a formal statement on March 9, 1948, to the effect that he would not actively seek the Presidency, but would accept it if offered. "No man could fail to be profoundly stirred by such a public movement in this hour of momentous import, national and international, temporal and spiritual," he announced. "I can say, with due humility, that I would be recreant to all my concepts of good citizenship were I to shrink because of the hazards and responsibilities involved from accepting any public duty to which I might be called by the American people."

His name was put up for the Wisconsin primaries, and he sent several messages to his adherents there. One, to the chairman of a farm group, said that American farmers must be protected against oppressive government controls and the "inroads of despotic ideologies." Was MacArthur referring to the New Deal, or what? It is revealing that in this particular message he did not even sign his name, but called himself "Supreme Commander."

No single Republican of any serious distinction came out for MacArthur in 1948, which must have shocked the General grievously. A few isolationist Democrats, like Mayor Curley of Boston, did come out for him. Also the fact that "Veterans Against Mac-Arthur" clubs were formed by G.I.'s all over the country hurt him; many who had served under him, he discovered, still disliked his very name. Meantime the basis of his support, financially and otherwise (people put up a good deal of money for the Wisconsin campaign, though he himself probably did not know the details), was unappetizing to say the least—disgruntled newspaper owners, last-ditch American Firsters, millionaires on the make, and an assortment of tatterdemalion Roosevelt-haters. It is only fair to say that MacArthur himself had never been an overt isolationist. But the dregs of the old isolationist movement spread over and smeared his band wagon.

A point of picturesque interest nowadays is that one of Mac-Arthur's most vigorous Wisconsin opponents was none other than Senator Joseph R. McCarthy, who at that time was a Stassen man. Mr. McCarthy, comparatively unknown then but notorious today, sent his constituents thousands of letters denying that MacArthur was an authentic native son of Wisconsin, dredging up details of his first marriage and divorce, asserting that he was an old man ready for retirement, charging that he had spent fifty years in the Army and hence knew nothing of civilian affairs, and pointing out that he had been out of the United States so long that he could not adequately fill the role of President.

All this had strange repercussions in Japan. The dutiful Japanese hung Tokyo with signs, "We Japanese Want MacArthur for President," and proudly wore MacArthur emblems in their buttonholes. But they were not allowed to get full details of the campaign. Censorship of the local press still existed in Japan as of that date, and the supersensitive, nervous press officers on MacArthur's staff carefully screened what Tokyo should read. A dispatch reporting that responsible Republican newspapers like the New York *Sun*, the Denver *Post*, and the Buffalo *Evening News* called the General "a dark horse whose political views are unknown" and that he was "an enigmatic candidate" was held to be "objectionable" for publication in Japan. The biggest Japanese newspaper, the *Asahi*, was not permitted to reprint an editorial from the New York *Times* suggesting merely that "General MacArthur should speak out on the campaign issues."

These developments were, to an extent, not MacArthur's own fault. He was the victim, as he has been on several other occasions, of a wildly overzealous staff, members of which were not only sensitive themselves but terrified of the General's own sensitiveness. And Japanese editors were in a quandary, since they could not easily print American criticism of MacArthur without becoming subject to the ironclad rule in Japan forbidding criticism of the Supreme Commander. American news agencies were in a quandary too—when for instance the MacArthur press office complained that they gave their Japanese clients news of the formation of anti-MacArthur clubs in the United States. But this *was* news. The Columbia Broadcasting System polled nine correspondents in Tokyo about their forecast of press relations in the White House if Mac-Arthur became President. The replies were not sanguine. Shocked by this hubbub, the General then sensibly forbade any "political activity" at his headquarters; he said he would "slow up his pace" for photographers, but not pose for them. The confusion was such that SCAP finally worked out a compromise—news of the campaign could be printed in Japan so long as it was "factual."

MacArthur was roundly beaten in Wisconsin, getting only eight out of twenty-seven delegates. The General was, it seemed in Tokyo, disappointed and defiant. Two days later he cabled a lady who was president of the Nebraska-for-MacArthur organization that he was still definitely in the race. "You may be sure . . . that my statement of March 9, that I was available for any public duty to which I might be called by the American people, was not limited to any particular political test." But the MacArthur boom never recovered from the Wisconsin defeat. He ran fifth in the Nebraska primary, and only the Hearst papers kept the movement feebly alive until convention time. In June the General was put in nomination at

Philadelphia after midnight when the hall was empty; it was a forlorn spectacle. He got 11 votes out of 1,094 on the first ballot; these 11 sank to zero on the third. So does the American public turn sometimes on its heroes.

All this was greeted with polite, guarded amazement in Japan itself; the Japanese could not understand how "their" General should have experienced such a setback. The Tokyo correspondent of the New York *Times* wrote, "The shock to the Japanese . . . is probably greater because Japanese newspapers were forbidden by censors for the first few days after the announcement of MacArthur's availability to publish anything but favorable comment from the United States—giving the impression that the General was virtually without opposition."

A final word on this subject: many people in Tokyo think that MacArthur still has strong political ambitions, and has not given up hope, despite his age, for the Presidency in 1952.

MacArthur and the Press

For some years MacArthur was heartily unpopular with the newspaper colony in Tokyo—and vice versa. Nowadays relations are much better. The Supreme Commander did not have much use for journalists in the large anyway (though he was not above playing favorites among them) and his attitude seemed to be that the Tokyo correspondents were a gang of illiterate police reporters who should be subject to his orders.

Once Roy Howard visited Tokyo and MacArthur asked him why American newspapers gave such prominent space to crime news, scandals, and the like. As the Supreme Commander himself relates this anecdote, Mr. Howard's answer "completely floored" him. Howard said simply, "Douglas, American newspaper publishers and editors have to eat too." MacArthur thought that this answer, shunting off responsibility to the newspaper-buying public, was masterful. It did not occur to him that there are a good many newspaper publishers and editors who do not sensationalize and vulgar-

64

ize their front pages and who nevertheless manage to eat quite well. The proprietors of the New York *Times*, the Washington *Post*, the Washington *Star*, the New York *Herald Tribune*, the *Christian Science Monitor*, the Louisville *Courier-Journal*, the Baltimore *Sun*, and countless other good newspapers are not starving.

It is, oddly enough, some of these same sound and respectable newspapers that have at one time or other aroused the particular ire of the Supreme Commander. Once a distinguished visitor from the *Herald Tribune* was told coldly—and explicitly—by none other than General Whitney that she would not be "received" or otherwise assisted in Tokyo. Conversely MacArthur seems to go out of his way to applaud the sensationalists. He sent a telegram of condolence on the death of Capt. Joseph Medill Patterson, editor of the New York *Daily News*, that has to be read (with the eyes popping) to be believed. One sentence is, "Patterson threw his untiring energies and brilliant mind into the advancement of journalism, invincibly standing for *those higher ethics designed to ensure propagation of the truth.*" Whether this was the innocence of a backward child on MacArthur's part, or not, I do not know. When Mr. Hearst celebrated his eighty-seventh birthday in 1950, MacArthur telegraphed him, "As you round another year in the dedication of your firm voice, indomitable will, and great moral courage to the building of an invincible America in an uneasy world, I send my warm admiration and my gratitude."

MacArthur alienated a good many correspondents during the war not merely by his high-and-mightiness but because his communiqués did not always tell the truth. The censorship in his command made it incomparably more difficult to work there than, say, in Eisenhower's theater.

The General almost never holds press conferences, and correspondents stationed in Tokyo may find it difficult to see him at all. A new arrival for an important agency or paper is, however, received as a rule for a courtesy talk. But not always. For instance one bureau head for *Time-Life* (an organism highly favorable to

MacArthur and one which he customarily favors) was not received for many months, largely because the General resented so deeply an article in *Fortune* on "Scapitalism" that severely censured the economic policies of the occupation.

Only once has MacArthur visited the Tokyo Press Club—in 1947. He talked sitting down with candor and informality for an hour, and then a correspondent asked him, "General, may we ask questions?" "Certainly," he replied. "Is it on the record?" To everybody's surprise the General said "Yes," whereupon a violent scurry took place for paper and pencils. It was on this occasion—back in 1947 —that the Supreme Commander said that Japan was ready for a peace treaty "now." This remark was widely interpreted at the time as meaning that he thought that his job was more or less completed, and that he would return presently to the United States. Later it was explained that he meant, not "now," but "as soon as possible."

MacArthur may appear to be distant to journalists, but he is attentive in the extreme to what is written about him. If a correspondent in Tokyo gets a commission for a magazine article and takes a draft of it to SCAP, it will be read and checked with almost excessive care. There is no censorship nowadays, but the cable correspondence of correspondents may be read later. A lady correspondent new to Tokyo wrote a cable about Formosa just before the Korean war; two days later its substance had been transmitted back to SCAP and General Whitney himself called her in to administer enlightenment. Once, during the war, when MacArthur was at advance headquarters somewhere in the South Pacific, an Australian journalist brought him the manuscript of an article. The General took the greatest pains to read it, and at the end changed one word; he did not like "remote" in description of himself, and altered it to "austere."

(Perhaps I should interpolate at this point that nobody in Japan, from MacArthur down, ever put the slightest pressure on me while I was working there—except that of helpful courtesy—nor was the slightest suggestion ever made that I should submit what I was

66

writing to scrutiny of any kind. Doubtless this book will be greeted in Tokyo with pained silence, but I have written nothing except the exact truth of what I saw and felt. It will be interesting among other things to see whether SCAP permits what I write to be translated into Japanese.)

Newspapermen resident in the theater have had, on their side, several grievances. They did not like to be treated like G.I.'s, spies, or would-be courtiers. They found it disagreeable that the Supreme Commander was so inaccessible. They did not get along well with several of his press officers. One of these, General Frayne Baker, got into the habit of writing letters of protest to publishers or employers over the local correspondent's head; nothing could have been more calculated to make the whole press corps furious. General Baker saw the light and gave this up, however, when, after complaining to Edward R. Murrow of the Columbia Broadcasting System about William Costello, the Columbia representative in Tokyo, Mr. Murrow sent the tart reply, "Your letter has greatly increased our confidence in Mr. Costello's work."*

No American correspondent has, so far as I know, ever been expelled from Japan, but several have had grave difficulty getting back if for instance they left the theater on home leave or for assignments elsewhere. The most famous case in point is that of Compton Pakenham, the correspondent of *Newsweek*. Pakenham was charged with associating "with the wrong kind of Japanese" and "being critical of the occupation," partly because he wrote stories attacking SCAP's purge of the big industrialists. In other words a correspondent for a conservative organ got into trouble for taking what might be called a rightist attitude—something that some of MacArthur's radical detractors will find it hard to believe. It took *Newsweek* the better part of a year to get Pakenham back into Tokyo.

Also the MacArthur headquarters got into a crisis by a ruling

* Cf. "The MacArthur Censorship," by Robert P. Martin, *Nieman Reports*, April, 1948.

to the effect that any correspondent who left Japan—even temporarily—must forfeit his credentials and apply for accreditization all over again; moreover, his family, if he had one, must leave Army quarters. Struggle over this decree was carried all the way to Washington; in the end MacArthur was flatly overruled, and the regulations modified. Resentment over this and much else led to an open "revolt" of the Tokyo press corps. A manifesto was drawn up, charging that correspondents who did no more than report facts were subject to attack on security grounds; that the Tokyo police had raided the home of at least one newspaperman who had criticized the occupation and subjected him to threatening interrogation; and that members of SCAP tried to get correspondents fired. In conclusion, the newsmen asked the American Society of Newspaper Editors to investigate "intimidation, coercion, and censorship in Japan."

After this things went smoothly—more or less—till the Korean war. Several perfectly reputable reporters were barred from Korea during the first weeks of the war, on the charge that they "had given aid and comfort to the enemy"; actually, they had performed high patriotic service by writing the truth, which badly needed to be told, about American and South Korean weakness. Then the celebrated Miss Marguerite Higgins of the New York *Herald Tribune* was, by a stupid order, similarly barred; MacArthur promptly reversed the order. The officer thought to be responsible for much bad feeling with correspondents is Major General E. M. Almond, a hot-tempered southerner with little experience of the press (he commanded a Negro division in World War II), who was MacArthur's Chief of Staff and who later led the masterful operation at Inchon. A recent bulletin of the American War Correspondents Association prints an article about Almond, under the title "The Man Who Hates Correspondents," which reads in part, "Time and experience have proved that many of our difficulties boil down to the fact that General Almond has an organic hatred and distrust of all correspondents. It is next to impossible to reach Mac-

Arthur himself . . . but on normal yet important matters there is no one who can go over Almond's head and get at MacArthur."

A few weeks earlier, before the Korean war, Almond got into a fine fracas over the case of Frank Hawley, the Tokyo correspondent of the London *Times*. Hawley wrote a story, to which SCAP took severe exception, describing a Japanese communist demonstration which the police broke up; he stated that the police had violated an article of the constitution, and that some police officers, out of fear of later retaliation by the communists if they should ever form a government, had turned in their arms. General Almond took the unprecedented step of peremptorily summoning to his office Sir Alvary D. F. Gascoigne, the chief of the British Mission in Japan—what is more, he summoned him from amidst his guests at a party at the British Embassy celebrating the King's birthday, than which no procedure could have been more tactless—and notified him that Hawley had displeased the Supreme Commander and was "persona non grata." Almond's rage during this interview has been vividly described, particularly when the imperturbable Sir Alvary, than whom no man is more imperturbable, responded that His Majesty's Britannic Government had nothing whatever to do with the London *Times*, and that the Foreign Office could not possibly be asked to withdraw Mr. Hawley from his post. The upshot was a confused medley of protests, statements, and counterstatements. The London *Times* refused to withdraw Hawley, and Almond had to eat his words. But not before he had a stormy interview with Hawley himself, in which he went so far as to state that any correspondent who wrote dispatches contrary to SCAP policy would be classified as a *security* risk and would be subject to expulsion. Hawley was, however, not expelled.

*

People sometimes say that MacArthur has a "Gestapo." This is nonsense of course. Nothing remotely like Hitler's Gestapo or the Russian secret police exists in Japan—the idea is wholly unthinkable—but just the same pretty nearly everything about everybody *is* known in Tokyo. There is no censorship of the mail or telephone, and I do not know what agents may, or may not, be employed by G-2 or Government Section or, for that matter, what the role is of the Japanese police. But little goes on that SCAP does not hear about.

Even in the most innocent of fields people may be carefully watched. When my wife and I wandered alone about Tokyo I am certain that we were not followed, and I know that we talked to some people SCAP did not particularly care to have us meet, without SCAP's knowledge. On the other hand the correspondent of an important American newspaper (an extremely conservative newspaper at that) went to Kyoto for a trip recently; within a week, every Japanese he called on was interrogated by Japanese detectives. My friend was furious, and made a bitter complaint to SCAP, which utterly denied any knowledge of (or complicity in) the event.

Theoretically no censorship of any kind exists in Japan any more. General Whitney told me that in the whole history of the occupation only two books were not allowed to be translated into Japanese, *Mirror for Americans: Japan*, by Helen Mears, and *The Case of General Yamashita*, by Frank Reel. (SCAP doesn't like Miss Mears, and MacArthur himself once took the trouble to write a letter to Ben Hibbs, the editor of the *Saturday Evening Post*, protesting at one of her articles.) In April, 1948, the Author's League of America announced in New York that four books by Edgar Snow—also John Hersey's *Hiroshima*—had been refused publication in Japanese. MacArthur vigorously cabled back that this was untrue, and blamed "a maliciously false propaganda campaign" for the rumor, which aimed at producing "the completely fallacious impression that an arbitrary and vicious form of censorship exists here, whereas American literature, even though critical of the occupation, is subjected to no censorship control whatever."

A minor SCAP official once held up the license for the translation of Mr. Churchill's memoirs some months, for a reason nobody has ever been able to figure out. Churchill's agent finally got to Mac-

Arthur himself to protest; of course the General had never known anything about the matter, and the license was granted within an hour.

Men Around MacArthur

There are, as they say in Tokyo, three "doorways" to the Supreme Commander. One is Col. L. E. ("Larry") Bunker, his chief aide, the channel for diplomatic contacts and the like. The second, for strictly military matters, is the Chief of Staff. The third, and most important, is Brig. Gen. Courtney Whitney, his chief political adviser and, so to speak, his secretary of state.

Whitney and Bunker are both very close to MacArthur; on a personal rather than an official level several others are almost as close, like Mrs. Gibbons, Colonel Huff ("Old Sid," who has been in his service longer than anybody else), and Major Anthony Story, the pilot of his private plane, once the *Bataan* and now the *Scap*. Then there are others, again on a different level, like Maj. Gen. Charles A. Willoughby, his chief of G-2 and an extremely picturesque officer, and Maj. Gen. William F. Marquat who is the accomplished head of scap's Economic and Scientific Section.

Some of those intimate with the General are known as members of the "Bataan Crowd" or "Bataan Gang"; i.e., they were with the Supreme Commander in Manila at the outbreak of war or before. The highest eminence in this restricted circle belonged, naturally, to those whom MacArthur took out with him on the flight from Corregidor. Incidentally, officers who *stayed* in the Philippines, under General Wainwright, never had much of a subsequent career with MacArthur. The original Bataaners have thinned out. Huff was in the General's party, and so were Willoughby and Marquat, but these are the only ones of consequence left. Whitney knew MacArthur closely in Manila, and in fact was his lawyer there, but he was in the United States when war broke out. Similarly, though his service dates back, Bunker (also a lawyer) was not of the original Bataan group.

71

These men, though their names are hardly known in America, are important to all Americans—especially since the Korean war. Their distinguishing mark is reverence—even adoration—of the Supreme Commander. I heard one of them say, with perfect genuineness, when I asked him about MacArthur's character, "I honestly can't tell you anything. He's too enormous, too unpredictable. I don't really understand him myself. No one could." Another told me, "I lived under his *domination* [sic] for so many years that I do not know what to say."

These officers are acute, lively men with strong personalities, and though their allegiance to the General binds them together they have sharp tensions and jealousies amongst themselves. MacArthur is perfectly aware of this, and feels in fact that such a situation is useful in that it drives each man to do his best. He is not above playing one off against another, and scap has its cliques and camarillas. But—a basic group fealty binds *every*body to MacArthur. One officer, who dislikes another heartily, will talk about his rival with a lofty sneer, "Of course the Old Man has to have that fellow— he needs somebody to do things that he wouldn't touch himself, or let *us* touch!" The most famous intramural feud is that between Willoughby (whose real name is Tscheppe-Weidenbach and who speaks with a strong German accent) and Whitney. Bunker, an adroit and sophisticated personage, is more friendly to Willoughby than to Whitney, but plays a lone, careful game. I asked somebody why neither Willoughby nor Whitney went to Marquat, the third member of the triumvirate, to use him as an ally against the other. Answer: "Probably they never thought of it. Anyway Marquat is such a nice guy he wouldn't play ball."

In another category are the strictly military men who serve MacArthur in his role as CINCFE, like General Walker, commanding officer of the Eighth Army; Admiral C. T. Joy, the navy commander; and two superb air officers, Lt. Gen. George E. Stratemeyer, boss of FEAF (Far Eastern Air Force), and the commander of the Fifth Air

Force, Maj. Gen. Earle ("Pat") Partridge, one of the ablest and most attractive airmen I ever met.

*

General Whitney, who is described as a "soldier-statesman" in biographical material prepared by SCAP, was born in Maryland in 1897. He is an exceptionally shrewd lawyer, with a sharp, fluent mind, who had a big corporation practice in Manila—where the MacArthurs first met him—in the 1930's. Before that he had been an Army officer; he resigned from the Army and lived in the Philippines from 1927 to 1940. He was on holiday in the United States in 1941, and reentered the armed services with a commission in the Air Corps. MacArthur summoned him to Australia in 1943, and they have been inseparable ever since. It was he who organized and directed the Filipino resistance movement against the Japanese after 1943, and who superintended the transfer of authority from the U.S. Army to the Philippine Commonwealth when the war was over. The Supreme Commander likes him so much because "their minds just meet." MacArthur never has to ask or explain anything twice; Whitney knows, as if by intuition, exactly what his master wants. Many in Tokyo dislike him almost as much as the General likes him, for the most part because they resent his role as *éminence grise*, and are jealous of his omniscient power.

General Marquat, the director of the economic life of Japan, is fifty-six. He was born in St. Louis, and brought up in Seattle; his personality is cheerful, vigorous, and modest. As a youngster he worked as a reporter on the Seattle *Times*, and for a brief period was its automobile editor; he told us that there is still printer's ink in his veins, and that "they spoiled a good newspaper man to make me a lousy officer." He is far from being a lousy officer. Marquat went into the Army in 1916 as a second lieutenant in the National Guard, and served well in France; with one intermission he has been an officer ever since. He told us that he was the only general in the Army, except MacArthur, who has never seen the Pentagon;

he has had only one brief period of home leave since 1937. General Marquat "just migrated" into being a specialist on antiaircraft, which was his function in the Philippines. People tell plenty of stories about him, mostly with affection, because he pays little attention to the jargon of his present field; once he is supposed to have turned to his first assistant during a heavy conference on economic affairs, saying "What *is* marginal economy, anyway?" Marquat has been chief of SCAP's Economic and Scientific Section since 1945.

General Willoughby is still another and very different type. This stupendous officer—he is tall and stout as an ox, with what seems to be a square yard of decorations on his cask-like chest—was born in Heidelberg, Germany, in 1892; his mother was an American, his father a German aristocrat. Naturalized as an American citizen in 1910, he assumed his mother's name. Nobody could be a more civilized host than Willoughby; with nobody in Tokyo is it possible to have more peppery arguments. He gives a note of the old Central Europe still—a man of the world, gay, clever, irreverent, and possessed of some remarkably parochial ideas. MacArthur is the only man in the world about whose opinion he cares anything. The Supreme Commander thinks that some of his eccentricities may be annoying, but he has complete confidence in him as an officer; Willoughby became his head of intelligence in 1941, and he has held this job ever since; the General has never had any other boss of G-2. Willoughby entered the Army at the bottom, and rose to be major general. He met MacArthur in the middle 1930's, when he was a captain teaching military history at Fort Leavenworth. Previously he had read carefully and admired MacArthur's annual reports as Chief of Staff—he likes to say debonairly that he is the only man in the entire Army *ever* to have read fully a report by a Chief of Staff—and had been the author of a column in the Army-Navy *Journal* which provoked correspondence with MacArthur. I asked Willoughby what chiefly impressed him about the General when they first met, and his answer was, "Not just his shiny boots." MacArthur took to him at first sight, and presently summoned him to the Philippines.

Willoughby encountered some extremely severe criticism when it seemed, early in December, 1950, that our forces in Korea were facing possible catastrophe as the result of Chinese intervention. Willoughby was responsible for what information MacArthur was receiving; most other sources of intelligence were frozen out. The blunders involved seem so monstrous (as of the moment this book goes to press) that it is wise to defer judgment till the whole story can be known. Yet nothing can minimize the fact that, a few days after MacArthur opened what he thought would be the final offensive of the war, up to the Yalu river, the American and United Nations forces walked blindly into huge Chinese armies (which were fully known to be there—they were not invisible) which not only halted our momentum, but pushed us back in as potentially grave a disaster as has ever afflicted American arms.

MacArthur is, as I have said, fanatically loyal to Willoughby and many other officers, and demands the most scrupulous loyalty in return. Loyalty breeds loyalty, up to a point. But he will not permit any abuse of privileges by an officer, and is constantly on the alert to see that he himself does not become a screen for anything improper.

Summing Up: Philosophy and Belief

MacArthur, a profoundly religious man, really believes in Christianity, which is one reason why, even in the face of possible disaster, he relishes his role as a defender of the Christian faith and way of life against the ravages of communism. Both he and his wife are Episcopalians. He does not, since he works every Sunday, attend church; his wife, accompanied by Arthur, goes in his place. As everybody knows he uses the word "God" frequently in his speeches. Of all the gifts and tributes that came to him on his last birthday, the one that pleased him most was an autographed portrait of the Pope. He even goes so far as to think of himself and the Pope as the two leading representatives of Christianity in the world today. The Pope fights on the spiritual front, so to speak, while he tackles communism on the ground.

MacArthur did attend a church ceremony when a memorial service was held for George Atcheson, his State Department advisor who was killed in an airplane crash in the Pacific. He asked one of his junior aides for a black arm band, and the aide replied that regulations forbade using such an arm band except for the President of the United States. MacArthur replied gently, "Listen, son, I'm wearing one."

I was privileged in Tokyo to read through the whole file of MacArthur's communications and pronouncements since the occupation began, and many of these touch, at least indirectly, on religious themes. He constantly associates Christianity with both democracy and patriotism. He wrote the editor of a religious journal in March, 1948:

I am absolutely convinced that true democracy can exist only on a spiritual foundation. It will endure when it rests firmly on the Christian conception of the individual and society.

At about the same time he addressed a communication to the editor of the Brooklyn *Tablet*, a strong Catholic organ:

We shall, of course, do all in our power to encourage study of the historical development of the Christian concept. As a powerful corollary is the fact that its rudimentary understanding will come from the living example of the application of its immutable tenets to which every phase of occupational policy is attuned—of which every member of the occupation force is a daily practitioner. . . . Through daily contact with our American men and women who are here engaged in the reshaping of Japan's future, there is penetrating into the Japanese mind the noble influences which find their origin and their inspiration in the American home. These influences are rapidly bearing fruit, and apart from the great numbers who are coming formally to embrace the Christian faith, a whole population is coming to understand, practice and cherish its underlying principles and ideals.

As to patriotism this is the concluding paragraph of a message sent to the Los Angeles *Examiner* in May, 1948:

And today, as on bended knee I so reaffirm my faith and rededicate myself, I humbly give thanks to Almighty God, the divine Father of us all, for that greatest of blessings, the birthright proudly to say—I am an American!

MacArthur believes, it goes without saying, in freedom of worship; later we shall go into his position vis-à-vis Shinto, the militant Japanese religion, on the one hand, and birth control (a great issue in Japan, which has its religious overtones) on the other. Once he had a Christian prime minister in Japan, by name Katayama; this pleased him greatly and he pointed out what a good augury it was for the future—the prophecy was somewhat rash—that three great countries in the Far East all had Christian leaders, the other two being Chiang Kai-shek in China (as of that date) and President Roxas of the Philippines.

To try to define the substance of MacArthur's political views, underneath his broad concept of democracy, is somewhat difficult. He would certainly resent being called a reactionary. He has a Wisconsin frontier heritage, and he dislikes heartily economic injustice and the abuse of privilege. In plain fact, though he once applauded the results of a Japanese election as showing a trend toward the "conservative philosophy of government," he considers himself to be a distinct liberal in many fields. He even said once that he hoped that after the occupation Japan would be "a little left of center." Above all he has the social optimism of the nineteenth century philosophers, and believes firmly in evolutionary progress by reform. On the other hand MacArthur is, of course, horrified if anybody thinks that he and SCAP are overtly leftist; he even took the trouble on one occasion in 1948 to write an indignant 1,600-word letter to a man in Idaho denying that he was an enemy of private enterprise. Once when he was about to receive the president of a celebrated university, he whispered to an aide, "Isn't the man somewhat pink?"

The following is from a SCAP memorandum summarizing the measures taken to break up the old feudal oligarchy, and defending MacArthur's policy. It is worth quoting for several reasons. The General's men hate him to be called a socialist, and, believe it or not, he was being attacked in the United States on just this ground:

77

The attack, spearheaded by *Newsweek*, used for its main vehicle a "confidential" report circulated by one Mr. James Lee Kauffman, lawyer, upon his return to the United States after a few weeks in Tokyo in August 1947 as technical advisor on reparations and restitution matters to SCAP's Civil Property Custodian. Kauffman's report attacked a number of Occupation policies, such as the emancipation of labor and the purge of militarists but turned its heaviest guns on the program to dissolve the combines. . . . The Kauffman report must be read in full . . . to reveal the reckless misuse and misinterpretation of language utilized in the attack. According to this report, General MacArthur's staff, packed with an assortment of impractical theorists, "refugees from the New Deal" and military men who know nothing about economics, was engaged in a "great experiment," the object of which was to turn Japan into a Socialist State. The Japanese economy was being recklessly fractionalized, recovery was being delayed and the taxpayers of the U. S. were being saddled with great unnecessary costs. [Then SCAP proceeds to answer Mr. Kauffman, point by point.]

Above all MacArthur is interested in democracy not in the abstract but in Japan. He said in his 1950 New Year's Day message:

The myth of an unbridgeable gulf between the ways of the East and the ways of the West has been thoroughly exploded by the lesson of experience. . . . For men now know that humanity, whatever the origin, race or cultural environment, is fundamentally the same in the impelling universal desire for higher personal dignity, broader individual liberty and a betterment of life.

And in his third anniversary message commemorating the new Japanese constitution:

Above all, there has been [in Japan] an increasingly healthy awareness and acceptance of that individual political responsibility which exists where sovereignty rests with the people. In this, indeed, lies best assurance for Japan's continued advance as an exponent and practitioner of repre-sentative democracy. *And as Japan goes, so in due time may go all of Asia.* For men will come to see in Japan's bill of rights and resulting social progress the antidote to many of Asia's basic ills. If Japan proceeds firmly and wisely upon the course now set, its way may well become the Asian way, leading to the ultimate goal of all men—individual liberty and personal dignity—and history may finally point to the Japanese Constitution as the Magna Charta of Free Asia.

Let us reiterate in conclusion MacArthur's loftiness and sense of justice. After all he does not claim to be a philosopher, and his views on politics in the abstract may lack precision, but no one should doubt his tenacious and indisputable idealism. The loftiness does genuinely come from within; he is that rare thing in the modern world, a genuinely *high* person. This is not put on. It is part of his marrow and essence, and this is one reason why he is such an exciting man to meet.

*

But it is time now to turn to the theater where the multifarious MacArthur talents and predilections are displayed—in Japan and Tokyo today.

Chapter Five

TOKYO TODAY

THE first Japanese I met in Tokyo was a youngish newspaperman who had gone to an American university. He told me, "Never believe anything that any Japanese ever tells you. Even I cannot know when my compatriots are telling the truth."

That day we had lunch with a veteran American correspondent. He said, "You never know the whole story, when dealing with a Japanese."

That afternoon we had tea with an American admiral who declared, "Nothing you have ever heard about these people is true. They simply do not think the way we do. It is because of their religion and aesthetic sense. Often they do not tell the truth because the truth may be so ugly."

Now with all respect to these worthy informants and others I would beg to put in a small disclaimer. We may have been lied to often but, in general, we got much the same point of view from almost all the Japanese we met, and it is hard to believe that the entire nation had been secretly mobilized into a conspiracy to deceive us. Nor could anybody keep us from seeing what we wanted to see, which was a lot.

I have never been particularly partial to the Japanese, but on this trip I found them much changed and chastened—a difficult and prickly people perhaps, but full of admirable qualities, of the greatest importance to us in these days of acute crisis in Asia, and, so far as we were concerned at least, intensely hospitable, eager to be informed, industrious, polite, and equipped with a surprising amount of agility and charm.

Hotel Imperial

There is no such thing as a freely available hotel room in Tokyo; all living space is controlled by SCAP and everybody lives in billets. If you are lucky enough to have a V.I.P. status, life is comfortable. Several friends met us at Haneda Airport at 2:30 in the morning, and, after a period of amiable confusion, whisked us into town in a nimble Army limousine. I did not know till we arrived where we were to be put up, and naturally it was a pleasant surprise to find that we had rooms in the Hotel Imperial, which is normally restricted to senior officers and a few civilians.

The Visitors Bureau, under the friendly, efficient direction of Col. L. G. Clarke, has headquarters just off the lobby, and by a flick of the finger it will turn Tokyo inside out for you.

The Hotel Imperial is a very odd hotel indeed. It was, as everybody knows, built by one of the greatest of all architects, Frank Lloyd Wright, and, an important consideration in Japan, is earthquake proof. The story is that Wright built it on a bed of vaseline, so that if a shock comes, the building simply oscillates back and forth. (As a matter of fact I myself happened to be in the Hotel Imperial during an earthquake years ago and this is exactly what happened, though I do not vouch for the vaseline.) In architecture and décor the Imperial—with all respect to Mr. Wright—is a kind of Aztec or Mayan nightmare, full of protruding cornices, lumps of rough lava, lights hidden behind stones, doors that don't open, miniature furniture, and thousands of small, eccentrically designed windows which do everything except give light. Wright, people told us in Tokyo, was new to Japan and thought that he was building in the Japanese style when he created the Imperial. He was wrong. But he learned a lot about Japan during his stay, and when he returned to the United States he designed a number of buildings that do have a Japanese style and spirit, with wide windows, spacious clear walls, and an uncluttered atmosphere of harmony.

Almost at once the visitor to the Imperial learns about Army nomenclature. On the bulletin board I saw the following announcement:

GENERAL HEADQUARTERS
FAR EASTERN COMMAND
OFFICE OF CHIEF OF STAFF

Office Memo				Date
Record of Conversation				Time
Subject				Group
To	From	Name	Section	Phone

Message:
Iris flowers in the Meiji Shrine Park will be in bloom between the 10th of June and the beginning of July from hours 0800 to 1600.

Outside the hotel is a neatly framed document in English and Japanese, the instruction to the sentry:

1. My post is located at the front door of the Hotel Imperial.
2. My post is maintained 24 hours a day.
3. My primary mission is to prevent unauthorized persons from entering.
4. The only persons authorized are occupation personnel of the Hotel.

In orange ink at the top of the telephone book in every room is the following notice:

No security against line-tapping and listening in is afforded by the telephone. The use of this instrument in discussing classified matters should be governed accordingly.

Even the walls of the bedrooms assigned to major generals, I found, are stenciled (not just printed but actually stenciled) NO SMOKING IN BED.

Getting money is a process. You go to the front desk and exchange American Express checks (the use of actual U.S. currency is forbidden) into Army scrip. With this you buy $5 chit books, in denominations of 10 cents (red) and 5 cents (white) in a green cover, which pay for drinks or snacks. Next you get white meal tickets for 44 cents each; with these you buy breakfast, lunch and dinner in the regular dining room, the price of meals being 44 cents no matter what. Finally, if you wish to buy yen—Japanese currency —you may do so by converting military payment certificates at the official rate, 360 to the dollar.

One day in the PX I happened to pull out of my wallet a forbidden $5 bill. An Army wife standing in line burbled in astonishment, "My goodness, I haven't seen actual American money for three years!"

The Imperial is cheap; the best suite it can provide will come to about $4—a week! In the bar a cup of soup costs 10 cents, a cup of tea 5 cents, ham and eggs 25 cents, a dry Martini 20 cents, and a bottle of good Scotch $2.20. Incidentally—I have the menu before me now and can prove it—the chief eating place is called the "Main Dinning Room." Some items are marked with asterisks, which indicates that they are not American in origin, but have been procured "from approved indigenous food outlets," that is, may be presumed not to be poisonous even if Japanese. Actually the meals in the main restaurant run a gamut from the merely obnoxious to the horrible. But an à la carte restaurant exists in the Imperial, called the Maison Française, where a heavily elaborate seven-course meal is served at astonishingly low prices—the full lunch is 50 cents.

Japanese are of course not allowed inside the Imperial except as guests in somebody's room, and are seldom seen. They are not permitted in the public rooms or restaurants. I will not forget how, when a sedate, dignified old Japanese gentleman called on us the first day, we had to sign for him as if he were a criminal.

First Impressions of Tokyo

Between 60 and 65 per cent of all buildings in Tokyo, a city with more than six million people, were destroyed during the war and large sections were completely gutted, yet there is little concrete indication of destruction today. At first I thought that the reports of damage caused by our great fire raids must have been exaggerated. We drove for miles through streets that showed no signs of damage whatever; I assumed that these had never been hit, but I was wrong. They were hit—and badly—but the methodical and busy-bee Japanese have rebuilt at such a pace that few scars remain. We lunched one day in a house, formerly belonging to the Mitsuis, that had twenty-three bomb hits; nothing untoward was visible. Of course it is comparatively easy to rebuild quickly in residential areas of Tokyo and elsewhere in Japan, since almost everything is made of wood.

Next, any visitor will see at once the obvious evidences of Americanization. Parts of Tokyo look as Oriental as Peoria, Illinois. Many streets have been given American names—Avenue B, Sycamore Street, and so on—and are identified by black and yellow signs. A few main arteries like the Ginza retain their Japanese names; hence you see oddities at intersections like signs reading "12th St.—Hashimoto Avenue." Houses in Japan are not numbered —I would hate to be a Tokyo postman—and so nowadays all those occupied by Americans have their own numbers—House No. 26, House No. 107 and so on; for instance General Whitney lives in No. 330, Mr. Sebald in No. 525. The numbers have no relation to seniority or even to geography. Big buses rumble up the streets marked "Red Route B" and "Black Route A," so that G.I.'s can find their way around; such phenomena exist as Doolittle Park, Washington Heights, and the Roosevelt Recreation Area; drive-in bakeries, milk bars, and filling stations look like Boston or Sacramento. The streetcars are marked with signs in Japanese and English, "DDT," to show that they have been sprayed; at one busy corner something called a "Death-o-Meter" registers the number of traffic accidents; and everybody laughs at the conspicuous signs before headquarters buildings, PARKING FOR GENERAL OFFICERS ONLY.

The fantastic charcoal-burning taxis with a stove tied on behind and buckets full of wood for fuel, chugging, hissing, steaming, and

84

all but blowing up in clouds of smoke; the pedicabs or bicycle rickshaws, colored white; children carried on their mothers' backs like papooses, and women clamping along in wooden clogs; occasional bright kimonos and the barefoot newsboys ringing a bell to announce an extra—such items present some Asiatic touches. The portable ramshackle stalls on the Ginza, under their long awnings, are as crowded as they ever were. You can buy anything from a refrigerator to a miniature camera, from ingenious toys to cigarettes—the two most popular brands are, significantly enough, named "Peace" and "Happy."

Japanese shop signs seem to be what they always were—a picnic. Some of the more famous have passed into legend like:

CURIOUS ANTICS (the shopkeeper meant "Curios and Antiques")
PEARLS, CURIOS, AND FRESH FISH
OFF LIMITS—VENEREAL DISEASE—WELCOME FOREIGN TRADERS!

Some that I saw were "Forgive and Forget, Swan Radio Company," "Curb Service for Shrimps," a hospital called the "Digestive Clinic," and a sign near the Imperial, "Doctor of Births and Skin." One American lady was stunned recently at finding "Sanitary Manure Only" in the American commissary, next to piles of fresh vegetables.

The weirdest use of English we encountered was in a new, excellent French-Japanese restaurant; here are some items on the menu:

SKEWERD OR GILLED LAMB
SAUTED OF MASHROMS
CUSTARED PUDDING
ASSOARTED FRUT

One thing impressive is the technique of the traffic cops. They faithfully imitate and exaggerate the gestures of our MP's, and have transformed the simple process of stopping a line of cars into something that is a cross between a dance by Isadora Duncan and calisthenics by an Indian contortionist. The effect is heightened at

85

night when the modern cop, operating at a modern intersection, directs traffic with a paper lantern illuminated by a candle. One joke in Tokyo is that everybody will know that the occupation is really over when a Japanese cop first dares to arrest an American for a traffic violation.

Night life is copious and lively. The Japanese get drunk easily and when they drink, they make noise. There must be at least 10,000 bars and *boîtes de nuit* in Tokyo, and some are as rough as anything I ever saw, Port Said and Marseilles included. The Yoshiwara is still going full blast (of course it is off limits to G.I.'s); prostitution is a tremendous business in Japan. The signs enticing customers into the bars have quality; we passed one equivalent of the Stork Club that called itself "EXOTIC," "PLENTIFULLY," "SHARMING," and "BOTTOMLESS." I still have a program from the Cabaret Mimatsu; I am staggered by what it says but here it is before my eyes:

GIRL'S CHARGES
¥   300.00 per head
¥   500.00 per two or three girls
¥ 1,000.00 per five girls
Boy's Service Charge Included in Bill.

One day we went to the Kabuki theater, and between the acts met two of its most celebrated players, Ennosuke and Mitsugoro. The theater was jammed; it holds 2,500 people; we were the only Americans there, though the Kabuki is not off limits. The Japanese audience moans, howls, and shrieks as the fantastic pantomime proceeds; we thought we were seated among savages. On the way out I saw the single most astonishing thing that I ran into in Japan—a tall half-naked man holding a banner aloft and advertising something by means of large Japanese characters painted on his naked chest. He was the son of an admiral and he gets good pay for this display—1,000 yen a day.

We proceeded to visit "Theater Street" in the Asakusa district, saw some tawdry American-style burlesque, and went on to a dinner party where we met two of the leading movie stars of Japan—Miss

86

Kinuyo Tanaka (teen-age daughters of American generals admire her greatly, as does the entire populace of Tokyo) and Miss Hideko Takamine, who is younger, an ingénue type, and practically the prettiest girl anybody ever met. They told us the plot of their new picture, *Powdered Snow*; it deals with sisters of a family in Osaka once rich, who have to adjust themselves painfully to the rigors and uncertainties of the modern world.

Japanese dinners, with their calm ritual, are a story in themselves. We went to half a dozen, of the most varied kinds, and loved every minute of every one.

Interviews and Letters

I have had half a dozen books translated and published in Japanese, some before the war and some after; hence we had the good fortune to meet many Japanese publishers, editors, authors, young intellectuals, artists and the like. Also I was interviewed a good many times, with results somewhat astonishing. Here is a translation of one in Kyoto, as prepared by the youthful Japanese (he was an ardent admirer of T. S. Eliot) who accompanied us most of the time we were there:

Since Mr. Gunther came to Japan, who is very famouse writter as a author of the "Insight of America," he met General MacArthur, and the top officers of G.H.Q. and had interview with the prime minister, Sigeru Yosida, chair man of parliament, Kijuro Shidehara, and visited the visiting places, Hakone and Nikko. He arrived at Kyoto on the 20th, at 5:30 a.m.

On that day, by the guide of Mr. Nishi who had receipt of the wire from Prime Minister, Yoshida, he visited Zohiko, Inaba, Yokoyama, and another curious stores. Mr. and Mrs. Gunther stay at Japanese Hotel, Tawaraya, and firstly had a night at Japanese Hotel. He said, "I came to Japan, having the purpose to write the Japanese condition after surrender. I will publish a book entitled the "Insight of Japan" on next January. In that book I'll write that in what way democratization in Japan has been doing. American people does not hope to keep the occupation for a long time. But Japanese conditions under the occupation of the American army are much better than those of Germany. Communism is the child of poverty, so that, the Communism in Japan depends upon the economic condition.

Japanese rooms are very comfortable and wonderful. Breakfast in Japa-

87

nese style is very delicious, which is at the first experience for me. But I and my wife are surpride that some rats run on the ceiling through a night.

We got many letters from Japanese, which taught me much. The day after we arrived, the night porter at the Imperial telephoned our room saying that a Japanese was calling on us in the lobby. It was midnight and I was half undressed. But I put on shoes and a jacket and went down and found that my caller had prepared for me a seven-page letter in exquisite handwriting. He refused to enter the hotel proper on the ground that he was "not fit to be seen," and indeed he looked grimy, with shabby clothes. He spoke perfect English, and had been educated at Columbia. The gist of the letter which he asked me to read while standing in the deserted lobby was that I should accompany him to some of the "shadow places," the "dark places" and slums, so that I could see for myself what Japanese poverty was like. I asked him to come around the next day. Early in the morning a second letter came, shorter but to the same effect; it announced that my caller would wait for me on a bench in the park opposite the hotel. I was busy and could not get there. The next morning at 7:30 came another message containing the single somewhat menacing sentence, "I am waiting at the appointed place." Finally I got hold of him and we talked for a while. Thereupon he said he would take a walking trip through Japan to send me daily reports by postcard on what he saw. But only one postcard ever came. Its sensible gist was what his other communications had suggested—that I should keep my eyes open, remember that Japan was an appallingly poor country, and see something of the economic misery that gripped the great mass of the population.

One letter we received began, "My brother was executed as a war criminal"; another, "I am a purged school teacher." Several correspondents asked me to excuse them for their "audacity" in daring to write me, and half a dozen enclosed long manuscripts and told the stories of their lives. They prayed for my good health, offered to set up secret means of communication with me, and suggested titles for my new book, among them *A Peep Hole Through Paper Screen* and *Through MacArthur's Buttonhole*.

One letter from a writer (in English) said:

No doubt you have enough routes to get materials, but can't I be of a little help to you on one point—that is, about the underneath psychology of the common Japanese people. I, myself, not a person of any publicity, but a most commonplace citizen, can boast to understand this psychology most well.

Another:

I am just an ordinary uneducated man, 53 years old. I have no vices for drinking, smoking, and women for the past twenty-five years. . . . I sincerely hope your tenacious business as an excellent journalist, and I never doubt almost all Japanese is expecting your advice for the path of this nation.

The most interesting of all came from a retired banker, who wrote that he was sorry for the sorrowful plight of his nation "but I am enduring the misery with no grievance against anybody, accepting it as a punishment for the folly committed by our country, for which every adult Japanese must be responsible," and expressing the view that the trouble with MacArthur was that he did not "impose" democracy with a strong enough "overall discipline." He wrote about the land reform, saying that at first he thought this revolutionary undertaking would weaken Japan "by bringing down the social position of landowners of conservative inclination," but that he now understands its wisdom, even though he himself is a sufferer as an absentee landlord. The Japanese people, he went on, were in "a stupor" as a result of their defeat, and he feared that they would inevitably turn left. He heard the news of the end of the war with "mingled feelings of sorrow and relief," and "has never been oppressed by the presence of the American army." But:

I have seen an American soldier running on a jeep was brutally chastising a Japanese who had crossed right ahead of the jeep, notwithstanding his repeated submissive apologies. It was very hard for me to see the sight without being able to interfere with the soldier because of my being a vanquished nation.

It is not unusual case that American soldiers are smoking in a bus or street car where smoking is prohibited or dead drunk making passengers unpleasant. It is hard for me to have to overlook the misconducts because of their being the occupation army. They are likely young men of around twenty, so it is too much to hope perfect conducts to them. But, American soldiers should know that they are looked upon here as the specimen of a democratic man.

The author of this letter was particularly illuminating about the position of the Emperor. "Every Japanese with the exception of communists is very much grateful to the Allied Powers for allowing Japan to retain the Emperor as her symbol. I cannot imagine Japan without the Emperor, though I do not know why." He proceeds to say that he attended the palace celebrations on the Emperor's last birthday. "The Emperor returned our salutations, waving his hat to all around. It was indeed an impressive scene. I felt the Emperor very near to us; I thought of him as our own, not as a person above the cloud as he used to be." The Emperor, he feels, is himself a much happier man nowadays, because he can behave like a normal man, "though he may be afflicted with his sorrowful fate of bringing Japan to the present unhappy predicament."

And as to MacArthur:

What impressed me most is that the general does not make himself conspicuous at all, leading a very quiet life. . . . Except being out to Haneda air port to greet notables, I have not heard of his having ever been out. He seems to be denying himself every pleasure outside of his home. Mrs. MacArthur goes to the theater, attends party and sometimes goes on a trip. But the general never does. He reminds me of a stern Japanese warrior of the olden times. Such may be the nature of the general. But his self-denying life cannot but contribute to win the respect of the Japanese.

The mood of these letters was interesting in the extreme to me, though it is dangerous to generalize from such small particulars. I got a sense of humble, well-meaning people in total ferment—people who were undergoing a profound spiritual crisis, who wanted

90

intellectual succor and emotional advice, people who, having survived one terrible catastrophe, were exhausting their last emotional reserves in a desperate effort to stave off another, in the hope that they could somehow manage to achieve stability.

What a Japanese Cannot Do in Tokyo

No Japanese is allowed into the Imperial or other billets reserved for SCAP personnel. No Japanese may take one of the comfortable new taxis which are neatly marked "Foreigners' Cab." No Japanese may go into a PX or the American commissary. (But, to be fair, one should mention that no American civilian would be allowed in a PX in the United States.) No Japanese may go to a G.I. movie or carry G.I. money. No Japanese may shop at the foreign traders' stores or in the Imperial Arcade. He can move around the country —within Japan—more freely than before the war, but he is not allowed to leave Japan itself without permission.

Several of the express trains across Japan are reserved for occupation personnel only, and most suburban trains carry one first-class car from which Japanese are excluded.

What a G.I. Cannot Do in Tokyo

G.I.'s are not permitted to go into any bars or night clubs unless they are specifically marked "On Limits," and these are few. All over Tokyo are signs, "Not Approved for Military Personnel." G.I.'s are not allowed to stay in a Japanese house after 11 P.M. except by permission of the commanding officer. Americans (and this applies to officers as well as G.I.'s) have recently been permitted for the first time to eat "indigenous" (i.e., Japanese) food if they buy it in the shops, take it home and cook it themselves, but they are not allowed, by and large, to go into Japanese restaurants—that is, they cannot eat indigenous food prepared by the indigenous.

The order forbidding Americans to eat Japanese food illustrates sharply one aspect of MacArthur's subtle genius as an administrator. It was done not merely as a sanitary precaution (dysentery was rife in the early days) but to forestall any charge of exploitation

91

The principle was established at once that Americans should provide all their own food and thus take none from the Japanese, who are a food-short and hungry people.

Sometimes a G.I. with a drink under his belt will behave badly in a crowded train, as indicated above, but this is rare, and getting rarer; most members of the occupation have behaved with propriety and rectitude. Should any American assault or otherwise molest a Japanese, punishment is severe if he is caught. To slap a Japanese publicly could bring an American a sentence as stiff as five years. While I was in Tokyo a cavalry private was found guilty of forceful entry into a Japanese tea-house and armed robbery. He took ¥ 500 ($1.30) from one Japanese and ¥ 23 (6½ cents) from another. The private was sentenced to ten years at hard labor and was dishonorably discharged.

Fraternization

MacArthur's attitude toward fraternization is quite simple—that soldiers will be soldiers no matter what, and that people of different nationalities ought to get to know one another. Hence fraternization was never forbidden in Japan and in fact there has been only one public pronouncement about it in the whole history of the occupation. This was an early order by General Eichelberger that there should be no "public display" of affection between Americans and Japanese. Actually, this order is mildly violated all the time. In Gifu, where a Negro regiment was stationed before the Korean war, we saw black G.I.'s and pretty Japanese girls driving in pedicabs together and otherwise being companionable.

Intermarriage between members of the occupation and Japanese is not forbidden but it is certainly not encouraged. Most such marriages that have taken place were between Japanese girls and Nisei.

American Attitude to the Japanese and Vice Versa

Odd and striking as the point may seem, most Americans in Japan appear to have forgotten completely that the Japanese were ever our implacable, mortal enemies; there is practically no evidence of hostility, resentment, or even suspicion. This is not to say that Americans by and large actually *like* the Japanese, nor do they understand them well; most are baffled day by day by peculiarities in Japanese behavior. And indeed the Japanese are a profoundly impenetrable people.

Most Americans find them very slow. They find them dull—and, as I heard it nicely put, it is indeed true that most Japanese are dull *in English*. Scarcely a handful of Americans in Tokyo have bothered to learn even a few words of the Japanese language. Many Americans are arrogant; I even heard one occupationer snort, "They really ought to do something about fireproofing. We burn down their

THIS IS THE WAY THE WORD "DEMOCRACY" LOOKS IN JAPANESE.

hotels all the time." MacArthur himself is an exception, but many of his men seem completely out of touch with what is going on. Our motives are worthy, but nobody makes much attempt to get out into the grass roots, see and learn, and find out something about Japanese *people*. The Americans came in with the attitude, "We'll show 'em!" but this is not enough. SCAP ought to have a section called "How to Understand the Japanese."

Of course—to repeat—they *are* distressingly hard to understand. How is the average American to cope with an Osaka businessman who says proudly, "Come and see the magnificent damage you did

93

to our unworthy docks!" It takes some time to get on to the fact that, if you ask a Japanese a direct question, such as "Do you like beefsteak?" his answer may well be, "In the French literature of the eighteenth century much attention is paid to food."

At a cocktail party one day, in a luxurious house occupied by an American officer, we met a chic, cultivated Japanese lady. We admired the house and then discovered that it was her own! This was the first time she had been in it since she was dispossessed three years before, and her eyes were alive with polite curiosity. When an occupationer takes over a Japanese house the Japanese owner is duly recompensed, of course, but the compensation is paid for by the Japanese government, not by the Americans. At this same party another guest was the widow of a distinguished Japanese general killed in the war. In the same room were American officers of the squadron that had shot him down. No one paid attention.

Free social contact between Americans and Japanese is, however, comparatively rare. If a SCAP official conspicuously entertains Japanese over a long period, he is likely to be rebuked. Even those Americans prepared to risk this and who admire the Japanese seldom give hospitality to their Tokyo friends because almost all Japanese are too poor to reciprocate; it is an acute embarrassment to a sensitive Japanese to be asked out to lunch if he knows he will never be able to pay it back. Take an official as important as the secretary to the prime minister. His salary is forty dollars a month. You cannot do much entertaining on that, particularly if you have a lot of children, as almost all Japanese have.

It horrified our American friends in Tokyo when we announced that we would stay in a Japanese hotel in Kyoto, rather than an Army billet. Two reasons account for this: (1) Genuine solicitude for our comfort. The Americans thought that we would be miserable sleeping on the floor. (2) They could not get over the feeling that it was somehow wrong and undignified for an American to "go native" even to the extent of spending a night or two in what turned out to be one of the most entrancing hotels I have ever been in.

As to the Japanese attitude, it is not easy to define, and I hope to

94

touch on it in detail later. I never came across any example of discourtesy to an American. But this may not mean much; notoriously, the Japanese are a courteous people. When the occupation began the Japanese—who had never lost a war and who had never been invaded—were dazed, tottering, and numb with shock. The bitter sting and humiliation of defeat persists to this day, but few people take this emotion out on individual Americans.

If the Japanese were a surprise to us, so were we to them. They expected G.I.'s to rape their women and slaughter their infants, but instead, after one of the most savage wars in history, we arrived—with chocolate bars.

I met one Oxford-educated Japanese, a sophisticated person, who provided a note somewhat different from the ordinary. I happened to ask if he thought that our possession of Okinawa was a live issue to the Japanese and whether Japan wanted Okinawa back. "Of course!" exclaimed my friend. "The Okinawese are our own people. I would cut my ten-year-old daughter off without a cent if, when she grows up, she should marry an Englishman or an American, but I would be happy to have her marry an Okinawese."

The Forlorn "Traders," and Life of the Diplomats

Japan was reopened to foreign trade in August, 1947, and businessmen from the United States and elsewhere began to filter in. Every entrant had to have SCAP permission. All—whether bankers, merchants, advertising men, attorneys, airline officials, art dealers, or even professors—were designated by the blanket word "trader."

This term rankles with most of them; I never met a trader who did not resent being called a trader. Traders are segregated in their own hotels, which are converted office buildings in some cases and pretty miserable; they pay an average of $10 per day for hotel space, whereas army officers and V.I.P.'s pay 40 or 50 cents; until recently, when they were allowed to operate in yen for the first time, they were restricted to the use of a special type of Army currency; they paid—to cite just one instance—60 cents for a gallon of gas, as against 10 cents paid by Army personnel. Other irritants exist too.

95

Traders are not allowed in Army hotels, cannot buy in the PX, and cannot use the Army mail or other facilities which make life in Japan so comfortable for nontraders. They are not allowed to make use of the magnificent resort hotels in the environs of Tokyo (or elsewhere in Japan), skiing resorts, or golf courses, except by special invitation and on paying through the nose. Sport and holiday facilities that could handle 150,000 people are usurped near Tokyo by an Army population of 30,000, one bitter trader told me. Even so eminent a local personage as the resident manager of the National City Bank, say, or of the biggest American oil or airplane company, is a trader in the eyes of SCAP, and hence is not permitted even to enter the sacred precincts of the Imperial Hotel (unless invited as a guest) or to buy a drink at the bar.

On the other hand traders had a field day in one highly important respect until July, 1950—they paid no local taxes, nor any Japanese tax on their American income; moreover if they were nonresidents of the United States they paid no American taxes on whatever income they made in Japan. Recently, however, the tax law was drastically changed, largely on the recommendations of a tax expert SCAP brought in, Professor Carl Shoup of Columbia University. This caused black fury in trader circles. Traders are obliged nowadays not only to pay Japanese taxes on their earnings in Japan (and the basic rate is around 55 per cent) but also Japanese taxes on their dollar income in the United States. No trader with much conscience could put up a case that he should continue to live totally tax-free. But the new system seems to many to be unjust. I heard one indignant banker snort, "I, an American, who helped beat this nation in warfare, am now obliged to pay taxes on my *American* income to the Japanese government which, since there is no peace treaty, is still technically my enemy."

If you ask why MacArthur permits this the answer is simple; it is a tribute to his statesmanship. He wants an absolutely immaculate occupation. His policy is to lean as far backward as possible, in order to avoid any possible charge or shadow of a charge that SCAP permits exploitation of the Japanese by foreigners. Communist propaganda in the East rests largely on the case that the capitalist West has always exploited the Orient; every foreign power except the Soviet Union (say the Soviets) is an exploiter. That MacArthur limits severely the amount of profit a foreign trader can take out of Japan and otherwise keeps business under strict controls is his most effective answer to this type of communist propaganda, because nobody in his right mind can accuse SCAP of economic exploitation.

*

Another forlorn community is that of the foreign diplomats. These are accredited, as I have already mentioned, not to the Emperor or the Japanese government, but to MacArthur himself. They can make no contact with the government except through SCAP and, unless they happen to have special permission, they are not permitted direct access to any Japanese, *officially*. I ran into the chargé d'affaires of an important European country, and he put it this way: "I have never 'met' Prime Minister Yoshida. But I know 'Mr.' Yoshida quite well, and I see him occasionally at parties."

All foreign heads of missions present their credentials to MacArthur. He never returns their calls, since he is acting as head of state. "The actual *sovereignty* of Japan is subject to the authority of the Supreme Commander," an Army pamphlet states.

The State Department is represented in Tokyo by an able young official, William Sebald. He has a perfect knowledge of Japanese, is married to an attractive lady half-Japanese, and was both a lawyer in Japan and an American naval officer before entering the Department. Mr. Sebald is well liked, and his influence is considerable. Yet he is the State Department's emissary *to* MacArthur, and his whole organization, despite his rank of ambassador, is no more than a section within SCAP. Foreign diplomats in Tokyo would be glad to see Mr. Sebald given greater authority, and so would many of the Americans in Tokyo. On the other hand some SCAP officials think that the State Department is a nuisance around headquarters

97

and want its power cut down; considerable jealousy and bad feeling exist between some levels in SCAP and the Department. But Mac-Arthur himself is punctilious in the extreme—he always behaves with impeccable official correctness—in all his dealings with Mr. Sebald.

One odd point is that the Russian delegation, alone among the foreign missions, is not accredited *to* SCAP. This is because General Derevyanko stood by the letter of the early directives setting up the Allied Council, and insists that the Russians are in Tokyo today as *part* of SCAP, and are not subordinate to it; he insists that he is in Japan as Russian *member* of the Allied Council. The total number of Russians in Tokyo is about 250, and they live mostly in the old Russian Embassy. What hairs General Derevyanko may split about his theoretical status do not matter much, because MacArthur pays no attention to the Russians anyway.

How the Japanese Have Changed, If At All

Two foreign expressions have entered the Japanese language; how they are used tells much. The German *Arbeit* (work) came into use as a term to describe something fairly new in Japanese life—boys and girls working their way through college. This marked an important change from the old way of things, because a student paying his own way through school was no longer economically dependent, as in former days, on the parents. Now *Arbeit* also means, of all things, petting. Kids go to school on their own and earn their own keep; hence they are free to associate with the opposite sex and make love.

When you ask people in Tokyo how the Japanese have changed, the first thing you hear is that boys and girls make their own decisions, and are not completely subservient to their parents; second, that they hold hands on the streets and embrace on park benches, which would have been all but unthinkable before the war. In the country districts, however, these developments are less marked than in Tokyo, Osaka, and the great cities. Another point is that, nowadays, husband and wife walk together in the street, and, miraculous to state, the husband sometimes even carries bundles; in the old days the wife and children always walked behind. Still another is that the practice of ceremonial suicide, hara-kiri, has virtually disappeared.

The other term is a corruption of the French *après la guerre* (after the war); in Japanese pronunciation it sounds like "Appelagerra." It means, roughly, everything from nihilism in personal behavior, corruption, loosening of standards, and lost-generationism, to just having fun. Recently I saw a kind of Gallup poll printed in the Osaka *Mainichi*, one of the greatest of Japanese newspapers, which purported to tell what young people were thinking about. One question was, "Which do you support—platonic, realistic, or *après-guerre* type of love?" ("Realistic" love is defined as that which leads to marriage; "*après-guerre*" does not.) The students voted 118 for realistic, 71 for platonic, and only 2 for *après-guerre*.

Another question showed that *Hamlet* led all other recent films in popularity (incidentally a stage production of *Hamlet* was forbidden in Tokyo just before the war, because of its "tendency to promote disrespect for royalty"), and another gave the United States as "favorite country." Another mentioned the misery that almost all people feel about the fate of Japanese war prisoners—some 375,000—still held by the Russians in Siberia. Other results:

Q. Which do you prefer, the American type or the Soviet type of democracy?
American type, 107; Soviet type, 45; Don't know, 14; No interest, 4; Both, 2; No reply, 28.

Q. Do you support the capitalist structure?
Yes, 65; No, 121; Noncommittal, 12. [21 students wrote in "I support communism."]

Q. What is your ideal type of woman?
Intelligent and cultured woman, 75; womanlike woman, 61; Healthy woman, 17; Woman of willingness, 12; Good-looking woman, 2.

A whole lot of Japanese character can be gleaned from the last two answers!

Another phrase often heard in Tokyo is *Shikata ga nai,* which means roughly "The hell with it," "I don't give a damn," or literally "Nothing can be done." Then there is a phrase common in Kyoto, *Masakozi*, the equivalent of "All messed up" or "Snafu," and it is sometimes said that the people who have really messed everything up are the *Intelli*, pronounced "Interi," which means "Intelligentsia."

Democracy is a puzzling concept for the Japanese to absorb. I went to a party at General Stratemeyer's villa, just before the Korean war, at which the Prime Minister was present. One of the servants conspicuously did not bow when he entered, and later Mrs. Stratemeyer asked her why. "Under democracy we do not bow," was the reply. Then there is a baseball anecdote doubtless apocryphal. A player was ordered to bunt, but smashed the ball instead. The manager of the team rebuked him, whereupon the player replied, "You do not realize that Japan is now a democracy, and we swing at the ball when we like."

People have been shaken up; things have come too fast; it has been like giving a baby a box of matches. I met one American schoolteacher who said that before the war he would have implicitly trusted his life to any of several Japanese friends; now he would not. "Standards are lower; people are like flotsam, with their roots gone." For instance a true geisha, in the old days, could not possibly be proficient at her interesting job unless she had something like ten years of training. Now geishas are turned out almost overnight—and they speak smatterings of Army English.

"The movies we send to Japan are over the people's heads," I heard it said. "The pace is too fast—the Japanese become confused. Send them movies of simple day-to-day American life, showing that Americans too have small problems and distresses."

The wife of a Buddhist priest recently appeared on a Japanese radio show, an imitation of our "Information Please." This was as unprecedented in Tokyo as it would be in New York for a society dowager to do a strip tease in a burlesque show.

Only twice in Japan did I hear anybody hiss. This hiss, a quick sibilant intake of breath to show respect while addressing a superior or a foreigner, was one of the best known of all Japanese characteristics before the war. One of the hissers I heard this time was a former prime minister, the other a bus boy in the Imperial Hotel, which at least indicates that hissing exists in widely separated spheres.

But people still pray to their ancestors at the Meiji shrine; the Yasakuni shrine, devoted to the souls of those who were killed in battle, is still crowded. Cheerfully we heard an educated young man in an important political position say, "This week will tell whether I am a success or a failure." His wife was just about to have a child, and he would be a failure if it were not a boy.

Parents still count for a great deal in Japan, if only because almost all Japanese are ancestor worshipers. I have said that members of the new generation are freer of their parents than before, particularly in some such item as choosing a career. But one should not underestimate the formidable role that respect for age still plays in Japan, especially among the poor in the rural districts, where the parents (who need the child's work) have almost complete *economic* control of their families. One American, high on MacArthur's staff, told me, "We will have to stay here twenty years to do a real job, because when it comes to a showdown the parents still have final authority in the majority of Japanese families, the kids don't dare say No, and we will simply have to wait for the oldsters to die off."

On the other hand we met one youthful editor of a Japanese magazine patterned on *Reader's Digest*. He snapped, "Don't misunderstand—we Japanese are completely finished with any such mythology as Emperor worship—and all that stupid Kamikaze nonsense!"

Fermentation, a groping upheaval, shock, bewilderment, national self-interest—these are some of the hallmarks of the contemporary Japan. We should not forget that these people, for all their faults, are by far the best material in Asia at present, the most potentially useful and usable people on the whole giant continent of 1,200,-

ooo,ooo people, if we ourselves have the wisdom and concrete sense to know how to use them for their own betterment and ours.

Why Did They Think They Could Get Away With Pearl Harbor?

The answers are two: (a) ego, (b) ignorance.

The Japanese, after the Meiji Restoration in 1868, had things all their own way. They won a war with China, won a war with Russia, made considerable territorial gains, grabbed off Korea and Formosa, entered World War I with little risk, and were greeted by Britain and America at the Versailles Conference as equals and a Great Power.

Then came intensification of military greed and ambition, the gradual transformation of what had been at least a quasi democracy into a thought-controlled military dictatorship, the Mukden Incident, the machinations of the Kwantung army, the unprovoked assault on China, the spreading out of ugly tentacles further south and east, the ill-fated alliance with Hitler, growing avarice, belligerence, and—Pearl Harbor.

Pearl Harbor was, itself, no more than the climax to events the roots of which had been planted long before. To assume that it was merely a gesture of witless desperation is to miss the point. The Japanese were driven to Pearl Harbor, inexorably and inevitably, by their own expansionist aggression, which in turn produced American resistance. As we continued defensively to strangle Japan by embargoing shipments of oil and steel and to insist that a *sine qua non* of peace was Japanese withdrawal from China, we should have known that some such adventure as Pearl Harbor was altogether bound to occur. It was not an act of madness or provocation by the Japanese. It was the only thing they could do. Their theory was that, if they knocked out our fleet, they would have the whole Pacific to themselves. They could not risk having the American Navy on their watery flanks if they were to succeed with their conquest of east Asia. So, they struck. It was a maneuver, from their point of view, more defensive than offensive, strange as this may seem. Of course their great miscalculation, based on the most primitive ignorance, was that the United States would take the attack lying down, or, at worst, would be unable to retaliate except feebly and after long delay. Japanese Imperial Headquarters honestly thought that, even if we did fight, it would take us ten years to progress across the Pacific island by island and effectively strike back in their home waters. Ten years! They thought that the Axis was bound to win in Europe soon and that they and the Germans could easily divide the world and become utterly and permanently impregnable—long before we got started.

Smart Japanese knew that the game was up, and that they were irrevocably doomed to pay the cost of their gigantic and lunatic folly, by the time of the Battle of the Coral Sea in 1942.

I put the following to several Japanese—did they realize that by Pearl Harbor *they* made certain the entrance of the United States into the war against Germany, that they themselves ended the long period of American pusillanimity and isolationism, and that, in effect, it was they who wrote the doom of the Axis, ensured Russian victories in Europe, made the United States a united vertebrate nation, and elected Mr. Roosevelt to his fourth term in the White House? Most seemed bewildered by my line of thought.

*

I asked many Japanese, from men on the highest level to young officials who at that time were in their teens, what ended the war. One and all they replied, without the slightest dubiety or hesitation, "The atom bomb on Hiroshima." There can be no doubt about this at all. Resistance might well have continued briefly, but the Hiroshima and Nagasaki bombs smashed utterly the whole structure of Japanese effort, morale, and will to win. They might have struggled on a while longer, but they knew after August 6, 1945, that the fight was completely hopeless. Einstein won the war.

Chapter Six

BRIEF DISQUISITION
ON THE EMPEROR

I HAVE heard many stories about cabbages and kings, but this is the first story I have ever heard about a radish and an emperor.

A Japanese we met and liked very much, Kuramatsu Kishi, is Mr. Shidehara's close friend and secretary. He has a small farm outside Tokyo, and, visiting it one day, he was presented by his farmer with a particularly large and perfectly shaped daikon, or radish, which is one of the staple foods in Japan. (In Tokyo, in a crowd, you can smell daikon on almost everybody as, say, you can smell goulash in Budapest, or beer in Munich.) Mr. Kishi thought that the daikon was so handsome that he would present it to Shidehara, who exclaimed, "This is by far the most magnificent daikon I have ever seen. I have an idea. Let us give it to the Emperor."

The new constitution forbids anybody giving a gift to the Emperor, but, since this was only a daikon, the venerable Shidehara thought that he would not be impeached for violating the law. So, ceremoniously, he sent the daikon over to the Imperial Palace, and gravely asked for a receipt to transmit to Mr. Kishi's farmer. The Emperor responded at once with a note of profound thanks. Some weeks later Mr. Shidehara happened to meet the Empress Dowager, Hirohito's mother and a most formidable and picturesque old lady; she grasped him and said, "Thank you for that daikon. My son sent me half of it, and we are all enjoying it very much!"

Life for the imperial family in Japan is not, as one may judge from this small anecdote, all that it used to be.

Forty-nine-year-old Hirohito, the 124th Emperor of Japan in an unbroken succession that goes back 2,611 years, the Man-God of celestial Nippon, the descendant of the Sun Goddess in whose august being the entire spiritual life of the nation is consecrated, was at one time—before the surrender—by all odds the richest man in Japan, and one of the richest in the world. In a sense, he *owned* Japan. The mundane investments of the imperial house were, to put it mildly, grandiose. Now it would be an exaggeration to say that, today, Hirohito and his family are poor as church mice. They have enough to live on quite comfortably, by any reasonable scale. But the former standards have been enormously, unbelievably cut down. Most of the imperial palaces and other properties had to be given up on account of merciless taxation, the palace staff has been reduced by half and Hirohito himself was put on a civil list like any constitutional monarch. The Diet, while debating the budget, decides each year how big his appropriation shall be, and he is directly dependent on the elected representatives of the people for what money he may—or may not—receive.

Recently his second daughter, Princess Kazuko, got married. The story is told with a straight face in Tokyo that the royal family did not think it could afford to give her the type of expensive ceremonial kimono which is usual on such occasions, and so she was married in a kimono belonging to her older sister, Shigeko, which Princess Shigeko had used at her own wedding some years before.

Most members of the family—though, again, it should be stressed that none are what you would call exactly starving—live with simplicity and modesty these days. They have been forced to sell most of what they owned, to meet the capital levy and other taxes. Prince Chichibu, the Emperor's first brother, lives in a lonely farmhouse in the foothills near Mount Fuji; Prince Takamatsu, another brother, has a small house next to his former palace—the palace itself was sold to become a businessmen's club. Hirohito's mother, brothers, and children have been allowed to retain their titles; all other titles, even of other members of the imperial family, have been abolished. Prince (now "Mr.") Naruhiko Higashi-Kuni, who was prime minister at the time of the surrender, and who was purged by SCAP even though he is a relative of the Emperor's, both by descent and marriage, has successively tried to earn a living as a grocery dealer, cabaret owner, insurance agent, and founder of a new Buddhist sect.

Just as he was cut down financially, so has Hirohito been cut down politically. Under the Meiji constitution he was not merely head of state, he *was* the state. Sovereignty was believed by the orthodox to reside actually in the person of the Emperor, not in any organ of government. He had power to suspend the constitution, to initiate and veto legislation, and to determine the policies of army and navy. Of course he seldom exercised these powers. Japan was ruled, not "by" the Emperor, but in his name; what determined the course of Japanese politics, both foreign and domestic, was the nature of the advice he got from the army and the inner palace clique. Nowadays all this is completely changed. Like everybody else in Japan, Hirohito is subject to the authority of SCAP. This was made perfectly clear in the first directives to MacArthur, and it was formally written into the new constitution that the Emperor is merely the "symbol" of the state, "deriving his position from the sovereign rule of the people." As I heard MacArthur himself put it informally, "The Emperor's function is about that of the Stars and Stripes in the United States, or the Union Jack in England." Moreover the Emperor can perform no functions that are not specifically provided for in the constitution. "Never shall he have powers related to *government*," the constitution states.

The Diet watches the Emperor with some care, to see that he really does stay out of politics. (Of course the Diet is watching SCAP too, which is watching it.) When Joseph B. Keenan, the American prosecutor at the Tokyo war trials, returned to Washington he inadvertently let it be known that he had delivered to Mr. Truman the "personal greetings" of the Emperor—not a message of any political sort, but just greetings. The Diet at once took action, and asked the prime minister for an explanation, on the ground that Hirohito's "message" was an "intervention" into political affairs. (Incidentally Marquis Koichi Kido, the former Lord Privy Seal and for years the Emperor's closest civilian adviser, is actually in jail today, serving a long sentence as a war criminal.)

Whittling down the Emperor's prerogatives necessitated a good many changes in other fields, for instance legal matters. One chapter in the old criminal code, "Crimes Against the Imperial House," had to be abolished, and this provoked excitement, because the issue of *lèse majesté* was at stake. Under the old law the penalty for anybody who committed an injurious act against the Emperor or any member of the Imperial House was death. The SCAP authorities, when they supervised rewriting the legal codes, took the view that American law should be followed, and *lèse majesté* thrown out of the window. If anybody shoots the President of the United States, he is subject to the same legal procedure as if he had shot Joe Doakes. The same system is now in force in Japan.

Finally, and most important, the Emperor has been cut down from the religious point of view. The legend of his lineal descent from the Sun Goddess and consequent "divinity" was a political weapon of great power to those who formerly ruled Japan; it made the Emperor sacrosanct and united the nation in a blindly intense feeling not merely of loyalty but of actual kinship to the imperial house. Ancestor worship, patriotism, the conviction that the very soil of Japan was sacred, the devout belief that every soldier killed in battle becomes a kind of god himself—all this was knit together by the supreme, august symbol of the Emperor's divinity. SCAP knew that it must knock the props from under this structure at once. Few people, however, knew how wily its procedure was going to be. An amazed nation, on January 1, 1946, read an imperial rescript by Hirohito himself not merely announcing that he was *not* divine, but in effect stating that he never had been divine, and denouncing the myth of his own divinity. The text was, of course, prepared by scap, though people nowadays like to say that it came on the Emperor's initiative. The language is somewhat stilted:

Love of the family and love of country are especially strong in this country. With more of this devotion we should now work toward love of mankind. We feel deeply concerned to note that consequent upon the protracted war ending in our defeat our people are liable to grow restless and to fall into the slough of despond. Radical tendencies in excess are gradually spreading and the sense of morality tends to lose its hold on the people with the result that there are signs of confusion of thoughts. . . . The ties between us and our people have always stood upon mutual trust and affection. They do not depend upon mere legends or myths. They are not predicated on the false conception that the Emperor is divine and that the Japanese people are superior to other races and fated to rule the world.

Think back. Before the war a traffic cop gave the wrong signal in an imperial procession; he killed himself in shame. The court tailor could not measure the Emperor's clothes except at a distance, because touching the imperial person was forbidden. When the Emperor traveled, all blinds along the entire route had to be drawn, because of the theory that direct view of the Son of Heaven might cause blindness. No Japanese was ever supposed to look *at* him, or even at his picture unless it was covered by tissue. When a new foreign ambassador was introduced at court, the interpreters could not talk, but had to whisper. Once a cheerful American, about to be presented to the Emperor, told friends that he was going to take a dollar watch out of his pocket and say, "Your Majesty, here is *one* thing you folks can't imitate and undersell!" Horrified, his friends told him that he must not under any circumstances do this, because, if he did, the members of the imperial staff would consider that the Emperor had been insulted and all of them would at once have to commit suicide.

This type of nonsense is done with. The Emperor is still revered, but the rank and file of Japanese have translated their reverence into different terms.

I asked almost all Japanese I met what they thought of him. Ten years ago, even to ask such a question would have been impossible. The answers followed a general pattern. It is a very interesting thing in Japan (such a close-knit family the nation is!) to see how, to this and to other questions in different fields, the bulk of the answers are identical, whether you are talking to the chief justice or a bell-boy in the hotel. In remote rural districts men and women still prostrate themselves if the Emperor passes; even in the cities, many citizens still avert their eyes. Another classification of attitude is by age; men and women over sixty, by and large, may still worship Hirohito but do not admit it; between forty and fifty they treat him with deep respect, but not in overtly religious terms. I even met one sophisticated Japanese who said calmly, "It is something of a bore to have as Emperor a man whose hobby is marine biology." One newspaper reporter told me, "I think of him as my uncle"; another, who was trained as a Kamikaze pilot (the war ended before he made his first flight), said, "The Emperor? If I see him I go up and shake his hand, like any man's."

In the autumn of 1945 newspapers openly printed stories about whether Hirohito had been "contaminated" and should abdicate, which would have been unthinkable before. One of the most interesting photographs to be seen in Tokyo nowadays is that of Hirohito opening the first session of the Diet under the new constitution; he sits in the royal box overlooking the scene, and the speaker, at that time Mr. Yamazaki, is below and has his *back* to him. In the old days anybody who publicly turned his back on the Emperor would have been assassinated.

In the beginning strong sentiment existed in the United States—and elsewhere—for trying Hirohito as a war criminal. From several points of view he was just as much a criminal as other Japanese who were tried—perhaps more so. After all, Imperial Headquarters made the war and directed the Japanese war effort. Hirohito was commander in chief, and if comparatively minor figures, who only took orders from higher up, were hanged, it seemed illogical to let him off. The Russians were particularly intent on hanging him, and still are; recently, in fact, the Soviet Union has revived the cry that he should go on trial. Hirohito himself thought after the surrender that he would be tried, and never made any attempt to avoid what he assumed would be his fate—the gibbet. MacArthur told us that he had hoped that Hirohito would not be tried, but was not sure what the final decision would be; the decision was not his, but that of the Joint Chiefs in Washington. Politically, it would seem today, the decision not to put the Emperor in the dock was wise. That we spared Hirohito helped, among other things, to make SCAP popular and workable in the early days. On one occasion an organization came into being with the fine name, "Society for the Expression of Gratitude to the Occupation Forces for the Preservation of His Majesty." Yet that Hirohito should have got off scot free, except for the curtailment of his privileges and powers, is still a sore point to many.

Today the process whereby Hirohito has become "constitutionalized" continues steadily. He opens festivals, visits coal mines, goes to baseball games, and similarly shows himself more and more to the people, on the model of a British monarch; this is, of course, a shrewd move toward perpetuation of the royal house, a kind of insurance for the future. SCAP denies that it brings influence to bear on the Emperor in such directions. "We don't mix up in that kind of thing at all," I heard one high official say. But of course the original hint that he should popularize himself must have come from MacArthur.

Let nobody minimize the importance of Hirohito today. He has been bereft of his "divinity" but he is still a personage of great consequence in the life of the nation, temporal and spiritual; probably his influence is still as strong as, say, that of the Pope in Italy. Politically he has been of paramount help to SCAP, because the Japanese people follow implicitly any lead he gives. Part of the credit for the success of the occupation certainly belongs to the Japanese themselves, and one reason why they cooperated so willingly was that Hirohito told them to do so. Negatively, the Emperor could have been a formidable nuisance and difficulty if he had taken a different course; suppose he had simply passed the word along, "Don't be nice to the Americans." Particularly since the Korean war, the United States has had very few troops in Japan. Suppose the Emperor should, taking a leaf from Mr. Gandhi's book, suddenly declare a civil-disobedience campaign. He will never do so, but it could be an awful headache if he did.

Glimpse of the Son of the Sun

Though the Emperor has loosened up in some respects he does not often receive foreigners; even today, audiences are extremely rare. SCAP does not like to ask His Majesty to see visiting Americans, for fear that he will feel that he is obliged to do so, and nobody in SCAP itself (except MacArthur) ever sees him, because he is outside politics. Even so eminent an occupationeer as General Whitney has never once laid eyes on the Emperor. Unofficially, however, several nonpolitical Americans in Tokyo have become friends of the monarch. An outsider will, as a rule, only be received if General Mac-Arthur himself, in a quiet way, sends word to the palace that it would be a good idea; in our case he wrote the Emperor a letter. Then a reply came from the Imperial Household Ministry, relayed through Colonel Bunker, granting the audience and laying down the conditions under which it could take place.

We were told that, before our visit, Hirohito had not received more than four or five foreign journalists in more than twenty years. One stipulation with us was that we must not mention the fact that we had had an audience until after we left Japan.

Lieutenant Kan Tagami, a Nisei born in Fresno and an aide on Bunker's staff, picked us up just before eleven on a bright, gusty June morning. He came in one of the commander in chief's own cars, and the windshield carried a red chrysanthemum sticker, to denote that it was en route to the palace.

The imperial grounds lie in the center of Tokyo, surrounded by a broad outer moat and an irregular granite wall, some miles in length. The site, dating from the sixteenth century, is one of the most stately in the world. "With great pictorial impact," it was once written, "it symbolizes the austere and magnificent phenomenon it houses." Workmen in skiffs ceaselessly sweep the green iridescent waters of the moat, to skim off the leaves that descend from the twisted pines. The wall, interrupted by forty gates and a series of craggy towers, is built of heavy square gray boulders, set against a bank of earth and earthquake-proof.

The area was not, however, B-29 proof, and the palace where the Emperor lived for many years has been destroyed. This was not deliberate, since it was forbidden as a target; it caught fire and burned by accident when flames from one of the great incendiary raids were carried by the wind across the moat. It has never been rebuilt (it was a colossal structure) because the cost would be too great, and Hirohito resides nowadays in a nine-room "cottage" a half-mile or so from its bleak ruins. The new house—it was built on the foundation of a bomb shelter erected for the Emperor during the last days of the war, but which he never used—is concealed by a solid gray wooden wall, marked with gray squares, and may not be visited by anybody.

We strolled around, drove, and inspected various sights, including the experimental gardens and a startlingly picturesque collection of miniature trees, some of which are 700 years old. The area as a whole covers 240 acres. An automobile seemed to be approaching us eccentrically; in it was the Emperor's sister-in-law, the wife of Prince Takamatsu, taking a driving lesson. We climbed one knoll, and our guide pointed out the Dai-Ichi, across the moat, the great pyramidal structure of the Diet, and the dingy red building that houses the Metropolitan Police.

(A Japanese in our party recalled that in my book *Inside Asia* I had said that this was never completed because, if it had been made higher, people on top could *look down* on the Emperor's palace a mile away. I was astonished that any Japanese close to the throne had even heard of *Inside Asia*, much less had ever read it, because the first chapter contains sharp criticism of the Emperor. Later that morning somebody else mentioned this same chapter, calling to mind an item that I had completely forgotten having written—that one of the Emperor's closest councilors looks like a Chinese.)

The Emperor still spends two afternoons a week in his biological laboratory, and we dutifully visited this building. It is full of marine specimens neatly catalogued and well displayed, and heavy monographs in German and English on such arcane subjects as the gymnoblastic hydroids. One volume I noted was *Contribution to the Natural History of the United States* by Louis Agassiz. Then we were shown carefully a handsome book compiled by the Emperor himself, and published in 1949; its title is *Opisthobranchia of Sagami.*

Our audience took place in a building untouched by the war, the Office of the Imperial Household. We were met by a group of small, skinny, polite, young-old gentlemen wearing striped trousers and black coats, which—I mean no offense—seemed threadbare and shabby. Few Japanese are rich enough these days to buy new western clothes. They were Mr. Matsudaira, the Grand Master of Ceremonies; Mr. Mitani, the Grand Chamberlain; Mr. Kuroda, another Grand Chamberlain; Mr. Goto, the *Chef de Protocol,* and Mr. Akira Matsui, of the Foreign Office, who had been assigned to us as interpreter. Also a lady greeted us whom we had already met socially, Madame Tatsue Takagi, the Chief Lady in Waiting to the Empress; she was a Mitsui before her marriage, knows English perfectly, and is a person well known in Tokyo for her good looks, dignity, and unobtrusive charm.

The actual meeting with Their Majesties was arranged in this manner. We walked down a long, somewhat dingy corridor, the procession of officials following us, and entered a room decorated in the European style except for a large Japanese screen. The furniture, orange and green for the most part, was old-fashioned and run down. The Emperor and Empress then entered this room, and there was a moment of bowing and handshaking. I was then placed next to the Empress on one side, and my wife was given a position next to the Emperor on the other. Each conversation took place independently. Madame Takagi translated for me, and Mr. Matsui for my wife. Standing discreetly in the background were Mr. Matsudaira and others of the retinue. After twenty minutes a signal was given, and my wife and I changed places; she then talked with the Empress and Madame Takagi, while I moved over next to the Emperor and Mr. Matsui. There was no opportunity, except briefly at the end, for general conversation. The audience lasted fifty minutes in all. I had, in other words, about half an hour with the Emperor.

The Empress, named the Princess Nagako before her marriage, was the eldest daughter of Prince Kuninomiya; her blood was noble, but she was not a member of the great Fujiwara family which, by a tradition 1,300 years old, was the sole family group out of which an Empress might be chosen. But Hirohito fell in love with her when he was a youth, persisted in his suit against serious opposition, and finally married her. They have six surviving children.

Empress Nagako wore Japanese dress when we met her, a quite-plain green kimono with an unelaborate sash. She was once, it was obvious, an extremely pretty woman; now she has become somewhat stout. Her eyes, under heavy slanting lids, are veritable slits in an oval, ivory face; I thought she was the most typically "Japanese" woman I had ever seen; she might have come to life out of an early Hiroshige print. She laughed a great deal as we talked, and vividly described some of her problems with her children. She was interested in the life of American women, and mentioned with regret that she had never met Mrs. MacArthur and her son.

The Emperor keeps his eyes cast down when he speaks, and expresses his opinions with a firmness and vigor that surprised me. He is stockily built and youthful looking; he wears thick glasses, and shakes hands with muscular energy. He has a slight tic which is unobtrusive. He wore western clothes, an old suit of greyish tweed; a garter kept slipping down one leg. Direct quotation of the

114

Emperor's remarks is, of course, not allowed. But it may be said that he has pungent, discriminating views on a considerable variety of subjects, and expresses them with great pith. I have never met a king who did not, no matter what his circumstances, convey an instinctive atmosphere of command. And I am assured that it is quite in order for me to give my "impression" of what some of Hirohito's opinions were. He thinks, so I gathered, that our democratization of Japan *will* endure after the occupation ends, but that Japanese democracy will be of its own special type, perhaps quite different from that which exists in England or America; that MacArthur, whom he admires extravagantly, has done a magnificent, epochal job, and has not (as is sometimes charged) hurried things too much; that after the peace treaty Japan will manifestly need military protection, so that it can remain secure against both external and internal pressures; and that the last war, which he wholeheartedly laments, was a tragedy which he did everything possible to prevent. This last point was the one he stressed most. Then we talked about the United States.

A few days before we saw Hirohito I heard an irreverent American call him a celestial zero, a spook. I do not believe that this is true. My feeling, for what it is worth, is that the Emperor is a personage of powerful will and intelligence, who for good or ill may still play a commanding role in the future of Japan.

MacArthur and the Emperor

In September, 1945, immediately after the surrender, people thought that MacArthur would summon the Emperor to him forthwith. There was, in fact, a good deal of pressure on the Supreme Commander, suggesting that he should at once lay down the law to Hirohito, and put him in his place. MacArthur did nothing of the kind. He was much more subtle. He knew that, sooner or later, the Emperor was bound to come to him of his own volition, because, as he himself told us, Hirohito would be too curious about this new Power to stay away. Also, a gentleman with high regard for good blood and breeding, MacArthur did not want to humiliate Hirohito wantonly in the hour of his defeat. Finally, he thought that if he took too severe a line against him or behaved rudely, this might serve to martyrize him in the eyes of his prostrate people.

In any case the General took no initiative whatever. Presently an emissary came to him, asking if the Emperor might call. MacArthur was delighted. No one else was present at the interview, except an interpreter, and there was no excessive fanfare or publicity. The Supreme Commander did not, of course, return the call, nor has he ever done so, because to have made a return call would have led the Japanese to think that the Emperor had equal authority with his own.

Hirohito himself, to save face, gives it as his opinion now that MacArthur "met him half way" at their first meeting. This is a considerable exaggeration, unless he means merely to imply that the General was equally courteous, and equally eager to make the interview a success.

At their first talk the Emperor said that he deplored the war and had sought to stop it. MacArthur then turned on him with a fixed eye and asked him, if that were true, why he had not been able to make his desire effective. Hirohito responded, in effect, "My people like me very much. Since they do like me very much, they would simply have locked me up in a lunatic asylum until the war was over, if I had made any protest about the war or worked for peace. If I had done so and they had *not* liked me very much, they would have cut my throat."

MacArthur's relations with Hirohito are cordial in the extreme these days; he treats the younger man like a son. They never meet socially, and there is no contact between their families, but the Emperor calls alone at the Embassy twice a year.

It is often said that MacArthur is the real "emperor" of Japan today; an analogy closer to precedent would be that the Japanese royal family has temporarily reverted to the position it held between 598 and 1868 under the Tokugawa shogunate, when the shoguns,

hereditary military chieftains, ruled in the Emperor's name. Mac-
Arthur is Japan's new shogun.

The General's prestige with the Japanese is so enormous that—
as we shall see later—he is thought of almost as if he too had royal
blood. I heard one Japanese say early in the Korean war, before
the lamentable fact of Chinese intervention, "He [MacArthur] will
never lead us into any disaster or defeat!"

Crown Prince: Experiment in Education

One of the most interesting personalities we met in Japan was
Mrs. Elizabeth Gray Vining, an American lady who holds a unique
position as tutor to Crown Prince Akihito and other members of the
imperial family. Mrs. Vining is tall, distinguished, and good-looking—the word beautiful would not be a misnomer. She is a Quaker,
gentle in manners but packed with character and poise. She has
written several well-known children's books under the name Elizabeth Janet Gray, and has been in Tokyo since October, 1946.

The manner of her coming to Japan was this. Dr. George Stoddard, now president of the University of Illinois, came out to Japan
as head of an education mission on MacArthur's invitation. The
Emperor gave a reception for him, and, without warning or consulting his surprised advisers, asked him point-blank, "Can you find
me a tutor for my son?" Hirohito's stipulations were that the tutor
should (a) be an American woman, (b) be a Christian but not
fanatically so, (c) should not be an "old Japan hand." He added
that she should be "about fifty," but Stoddard succeeded in cutting
this age limit down. Back in the United States Dr. Stoddard set
about looking for someone. Mrs. Vining was at that time living in
Philadelphia, where she worked for the Friends Service Committee.
One of her colleagues told her about Stoddard's mission, and asked
if she would be interested in the job. She dismissed the idea as
fantastic, especially since she was told that her contact with the
Crown Prince would be restricted to one hour per week—to go
halfway around the world and take up residence in utterly new

surroundings in a strange land unknown to her for just one hour a week seemed too much. But, though she refused to ask for the job, she said finally that she would not object to having her name submitted to Dr. Stoddard. He saw her, liked her, and persuaded her to accept. What won her was his quotation of the Emperor's own words, "We want the eyes of our son, the Crown Prince, to be opened to the wider world."

Mrs. Vining arrived, and at once was received by the Emperor, the Empress, and young Akihito. The Prince had been carefully instructed to say to her (he was about twelve at the time), "Thank you, madame, for having come such a long distance in order to teach me." But Mrs. Vining had brought with her a box of American candy (everybody in the imperial family adores sweets); the boy was so excited by this gift that he forgot his speech, and only muttered, "Oh thanks for candy!"

Akihito already knew some English by this time, because for several years he had had another English teacher, Mr. Blythe. Mrs. Vining's function was not merely to be a tutor, but to teach English at the Peers' School, which the Crown Prince still attends. This school, celebrated in Tokyo, is where most of the Japanese aristocracy send their children; royal princes spend some years there, submit to its rigid disciplines, and live exactly as do the other boys, sharing their lessons and hardships alike. The school is, *mutatis mutandis*, something like Groton in the United States. The regime is frugal; for instance there is no heat in the classrooms in winter. The Crown Prince sleeps in the dormitory with a roommate three or four nights a week, and works side by side with the other 1,800 students with no favoritism or special privileges whatever.

Mrs. Vining's earnestness, good humor, and friendly Quaker sense quickly won her an extension of activity. The whole family, in fact, fell head over heels in love with her. First, shyly, the Empress herself asked if she would give *her* English lessons too. This was arranged, and the lessons still continue; for a time Madame Takagi was present during each lesson, sitting behind a screen so that neither the Empress nor Mrs. Vining could see that she was there; this was so that the Empress would not be embarrassed, and also in order that the lady in waiting might repeat the lesson later. The Empress came out of her shell of diffidence rapidly; her humor and spontaneity grow all the time. Next the young unmarried princesses asked if Mrs. Vining would teach *them*, and finally Prince Mikasa, the Emperor's younger brother, applied for lessons. So, at the moment, in addition to the class at the Peers' School, Mrs. Vining is teaching four or five members of the family. Every Thursday she entertains the royal children at tea, and invites other youngsters, both Japanese and American, to meet them; they play western games, romp around, and have a fine time generally. Recently the youngest princess, eleven-year-old Takeko, came to one of these affairs in her first real party dress—of course a kimono.

Crown Prince Akihito is a sturdy, smart, good-looking youngster, who is making full use of the opportunities Mrs. Vining gives him. She showed us snapshots of him taken during the past four years— he is sixteen and a half now—which vividly show his development. He ranked fourth in his class of 104 last year, but dropped to tenth this year, because of a minor illness. What he likes most, like his father, is biology. And surely it is encouraging that a child destined to be the ruler of a nation should be interested above all in science, the science of human life at that. Mrs. Vining and the boy have a close relationship. Last year she took a house for the summer at Karuizawa, the mountain resort near Tokyo; the Crown Prince was permitted to visit her, something utterly unprecedented, without his chamberlain or other escort. Even the bodyguard was done away with. The liberalization that all this shows is particularly pertinent when one keeps in mind that, for centuries, the Japanese court was by far the most ossified and tradition-bound in the world. It is great good luck that the young prince should have this splendid American woman as his teacher. And there are some in Tokyo who say that it might be a good thing if another notable youngster in the same city was getting something of the same treatment—a sound, American, democratic education.

Chapter Seven

THE RECORD OF THE OCCUPATION

JUST as the early fighting in the Korean war was a desperate, dogged race between the United States and communism, so, in a different dimension, the future of Japan is dependent on the struggle between American democratic ideals and the further rapacious growth of communist ideology. This is what makes the record of SCAP so important. It is not just a question of whether Japan has been "democratized," but whether, in the long pull, our reforms will be effective and permanent enough to keep Japan from being communized.

The high personnel of SCAP takes on, like a cloak, much of MacArthur's own idealism. I heard one official say, somewhat sadly, "When you ask an educated Japanese what he thinks we have done for Japan, he is apt to thank us for sending in food—for having kept him from starvation. Of course this is important but I do wish the Japanese would have more appreciation for the way we are *reforming* them!"

The analogy may make people in SCAP apoplectic with fury—for instance General Willoughby, who is an ardent admirer of General Francisco Franco—but Japan under SCAP reminded me a good deal of the Spain of the democratic republic in the early 1930's, before it was hijacked by the communists and then extinguished by Franco's counterrevolution. The Spain of those first days, the Spain of that earnest and immaculate Jeffersonian republic, is astonishingly like Japan in 1950 and 1951. Of course loyalist Spain did not have a MacArthur.

But the mood, the ambition, the very program, are much the same with certain qualifications—an attempt to end feudalism, drastic curtailment of ancient privilege, land reform, liberation of women, extremely advanced labor legislation, education for the masses, "bookmobiles" out in the villages, abolition of the nobility, wide extension of social service, birth control, public health, steep taxation of the unconverted rich, discredit of the former military, and, embracing almost everything in every field, reform, *reform*, REFORM.

Some Details of the SCAP Mechanism

The five SCAP sections that people talk about most are Government Section (General Whitney, with a remarkably able young civilian, Frank Rizzo, as his deputy), Economic and Scientific Section (General Marquat), Natural Resources Section (Colonel H. G. Schenck), Public Health and Welfare Section (a doughty officer, Brig. Gen. C. F. Sams), and Civil Information and Education Section (a Marine officer, Col. D. R. Nugent). Of course there are multitudinous other departments; SCAP is not merely a headquarters, but a government. If you thumb through the American telephone book in Tokyo you will find men charged with everything from procurement to statistics, from the custody of alien property to "cultural resources," from transportation to fairtrade practices and "document downgrading." And all have been busy for five years giving 83,000,000 people as cheap and efficacious an education in democracy as anybody ever got.

No group of several thousand vigorous Americans running a country can work without sharp divergences. Particularly in the early days when SCAP was supposed to be full of "New Dealism" the story was that "half of SCAP was giving out information and creating policy against the other half, with each half working behind the other's back." This was an exaggeration of course. On a perfectly proper level there are often disputes—for instance as to whether Civil Information and Education should get a bigger budget. MacArthur, on the top, makes all the serious decisions. Only twice have there been prolonged, exacerbated disputes on policy within SCAP; one had to do with the purges, the other with decentralization of the police. Willoughby and Whitney were the antagonists in each struggle, and Whitney won both, because the Supreme Commander took his side in the end. "The forces arrayed against us," one of Willoughby's men told me, "were terrific."

Direct military government, as I mentioned in a previous chapter, has never been introduced in Japan. It is the Japanese government that makes the laws, but a glance at an official chart will show where this stands in the picture:

CHAIN OF COMMAND, SCAP

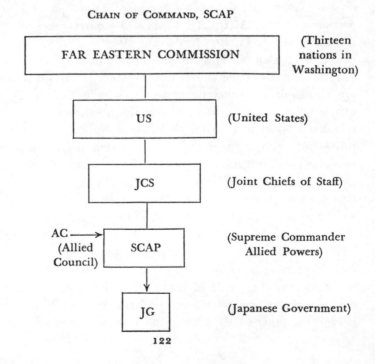

FAR EASTERN COMMISSION (Thirteen nations in Washington)

US (United States)

JCS (Joint Chiefs of Staff)

AC (Allied Council) SCAP (Supreme Commander Allied Powers)

JG (Japanese Government)

122

Or, to put it into the language of a SCAP document:

The Japanese Government, reoriented to insure that the requirements of the occupation would be met, has been permitted to exercise the normal powers of government in matters of domestic administration. . . . Policies and decisions of the Supreme Commander are transmitted to the Japanese government by formal written directives (memoranda known as SCAPINS) or informal instructions. . . . Japanese compliance with the directives of the Supreme Commander is checked by two methods: (1) Surveillance by GHQ staff sections in the area of their responsibility. (2) Observation and reports by the Civil Affairs Teams located at regional headquarters.

These teams do an interesting job; originally one existed in each of the forty-six prefectures of Japan. (Before the war Japan had forty-seven prefectures; Okinawa was the forty-seventh.) As conditions became stabilized the teams were reduced in number and at present there are only eight; they report on such matters as land reform, taxes, rice collection, public health, and so on. In effect they are supervisors of the local administration, but just as fast as the local authorities learn to do their job, pressure by the teams is lightened; the object is to transmit steadily just as much power as possible to the Japanese.

Only seldom does SCAP issue direct political directives these days. As long ago as 1946 Government Section abandoned formal directives in favor of "persuasion, suggestion, and advice." From the beginning MacArthur decided to use, in every way possible, the existing machinery of the Japanese government; nothing is overtly forced on anybody, and the forms are delicately observed. As a result people in Tokyo say that the present system is "government by telephone." There is no *written* record of what pressure, if any, still may be brought by a SCAP officer on a Japanese bureaucrat. Ostensibly, almost everything has been turned back to the Japanese, which acts on SCAP's behalf. "We won't do for them what they can do themselves," was an early MacArthur watchword. The technique is to say informally, "If you need advice on such and such my staff is always available to you." And the Japanese have certainly worked hard within their orbit; for instance the new Diet has passed no fewer than 700 laws.

Criticism of SCAP by Japanese is illegal and has been forbidden since the first days of the occupation. I distinguished myself for naïveté immediately after we arrived by asking all manner of Japanese, including the leaders of each party, whether they had any "grievances" against SCAP. They looked thunderstruck, and their first response was usually just to laugh. In fact they seemed scared to death at the question, and it took coaxing to get them to talk at all. Later, however, many Japanese did speak out to us with remarkable freedom and candor. The main grievances seemed to be (1) "Overnightism," i.e., the Americans have tried to push things through too quickly. (2) Japanese economy cannot stand the cost of some of our reforms, particularly in education. (3) Lack of understanding on the part of many occupationeers. (4) SCAP is not accessible enough, particularly in the lower echelons.

SCAP itself is not subject to the new Japanese constitution, odd as this may seem, and there are thus two laws in effect in Japan, our law and theirs. While we were in Tokyo four Japanese were sentenced to two years at hard labor each for "engaging in acts prejudicial to the objectives of the occupation." A member of the United States Provost Court announced severely when the verdict was given, "Remember, this is still an occupation!" In 1948-1949 about sixty Japanese, mostly communists, were jailed for criticism. As a matter of fact the point could probably be made that it is also illegal for *American* members of SCAP to criticize SCAP. If an American official consistently demonstrates a hostile attitude, he will be asked to leave Japan; I heard of one case in which an official was booted out on eight hours' notice. When, however, such an event occurs, the Army takes care to arrange the details so that no discredit will fall on the Army itself.

Another analogy to SCAP comes to mind, that of the old Indian Civil Service, the inflexible steel brace which ruled India until

World War II. I remember how astonished I was in Delhi in 1938 to learn that the Indian Civil Service contained exactly 591 Englishmen; yet it administered an entire subcontinent, and administered it extremely well. Similarly the total civilian personnel of SCAP, which rules 83,000,000 Japanese, consists of only about 2,200 Americans, and the number is steadily being cut down; moreover this number includes everybody—secretaries, messengers, chauffeurs, and the like. Even our armed forces in Japan are not numerous. At the outbreak of the Korean war there were only about 60,000 American military in the country, including GHQ, the Eighth Army, the Navy, and the Far East Air Force, and since Korea most of these have been siphoned out.

General Sketch of the Reforms and Constitution

At once, only thirty-two days after the surrender, SCAP issued the "Bill of Rights" directive (October 4, 1945), which instructed the Japanese government to release all political prisoners, and to remove all "restrictions on political, civil, and religious liberties on the grounds of race, nationality, creed, or political opinion." Then the government was required to abolish its notorious Kenpei-tai (a special secret-police organization), the "regular" secret police, and all public agencies concerned with censorship or "thought control," speech, religion, or assembly. There had been no fewer than 59,000 arrests in Japan for "dangerous thought" in the period immediately preceding the outbreak of war. Later, as a positive corollary, SCAP set up a "Civil Liberties Bureau," administered by the Japanese themselves, to see that the new guarantees were observed. Then the Home and Justice ministries were formally abolished; these ministries had been the chief agencies of repression, undemocratic procedures and reaction.

Among other reforms the Imperial General Headquarters, which made the war, was liquidated. The peerage was, except for a few members of the imperial family, done away with. A habeas corpus law was enacted; this had not existed in Japan before. The legal equality of men and women was established, something unknown previously, and a new law (aiming to break up the old family system) was passed covering the inheritance of private property, so that this can no longer be arbitrarily decided by the head of the family. Another early directive abolished categorically the system of indentured or forced labor. I remember in 1938 visiting textile factories near Tokyo and seeing girl workers, virtually slaves, who had been sold to the labor bosses and factory managers. This outrageous offense against humanity no longer exists.

The criminal and civil codes were redrawn, and the administration of government thoroughly decentralized. Local autonomy was encouraged—by a widespread group of new laws—so that nowadays the local communities elect their own officials, collect their own taxes, run their own police, and choose their own school boards, all of which was unknown before. The former dependence of the judiciary on the executive was abolished, and a new Supreme Court set up. In October, 1947, a public-service law was passed, establishing something totally new to Japan—an elaborate civil service on the merit system. Finally, militarism and war as an instrument of national policy were formally outlawed by the constitution. Japan is, I believe, the only country in the world forbidden by its own organic law to make war. The actual clause is "War, as a sovereign right of the nation and the threat or use of force, is forever renounced as a means of settling disputes with other nations. The maintenance of land, sea, and air forces, as well as other war potential, will never be authorized. The right of belligerency of the state will not be recognized."

General MacArthur, it is generally believed, wrote these words into the draft constitution with his own hand. He has said jubilantly that it would be impossible for the Japanese to rearm themselves for a hundred years. And Japan is, we all know, uniquely defenseless—the country has no military establishment whatsoever, not a soldier, not a tank, not an airplane, not a stick of bombs. But following Chinese intervention in the Korean war it may become im-

126

perative to rearm Japan. The Supreme Commander is extremely proud of "his" constitution, and he would hate to have it modified; on the other hand he would certainly dislike seeing Japan swallowed by an aggressor. As a matter of fact provision exists whereby the constitution may be amended without too much difficulty, and in time this will probably be done.

*

Technically—the point is not without interest—the allied powers have no legal right in Japan except that we are empowered to occupy it *until* it fulfills the terms of the Potsdam Declaration. Most people assume that the original United States directive to Mac-Arthur includes the instruction that he should "democratize" Japan; in actual fact the terminology is quite different, and asks merely that we "bring about the eventual establishment of a peaceful and responsible government . . . which should conform as closely *as may be* to principles of democratic self government." The directive proceeds, "It is not the responsibility of the Allied Powers to impose upon Japan any form of government not supported by the freely expressed will of the people."

Immediately after the occupation began it became necessary to work out changes in the constitution. The story of this, which I do not think has ever been written before, has its curiosities. One American news magazine has said that MacArthur "wrote" the new constitution himself; SCAP officials insist nowadays that the Japanese wrote it. The truth lies in between. In October, 1945, the Supreme Commander summoned Ex-Prime Minister Konoye (who later killed himself) and "suggested" that Japan should "liberalize" its old Meiji constitution. The American political adviser at the time was the late George Atcheson. Japanese emissaries from Konoye, who knew that the MacArthur suggestion was a command, called on Mr. Atcheson to ask him what to do. He told them to write some amendments to the old constitution, reducing the power of the Emperor and abolishing the army. This was all that MacArthur, as

I have heard the story from very high authority, had in mind at the time. The Japanese government set up a committee to investigate the matter; the newspapers got hold of the story, reported it inaccurately, and said that a *new* constitution was to be written. The Japanese committee then took the decision not merely to revise the old document but to start from scratch and draft one altogether new. After this, however, as if terrified by its boldness, it stalled, beat around the bush, and got nothing done.

MacArthur called in General Whitney and said, in effect, "That committee is not catching its cue. They're not moving. Step in and help them out."

Whitney thereupon, for some weeks, turned Government Section into what practically became a constitutional convention. Members of the Japanese committee and American personnel of Whitney's section, mostly legal experts, met every day in the Dai-Ichi and tussled until they got a draft. They read and analyzed, among other things, every other constitution in the world, including that of the Soviet Union. The actual drafting was for the most part done by Whitney's deputy, Charles L. Kades, who has now returned to legal practice in New York. Mr. Kades, his friends will always remember, is the author (for the most part) of the organic law ruling 83,000,- 000 people. Everybody had an excitingly good time at the "convention." There are few students of political science who have not wanted, at one time or other, to draw up a Utopia. Some violent arguments occurred—for instance as to whether the cabinet should sit in the Diet, and how exactly the Diet should choose the prime minister. Three different Japanese politicians of eminence like to assert today that *they* wrote the constitution. They didn't. In fact jokes were plentiful, when the document was published, about how it had to be translated at the last moment from English to Japanese. Yet the Japanese indisputably did have much to do with it. The committee had such a good time, drinking coffee and munching sandwiches late at night during the drafting, that members recently suggested to General Whitney that they should assemble once a year in the same room to celebrate.

One curious point is that the entire constitution is an *amendment* to the old one, which it abolishes. This was a bright idea of Mac-Arthur's. He wanted to emphasize the principle of continuity.

Before the new constitution could be promulgated it had to be approved by the Emperor, because it needed imperial sanction on being submitted to the Diet. For the first time in their lives members of a Japanese cabinet were given the touchy job of approaching Hirohito and asking his approval of a document that stripped *him* of most of his powers. Prime Minister Shidehara timidly went to MacArthur, and asked, "How will *he* [the Emperor] take it?" Mac-Arthur replied, "Mr. Prime Minister, have no fear. You will find that when the Emperor sees the draft he will like it very much."

The constitution was duly promulgated, and soon went into effect. Some of its language has considerable eloquence. Of course in no Oriental country do words matter much; it is quite possible for a nation to have a splendid constitution on paper and be a miserable dictatorship in fact—or vice versa. Nevertheless one should not minimize the seminal importance of this document. As I heard it put in Tokyo, "It transformed what had been a feudal, highly centralized state, ruled by a triple oligarchy of militarists, bureaucrats, and economic monopolists into what is on paper at least as liberal a constitutional democracy as exists anywhere in the world."

*

To implement their first directives, the Americans in Japan had a triple job. First, to change the actual legal structure of government; this was done by the new constitution and ancillary laws. Second, to try to encourage the growth of fresh personal leadership to our taste. Third, to create a *citizenry*—to try to get implanted into Japan a basic sense of responsibility by the people for the conduct of civil affairs and their government.

One day my wife and I went to a briefing in Government Section, and saw a series of charts showing pithily the Japan that was, the Japan that is, and the Japan that will be—if all goes well. Today the basis of power is the people, in whom all sovereignty is held to reside; the Emperor is a figurehead; the Diet rules. No longer can military personages break up any cabinet; no longer are the three major functions of government, executive, legislative, judicial, embodied in a single will.

Many of the new procedures governing the Diet were taken from the 1946 Reorganization Act of the United States Congress, but in some respects the Japanese Diet is a more supple and effective instrument of government than the American House of Representatives or Senate. For instance the Diet is organized into twenty-two committees, identical in each house; it would save much trouble and waste of time in Washington if we had the same system.

Another point is the average age of Diet members in comparison with before the war. They are a good twelve years younger.

At first SCAP did not know what to do with one old pernicious institution, the Tenari Gumi or "Neighborhood Associations." There was no local autonomy in prewar Japan; the Tenari Gumi were the indispensable feudal mechanism by which (a) control of the prefectures and communes was centralized in Tokyo; (b) the people were regimented down to their very thoughts. One group in SCAP wanted to abolish the Tenari Gumi forthwith. MacArthur said "No." In effect he proceeded, "Of course they're evil, but they are also an extremely deep-rooted national institution. If we order them out, there will be resentment. Suppose we let them alone, give the people something else, and hope that they will just die out." What the General hoped for has occurred; the Tenari Gumi may still exist, but nobody pays attention to them, because nowadays Japanese elect their own local officials and have complete autonomy in neighborhood and community affairs.

Women, Population, Birth Control, Abortion

Before SCAP, women had no political, legal, or economic rights in Japan; their position is vastly different now. MacArthur's philosophy about this was quite simple. Under Christianity women have souls exactly as have men, and even if Japan is not a Christian country, he did not see why the same theory should not apply. So it was carefully written into the constitution not merely that there should be no discrimination on account of sex, but that there was, as of basic right, "essential equality" between the sexes. I doubt if any constitution in the world goes so far.

Full and free women's suffrage was enacted, and thousands upon thousands of women who had never voted in their lives went to the polls. In the first general election under the occupation (April, 1946), women won no fewer than thirty-nine seats in the Diet. Mac-Arthur greeted each with a message of individual congratulation. Not so many sit now; the figure today is twelve in the House of Representatives, twelve in the House of Councilors. Ten of these are social democrats; three are communists. Every cabinet since 1948 has had at least one woman vice-minister and at present the chairmen of two Diet committees are women. In addition multitudinous women hold other political posts—there are 23 in the prefectural assemblies, 74 in city councils, and 707 in town assemblies. This was an important element in getting democratic procedures out to the rural districts.

People thought at first, when women were given the vote, that they would vote as their husbands directed, in other words that what woman suffrage really meant was two votes for the man, but it hasn't altogether turned out that way. One of the historic leaders of the emancipation movement for Japanese women, Mrs. Kanju Kato, told us that, in general, there were at least three types of Japanese women voters: those that did as a rule follow their husbands, those who were such ardent feminists that they voted only for women candidates, and the great majority, those who did think and choose for themselves.

It would be silly to pretend that, after only five years, women have been completely "emancipated" in Japan. A good deal depends on economics. Out on the farms, in the remote districts disfigured by the bitterest poverty, the status of women has probably changed little, except in theory. They are still a combination of womb and

131

beast of burden. But, looking at the national picture as a whole, and in long perspective, there can be no doubt at all but that the general condition of women has immeasurably improved.

One curious item is that the principle of equality, set forth in the constitution, made necessary many changes in the legal code. For instance under the old law adultery was a crime but the law provided for punishment of the wife and the other party to the adultery; a husband who committed adultery with an unmarried woman was not subject to punishment. To change this made a dilemma for the lawmakers. Either they had to make adultery equally punishable for both partners in a marriage, or "abolish it as a crime." After months of anguished discussion the Diet decided to abolish adultery as a crime.

In education a considerable advance has taken place. Before SCAP Japanese girls were segregated from boys and went to their own schools (if to any at all) after the sixth grade; coeducation in high schools scarcely existed, and there were no universities for women; they had different textbooks and in general their curriculum was pitched well below that of the boys. This has all been changed. Japanese girls and boys go to the public schools and state colleges as equals, and the girls have colleges of their own, twenty-six in all, considered to be on the university level. Of course one result of this, as indicated in a preceding chapter, has been to stir up more contact and fermentation between the sexes than ever existed before, and to make marriages without parental authority much more frequent.

The new labor laws go far, at least in theory, to protect women in industry. About 5,500,000 Japanese women are engaged in non-agricultural employment; about 1,500,000 belong to unions. The law limits overtime for women workers, restricts night work in certain industries, gives generous leave for illness and prematernal care, and embodies the principle of equal pay for equal work. There are even women police—1,900 so far—which is indeed unprecedented in an Oriental country, and some 14,000 women "Welfare Commissioners" work in the villages. Another item is that young women are active in sports, and you see girls in bloomers or shorts playing softball at a hundred street corners.

*

Population, a problem in any hungry country, is a terrific problem in Japan. The population was 82,600,000 in October, 1949, and is now estimated to be 83,500,000. This in a territory the size of California, of which only one sixth is arable! The density of population is enormous (569.3 per square mile—as compared to 49.7 in the United States) and the population has actually doubled in a little over fifty years. Since October, 1945 it has increased by no less than *ten million*, which is as if five cities the size of Philadelphia had been added in one decade. Not all this was, however, the result of natural increase, since it includes the considerable number of Japanese repatriated from overseas after the war. Even so, the natural growth proceeds at an extraordinary rate. The birth rate is the highest in the world, and has touched 34.76 per thousand. Meantime the death rate, as a result of modern sanitation and health control brought in by SCAP, has sunk from a prewar average of 17.3 to 11.6. The result is that the increase of births over deaths is something like 1,500,000 per year. One and a half *million* new mouths to feed every year— in a country that has to import at least 15 per cent of all its food! The population increases at the unbelievable rate of four to five thousand per day, and conservative experts think that by 1975 the total will be 100,000,000.

This does not alarm the authorities as much as it might. After 1975, they believe, the ratio between birth and death rates will stabilize, and the population will remain constant at about a hundred million. General Sams, the director of the Public Health and Welfare Section, thinks that continuing industrialization will be bound to limit the birth rate. This happens in all countries; when people move into the towns and become urbanized the birth rate drops. Out in the country a child, which is cheaper than a cow, is a useful object who can be put to work; in the city it is an expensive extra mouth. Rural families in Japan average four and a fraction children; urban families average only two and a fraction. Also Japan has had at least one period, roughly between the early 1920's and 1939, when the birth rate actually dropped; it may drop again.

All this serves to make birth control an acutely important and controversial issue. One of the most interesting hours we spent in Tokyo was with the Doctors Amano. Dr. K. W. Amano, an M.D. from the University of Pennsylvania and one of the best-known physicians in the city, and his wife, Dr. F. Y. Amano (who has medical degrees from Columbia and Yale), are veteran birth-control advocates, maintain a birth-control clinic, and have recently begun to publish a small magazine, the *Japan Planned Parenthood Quarterly*.

Birth control was legal in Japan before the war, but not conspicuously practiced or encouraged, and during the years of military control it was severely frowned upon, because the army wanted more babies. New laws passed under SCAP have stimulated the birth-control movement strongly. Every prefecture is, by law, supposed to maintain at least one "Marriage Consultation Office," where women (or men) receive free instruction in contraception. Of these offices 145 are functioning at the moment; the city of Osaka alone has 34; 19 out of 46 prefectures have not, however, got around to setting them up. In the *Parenthood Quarterly* you see advertisements for such devices as the "Pelvic Model for Contraceptive Instruction, Anatomical and Physiological Models, in Fiber or Wax," and doctors like the Amanos have taken the lead in showing how instruction should be given.

Contraceptives are big business in Japan; more than fifteen million items per month are sold. Nevertheless, the Amanos told us, progress in birth control has on the whole been slow. In one rural prefecture, only four women came to the Consultation Office the first month. Patients are not educated; neither are most doctors. Many women, particularly peasants, are too shy to come to the clinic to ask advice, or they come too late. Birth-control "rallies" with speeches and demonstrations by physicians occur in the big towns, and they are well patronized by young people, particularly young men, but not many mothers come.

One of the recent polls undertaken by the Osaka *Mainichi* throws light on these questions:

Question: Do you intend to depend upon your children?
Answers:
    a. Live entirely independent 11.1%
    b. Expect to depend on 29.1%
    c. Depend upon the heir 25.6%
    d. Live together without economic dependence 10.2%
    e. Want to depend, but not much hope 2.7%
Question: Since anyone can practice contraception freely and easily, what do you think about it?
Answers:
    a. Good thing 60.7%
    b. Not good 15.0%
    c. Others 24.3%
Question: What policy should Japan follow so as not to increase the birth rate in the future?
Answers:
    a. Limit the number of births 10.1%
    b. Make it disadvantageous to be prolific 1.8%
    c. Provide guidance to avoid too frequent births 41.3%
    d. Leave entirely up to individual's wish 31.2%
    e. Others 17.5%
Question: What do you think about artificial miscarriage (abortion)?
Answers:
    a. Approve when inheritance of bad disease is feared 65.8%
    b. Approve when mother's life is endangered 72.9%
    c. Approve when a poverty-stricken mother's health is
       feared to be endangered by childbirth 50.6%
    d. Approve when the pregnancy has resulted from rape ... 50.9%
    e. Approve when living is financially threatened 38.6%
    f. Approve when contraception has failed 18.4%
    g. Approve unconditionally 3.0%
    h. Oppose for fear of moral deterioration 8.2%

i. Oppose from religious standpoint 2.9%

j. Oppose from any standpoint 1.4%

Question: Are you practicing contraception?

Answers:

1. Practicing

   Urban 23.6%

   Rural 17.4%

2. Once Practiced

   Urban 10.3%

   Rural 8.2%

3. Never Practiced

   Urban 59.3%

   Rural 65.9%

Question: If you have never practiced contraception, why?

Answers:

a. Not worried by having children 12.2%

b. Want children 38.0%

c. No reliable contraceptive method 9.1%

d. Do not know any contraceptive method 4.6%

e. Practice is too troublesome 5.5%

f. No fear of conception 5.2%

g. Too expensive 2.8%

h. Oppose, as a principle 7.4%

i. Do not care either way 13.1%

Question: What method do you use?

Answers:

a. Rhythm 27.4%

b. Coitus interruptus 12.7%

c. Mechanical contraceptives 43.4%

d. Douche 4.8%

e. Drugs 29.6%

f. Others 15.0%

Question: For what reason do you practice?

Answers:

a. Economic 43.8%

b. For the mother's health 31.5%

c. To prevent inheritable disease 0.9%

d. To enjoy life 15.5%

e. For the children's health and education 38.9%

f. To leave each child more inheritance 0.8%

Abortion is, under certain circumstances, quite legal in Japan, following the Eugenic-Protection Law of July, 1948, which provides that a woman may have an abortion if childbirth will endanger her health, or for other medical reasons, upon the recommendation of a committee of doctors, and even on the ground of economic hardship. Abortion was illegal before the occupation, but countless illicit abortions did occur. *Mabiki* (infanticide) is a well-known Japanese institution; it means literally "thinning out" and for centuries it was the only form of Japanese birth "control"; a major cause of the relative stability of the population until modern times was *mabiki*.

One reason why many doctors in Japan support the birth-control movement wholeheartedly is their hope that this will check the number of legal abortions, which is alarming. (On the other hand unscrupulous doctors oppose birth control, because abortions are so lucrative.) In 1949, 246,236 Japanese women had abortions "through official channels," and the rate is going up steeply. The number of illegal abortions is prodigious, but unknown. A legal abortion costs 2,000 yen (roughly $5.50); this is the government fee. An illegal one can cost as much as 25,000 yen, or almost $70. Another point is that legal abortion may be authorized if a woman becomes pregnant as a result "of having committed adultery while unable to refuse or resist." Incidentally the Eugenic-Protection Law also provides for compulsory sterilization, both of males and females, in the cases of parents with certain hereditary diseases; 30 men were sterilized in 1949, and 5,749 women.

MacArthur's own view on birth control is that, roughly, the Japanese passed their own law and should be allowed to make it work. His basic feeling is that the problem of population will settle itself eventually through industrialization. There was considerable outcry when he refused to give Dr. Margaret Sanger permission to enter Japan. His aides explain this by saying that he did not mean to take a stand against birth control as such, since it was permitted by Japanese law, but that he did not wish non-Japanese to arouse controversy on a question the Japanese should settle for themselves.

137

Matters of Health

The chief of the Public Health and Welfare Section of SCAP is a remarkable officer, Brig. Gen. Crawford F. Sams. General Sams is an M.D. from Washington University in St. Louis, an expert in neuroanatomy, chief surgeon of the United States Army Forces in the Middle East in 1942-1943, a parachutist (he is a graduate of the Fort Benning parachute school), the veteran of half a dozen stiff campaigns in World War II, and one of the foremost experts of the time on public health. A compact decisive man, tough-minded, studious, he is, like many people of the top rank in SCAP, an idealist of realism. If a character like Sams were discovered by some journalist in Iceland, say, or Libya, books would be written about him. But he is an American working all but anonymously in Japan, and not one American in ten million has ever heard his name.

General Sams has superintended operations unprecedented in the whole field of public health the world over; mention the details to doctors newly arrived from the United States, and they cannot believe that figures of such magnitude are possible. For instance a smallpox epidemic broke out in Japan in 1946, with 17,000 cases. What happened thereafter is described laconically in a SCAP report: "The mass immunization of the entire population together with the routine vaccination and re-vaccination of all infants and school children, as required by the Preventive Vaccination Law No. 68 of 1948, has eliminated smallpox as a major health problem. During 1948 there was a total of only 124 cases in Japan. A re-vaccination of the entire population was again undertaken in 1949."

This means, in short, that on two occasions, *every* human being in Japan was vaccinated; twice, our medical service administered vaccination to something like eighty *million* persons. Nothing on this scale has ever been known to medical history before.

Tuberculosis, for various reasons, is a violent scourge in Japan. General Sams has pushed a program whereby, as of today, some thirty-five *million* Japanese citizens have been vaccinated with a new immunization agent known as BCG. "This control program" (again

138

I quote the staid official language) "has resulted in a 40 per cent reduction in deaths since 1945. Study of the deaths by age group indicates that the entire reduction has occurred in the age groups immunized with BCG. . . . Within the immunized groups the number of cases has been reduced by 79 per cent and number of deaths by 88 per cent." And every living Japanese under the age of thirty-five has been immunized.

Listen to some other figures. The Sams teams have dusted fifty *million* Japanese with DDT. The diphtheria rate—and diphtheria was a deadly menace—has been reduced 86 per cent under the occu-pation. Dysentery, very prevalent formerly, has been cut down 79 per cent, even though no vaccines exist conferring immunity against this disease. Typhoid and paratyphoid have been reduced a flat 90 per cent (and there were no fewer than 68,000 typhoid cases in the last year before the occupation) and cholera has completely dis-appeared. Not a single case of cholera has occurred in Japan since December, 1946. This was after the Sams organization gave thirty-four *million* people immunizations against it.

There is a widespread belief in the United States that the Japa-nese, in comparison with other Asiatics, are a "clean" people. They are not. Or to put it more precisely, "They are the cleanest people in the world in the most unsanitary way." They bathe—but in dirty water; they wipe with the utmost care the dishes and other paraphernalia with which they drink tea—with dirty cloths. "To bathe in a Japanese tub is the equivalent of bathing in a sewer," Sams told us.

General Sams has organized 80,000 Japanese to staff some 800 health-center districts (whereas before the occupation exactly two sanitary engineers existed in the whole of Japan), and no fewer than 60,000 six-man teams work out of these centers, going literally from home to home throughout the entire country teaching preventive medicine, checking water supply, using DDT, and demonstrating modern methods of sanitation. Also he is working elaborately on problems of nutrition. A cardinal lack in Japan is protein of animal origin. It will, he thinks, take a thorough reorientation of the economic and even the religious life of the country before nutritional reform can be complete—for instance grain-growing areas should be given over to cattle and the Buddhist tenet forbidding meat and milk as food is a serious obstacle to progress.

There is no such thing as a medically indigent person in Japan today, Sams says. Most observers believe that, if only because the results have been so spectacular, what we have taught the Japanese in public health will never be forgotten. Japanese medicine, opinion to the contrary notwithstanding, was not advanced; when we arrived we found it to be at least twenty years behind our own. The Japanese, a people who know value when they find it, have been eager to catch up. I asked one American doctor the question I asked everybody, "When we go, how much will stick?" The answer was, "There will be some backsliding in all fields. We teach a doctor to sterilize his instruments and then if we don't watch him for six months he forgets all about it. But there will be less backsliding in our field than in any other."

A Word About Religion

Sometimes it is said, "One thing that MacArthur has never interfered with is religion," but this is not literally true. The Supreme Commander's line on religious matters has, in essence, been more political than religious. He believes firmly in freedom of worship; he thinks that there is something good in almost all religions, and that Christianity is of particular merit because it grants dignity to the individual soul. To believe that the soul has dignity means that you must equally believe that a good life is worth living. In the old Japan, on the other hand, the state religion, Shinto, was a handmaiden to the power system; it taught that the individual human being did *not* count, but that everything was subservient to the state which was symbolized in the person of a "divine" Emperor. For predominantly political reasons, scap had to break this idea down.

Most Japanese (about 55 per cent) are Buddhists; some 15 per cent adhere to what is known as "Sectarian" Shinto; many are Buddhists and Shintoists at the same time. The basis of religious belief is—or was—a combination of ancestor worship, patriotism, and conviction that the Japanese race was divine. Buddhism is too complex a concept for us to define here, but it, too, could be said to have played into the hands of the militarists since its emphasis is not so much on individual effort and good works in the present life as on reincarnation in the future.

I met some Americans in Tokyo who thought that Japan could never be successfully democratized unless it was Christianized, in that democracy depends so much on ethical Christian values. There are, however, only a handful of Christians in Japan—about 130,-000 Roman Catholics (who proselytize actively), and 201,000 Protestants of various denominations.

First of all SCAP abolished State Shinto. This was done by specific directive on December 15, 1945; Shinto was disestablished as a state religion. People may think of this as a routine step nowadays, but it was fully as sensational as if a British government had suddenly been forced to disestablish the Church of England, fire the Archbishop of Canterbury, and abolish the ceremony of coronation.

The Japanese government was prohibited from the "sponsorship, support, perpetuation, control, and dissemination of State Shinto or *any other religion.*" Complete freedom of worship was guaranteed by the constitution, and we got to work in a number of adjacent fields; SCAP has a religious section with Catholic, Protestant, and Buddhist advisers. In the words of an official document:

The Japanese government [in implementing SCAP directives] has eliminated all Shinto doctrine from public school textbooks; has removed all Shinto symbols from public buildings, has ordered the removal of repositories of the Imperial portraits from school grounds and buildings, has prohibited school-conducted bowing toward the Imperial Palace, has revised the system of national holidays by dropping those most closely associated with Shinto, has eliminated the Imperial chrysanthemum from postage stamps and currency, and has deregistered certain historic sites.
Under supervision is the complex task, expected to take three or four

141

years, of transferring land titles from the state to religious organizations so that no vestige of connection with the state remains. Some 200,000 acres of state owned land at present occupied rent-free by approximately 110,000 Shinto shrines and 40,000 Buddhist temples are involved.

Militaristic and ultranationalistic movements and doctrines are not permitted to hide behind the cloak of religion. . . . Over 8,000 monuments objectionable because of Shinto ultranationalist connotations have been removed, and objectionable inscriptions have been erased from otherwise unobjectionable monuments.

All this has left something of a spiritual vacuum in Japan, as we know. People feel uprooted; they lack faith. A great many Japanese beyond doubt still believe in Shinto; the full evolution is going to take a lot of time.

Some strange cults have sprung up to satisfy theological yearnings, and these may grow to have considerable importance. One is called Seicho No Ie, and it includes in one amorphous "doctrine" the teachings of Buddha, Mary Baker Eddy, theosophy, some elements of Roman Catholicism, and Shinto too.

Some Economic Angles, Briefly Put

In economic fields MacArthur thinks more or less like this. Japan is a country only recently reclaimed from feudalism, with no substantial middle class and a background of the most grisly poverty. Its common people have known little except exploitation; they are prolific, crowded into a preposterously small area, and perpetually hungry. How, then, will it be possible for the average citizen to believe genuinely and forcefully in the idea of individual freedom, responsibility for free government, and intelligent participation in public affairs, unless he is given a true economic stake in the community? (Interestingly enough, the very word "community" did not exist in Japanese until recently; words existed for "town" and "village" but the concept of "community" was foreign to the language.) MacArthur's approach to economic problems, as to those in the religious sphere, is largely administrative and political. When people said that SCAP was New Dealish (and it was a healthy thing that it was) they meant simply that the Supreme Commander was trying to build up an economy in which people would feel secure, so that the political structure of democracy would be stable. Mac-Arthur never ceases to keep in mind that there will be a peace treaty some day, and that scap will then terminate. He wants to leave a situation in which every Japanese will have some sort of investment, however small, in the total life of the nation, in which labor will want to maintain the rights it has gained, and in which the peasant can feel that his new privileges are safe. In a word, to make Japan democratic it is necessary to make it prosperous, or, if not actually prosperous, healthy enough economically to stay alive.

Thus arose the two chief scap accomplishments in the economic field: (a) labor legislation, (b) the land reform.

The constitution specifically states that all people have the *right* to work, and that labor may organize and bargain collectively. This is guaranteed. As early as October, 1945, MacArthur "instructed" the prime minister to encourage unionization; before the war only about four hundred thousand Japanese workers were organized, as against a figure of roughly seven million union members now. On the other hand, strikes are certainly not encouraged—MacArthur nipped in the bud one attempt at a general strike—and since 1948 government workers have been forbidden to strike. Even so I heard Americans in Tokyo say that Japanese labor laws were so far advanced in protection of workers that they are "twenty years ahead of those in the United States." There is even a law limiting the weight a charcoal worker can carry on his back. A well-organized, comprehensive system of social security is in operation, and it is being strongly expanded all the time. scap itself has stated in an official announcement that the eventual objective of social security is to ensure "the well being of the entire nation from the cradle to the grave." Yet uninformed people call MacArthur reactionary!

As to the land reform the Supreme Commander himself states that "it is the most successful experiment of its kind in history." The basic figures are that before September 2, 1945, 54 per cent of the land of Japan was owner-operated, 46 per cent tenant-operated. As of December 31, 1949, 89 per cent was owner-operated, only 11 per cent tenant-operated. A total of 4,649,586 acres has been bought from former proprietors by the government, and 4,571,698 acres of this has been distributed to small tenant farmers. Properties worth 49 billion yen have been transferred from their former owners into 33,000 agricultural cooperatives which, as of today, have 8,200,000 members.

These figures are impressive, but they need careful scrutiny. The land reform has not been quite so effective as SCAP would like to think. You cannot totally transform and revolutionize the structure of agriculture in a country like Japan in five years. The reform itself was well planned and has been administered well, but the power of the landlords is not yet broken by any means; they have been softened up but not eliminated. For one thing the local committees that make the allotments are often in the control of the landlords themselves, because the peasants are still too timid to assert themselves, and many landlords deliberately evade or break the new laws because they feel sure that the tenants will not dare to sue them. The vessel of the land reform is admirable; but you have to analyze its contents. Be this as it may be, the reform certainly represents substantial progress, and already it is the object of wide attention throughout Asia. The Philippine government recently asked SCAP for guidance on a land-reform program (something the Philippines need desperately) and recently MacArthur had a letter from General K. C. Wu, the governor of the provincial government at Taipeh, Formosa, asking for similar advice. If the Kuomintang had made a land reform anything like MacArthur's, it might well be in Nanking today, instead of in the Formosa wilderness.

*

We have not the space to go into the work of SCAP's Economic and Scientific Section. General Marquat, an amiable creature, gave us a brief conspectus of his program, and we had a long talk with his chief brain-truster, Dr. Sherwood Fine, a youthful economist who reminded me of Washington New Dealers in the early 1930's.

Once he believed in deficit spending. Nor can we describe the work of the Natural Resources Section. Its able chief, Colonel Schenck, sat with us most of an afternoon; he and members of his staff showed us impressive charts and gave us orientation on everything from fisheries (85 per cent of Japan's animal protein comes from sea food) to shipping, from petroleum consumption to reforestation. It was interesting to hear that 37 per cent of all usable timber in Japan goes for charcoal and chopsticks.

Within SCAP there have been several substantial shifts in economic policy, and some strong quarrels. One shift came with the installation of what was called the "Dodge Plan" in the spring of 1949. This, worked out by Joseph M. Dodge of Detroit, a former president of the American Bankers Association, provided for stabilization, retrenchment, and balancing of the budget, with the general emphasis on recovery rather than mere reform. It was severely painful to many Japanese. One of the standard quarrels has been about cartels and trust busting. Dr. Edward C. Welsh, one of MacArthur's chief economic advisers until recently, led the struggle to break up the cartels and enforce fair-trade practices. Dr. Welsh is a former professor of economics in Ohio and has strong New Deal tendencies; the conservative Japanese fought him bitterly, and so did most of the American business community in Tokyo.

SCAP likes to say that Japan will be self-sufficient in 1952, but almost all non-SCAP experts (and many dissidents within SCAP itself) think that this estimate is wildly optimistic. To support itself in the next twenty years, Japan will have to create something like eight million new industrial jobs, since such multitudes of new workers come into the labor market each year and since agriculture is saturated. Japan cannot live, presuming the end of the occupation, except by paying for imports of food through its export trade; hence, the chief economic problem is to make exports expand. "You cannot," Mr. Shidehara told us quietly at lunch one day, "*order* prosperity." The country must, in an average year, import 15 per cent of its food; the figure has reached 25 per cent in some years,

145

Under SCAP today all staple food is rationed and distributed to the consumer by a government corporation; the average Japanese gets 1,975 calories per day. But what will happen after the occupation ends, and the United States no longer ships in enormous quantities of food? Will not the threat of communism increase, if the standard of living sinks?

The United States, i.e., the American taxpayer, supports Japanese economy and pays for the occupation in part by an instrument, utterly unknown to most Americans, called the "Garioa" dollar, which means dollars spent in "Government and Relief, Occupied Areas." About 54 per cent of all American expenditures are for food. The total bill to the United States for Japan in the fiscal year 1949 was roughly $517,000,000; the total since the beginning of the occupation is well over $2,000,000,000.

I heard an exceptionally well-informed and astute Englishman say, "The contemporary Japanese prayer is that God grant that the United States should cease to be their overlord but continue to be their underwriter."

Finally, Education

Above all SCAP has a tremendously ambitious program in education; upon this, in the long run, everything else will of course depend. Colonel D. R. Nugent, who was a schoolteacher in Japan in former years, told us about his work as director of SCAP's Civil Information and Education Section. One phase of the task is supervision, reform, and rehabilitation of a system that includes some 19,000,000 students, 42,000 schools, and 650,000 teachers.

First, SCAP decentralized. To break up the old system, whereby all education in Japan was rigidly controlled by Tokyo, we stimulated laws whereby the prefectures and other local authorities elected their own school boards, chose their own textbooks, appointed their own school superintendents, and the like. The job of local superintendent did not even exist in Japan before. Next, after considerable dispute, the Diet passed in 1947 the School Education Law, which sets up a new curriculum so that, in theory at least, every school child in Japan has equality of educational opportunity. The basis (many Japanese think it is too expensive) is the so-called 6-3-3 system, whereby a youngster spends six years in grammar school, three in junior high, and three in senior high. After that, he may go on to college and graduate professional schools. By law, the first nine years (as compared with six in the old system) are compulsory and free. For higher education at least one university now exists in every prefecture, and there are 350 government colleges and universities in all.

Colonel Nugent and his men took the decision at the beginning that a normally operating school system should be inaugurated without delay. This is in great contrast to what happened in Germany, where most schools were closed for a long period. Since the end of 1946, no direct orders in education have been given to the Japanese authorities; they sink or swim by their own efforts. Dr. Stoddard of the University of Illinois came out to Japan and his group, after surveying the field, made a number of recommendations; Stoddard's report was made available to the Japanese, but it was not a directive. A "Japanese Education Reform Council," with forty-seven members, works on cabinet level and cooperates with Nugent's section. There are plenty of rough spots and much argument still—which shows that a real fermentation is at work, not merely acquiescence.

Textbooks are a remarkable story. We do not impose new texts on the Japanese; they write them themselves. The old texts were discarded if they betrayed any militaristic or ultranationalist ideas— most did—and new ones were prepared. Even an elementary arithmetic text had to be discarded if for instance it used some such question as, "If one machine gun will kill ten Americans, how many will kill one hundred?" The writing and publishing of texts was removed from the Ministry of Education, and opened to the competitive publishing market. I saw some of the new texts, in fields like third-grade science, first-grade English and so on; they are very well done indeed. More than 200 *million* textbooks were printed and distributed last year, and this figure will be 250 million for the school year 1950-1951. Similar impressive figures are available in a multitude of other fields, for instance that of adult education; films called "selfy-helpies" have tremendous circulation. More than 8,156,000 Japanese have seen a documentary called *A Day at School*; more than 2,000,000 one on the Port of New York, and more than 1,200,000 one called *The Story of Local Government*.

As in other fields, the achievement is remarkable enough but figures are not what count; what counts is the reality beneath. Merely to revise curricula, achieve uniform standards, print good texts, and provide school lunches, however admirable all this may be, is not enough. The know-how is on paper nicely, but the system depends in essence on how good the actual teaching is. Hence the gist of the problem is the education and practical performance of the teachers themselves. How to teach the teachers? Great progress has undoubtedly been made, especially in the younger grades; much still remains to be done. By and large the older teachers cannot afford to admit that *they* have to be taught, or they lose face; final reform of the educational system cannot be complete until the present generation of older teachers dies out, retires, or is replaced. But— day to-day progress is continuing.

People sometimes ask about "Romaji." If the Japanese should adopt "Romaji," i.e., Latinize their language, their intellectual life would be much simpler. A strong movement for Romaji exists, and Dr. Stoddard's commission recommended its adoption. But this is one thing that MacArthur refuses to do anything about. He knows well how difficult and almost insanely unwieldy Japanese is, but he does not wish to destroy anything so basic to the national character, and before doing anything about Romaji he will wait until the Japanese themselves push him into it.

Americans in Tokyo should not feel too superior about our own superiority in education. Japan's literacy rate is very high, well over 90 per cent. But it is not common knowledge that between 60 and 70 per cent of G.I.'s in the Eighth Army have never gone beyond fifth grade.

Chapter Eight

JAPANESE SIDE OF THE PICTURE

SHORTLY after we arrived in Tokyo I asked somebody at lunch what
had happened to a Japanese statesman I had known before the war,
Seihin Ikeda, then minister of finance. "Oh," came the reply, "he's
been purged." This use of the word "purge" was new to me; I had
never heard it in political talk except in connection with Russia.
Later our hostess remarked, "Of course the trouble with Japan is
that all the really *nice* people have been purged." Still later I heard
a somewhat horrifying joke from an American. "Do you know the
difference between Stalin and MacArthur? Stalin purges *with* trials!"

We heard more loose talk about the purges than on any other
topic during our stay in Japan. The purges scraped off the top
cream. The purges removed from public life all the people who
knew how to run things. The purges took away most Japanese who
had higher education, who had been to America, and who spoke
English. The purges dislocated the entire economics of the country.
And so on.

We heard about the mythology of purgeism, its technical language, and its sociology. For instance it is not incorrect for an
American to be seen publicly with a purgee, but if he has purgees
and non-purgees together at the same function it is bad form. We
heard about people who had been "depurged" (the word is sometimes "unpurged") but these are rare; I met only one. We heard salty

anecdotes about clubs, chambers of commerce, and the like, the entire membership of which consists of purgees. We listened to the story of Count So-and-So, once rich and prominent, who, purged for no other reason except that he had a job in the steel industry, is destitute. We heard about the mayor of a small town who was purged after ten years in office because (allegedly) he asked to have a nearby road repaired. We heard about the big party leader, destined to be prime minister, who was ruthlessly purged because he once undertook a prewar mission for Prince Konoye (and for other reasons too). We heard about secret forbidden talks between members of the present government and ancient purgees now living in seclusion. And so on.

A memorandum submitted to me by an individual purged and then unpurged contains the following:

An ex-editor-in-chief of a certain influential newspaper was purged and to make a living, he became a tea peddler. In a shabby outfit so contrasting to his former looks, he is peddling from village to village, shouldering a large rucksack filled with green tea leaves. "I'm surprised at the small profit after train fares and expenses are paid," he wistfully remarked lately. "Goods are increasing these days, and it makes it difficult to sell. No use of working hard to be in reds. Tomorrow perhaps I shall go to the Inferno selling tea leaves!"

I myself got several letters from people purged. One contains this surprising sentence:

I have been purged as the last Diet member three years ago, perhaps by the demand of Derevyanko, the Russian delegate to Japan.

And:

I am purged though I had lectured American-style and published American-style educational research for twenty years till purged because of ultranationalist tendency of only three lines in three thousand pages of my writings.

These three lines were severely blamed by communist members of the committee of screening teachers in my university, but I was rescued from purge by sympathy of conservative members once. But I was purged afterwards by apathy of conservatives . . . and this purge was decided by MacArthur's too severe purge policy. I, as well as my wife and children, have suffered from miserable unemployed lives since then, and hence became anti-Americanists though we were pro-Americanists even in war time, and though we are not communists yet.

Let us go into the background of this and attempt to winnow the truth from all the nonsense. Everything dates back to a celebrated SCAPIN (No. 550) of January 4, 1946. On that date MacArthur sent a formal memorandum to the Japanese government, directing it to take action at once to identify and destroy all ultranationalist and totalitarian organizations, and "to remove and exclude from public office all persons who in one capacity or another had been influential in promoting militarism." The man who wrote the first purge directive was a young lieutenant commander who had done work on denazification in Germany. But the procedure adopted in Japan differed radically from that in Germany. It was more lenient, in that no people (except actual war criminals) went to jail or were otherwise punished except by exclusion from public life; on the other hand it was operated on an administrative basis, not judicial. Categories were set up, and all persons in certain categories were purged automatically.

MacArthur told us that the difference between German and Japanese war criminals was, in his judgment, considerable. He felt that many Japanese could be excused for their prewar conduct because of their ignorance of American and European values. "But the Germans should have known better. They were traitors to western culture."

It may be argued that the purges destroyed native leadership in Japan, but SCAP officials say that the contrary is true—leadership has improved. In fact the General's basic motive was not one of punishment, but a desire to shake and stir up the old structure, get rid of the archaic, and let new political blood come to the surface. Also he insisted that, so far as possible, the purging should be done by Japanese, not by Americans. A few personages were purged by direct order of SCAP, but by and large the Japanese were forced to administer the medicine themselves—of course under SCAP stimulus and supervision.

The purges lasted from January, 1946, to May, 1948, and passed through several phases. Purgees were of several classes; some people were removed from offices or jobs they already held; others were simply told that they could not seek jobs in certain fields. The grand total of purgees was 202,000, of which 54 were indicted war criminals; 160,000 were officers of army or navy. MacArthur took the personal decision that *every* officer must be purged, down to the lowest rank. The categories went from "A" to "G." In some "A" cases even sons and grandsons or other members of the family of the purgee were also purged. Category "C" included members of the various patriotic societies, of which no fewer than twenty-seven were listed, from the Great Japan Rising Asia Alliance to the Anti-Communist League to the Higher Ethics Society. Category "E" comprised anybody above the rank of auditor in any of a group of large banks and financial institutions "involved in Japanese expansions," which meant most of the important banks in Japan; the South Manchuria Railway Company was included, the North China Development Company, and several Korean organizations. Category "F" purged all senior officials who held posts during the war in Manchukuo, Korea, Formosa, China, the South Seas, the Dutch East Indies, Malaya, Indochina, Burma, Thailand, and the Philippines.

The first purge covered important officials of the national government itself, and 11,000 men were investigated; 1,100 of these were either removed from office or forbidden to run for office in the future. Next came the removal of 7,000 officials in local government —prefectural, city, and village administrators. Nobody could be a candidate in the 1947 elections until he had been screened; as a matter of fact, even today, nobody may run for office in Japan until he has what is called an "eligibility certificate." Moreover, in order to break up local bossism and the city machines, MacArthur decided that *no* incumbent in the April, 1947, local elections could succeed himself, though they might be eligible (if cleared by screening) to try again in the next elections in 1951. He wanted a clean sweep of all local officials—and got it.

The third—and most controversial and bitterly unpopular—phase was that which followed; it applied not to men in elective office, but to those who had jobs in what was called the "public service" field, i.e., journalism, radio, education, finance, and so on. People influential in these realms, SCAP felt, should be just as rigorously screened as those in government; about 240 institutions were involved. The upshot was that 250 men in commercial posts were removed, and about 170 in the media of information.

What are the specific punishments that a purgee faces? None except that he is excluded from government service and from employment in the field of public information or with any of 240 companies. Nobody goes to jail; there is no confiscation of property or interference with other civil rights. A purgee may not engage in political activity, and may not run for office. That is all—in theory. In actual fact a great many purgees have difficulty not merely in getting jobs in their own fields, such as banking, but in getting any kind of job at all.

How can a purgee become unpurged? Since the whole procedure was administrative, not judicial, SCAP felt that careful safeguards should exist, and what was called an "adequate" mechanism for review was set up. But the procedure of the appeal boards is laborious, and, even if an applicant for appeal is cleared by the Japanese, the case must be reviewed by SCAP itself. The result is that extremely few men have ever been successfully depurged.

I asked several Americans (and also Japanese) if the purgees tend to think of themselves as patriotic martyrs. The answer is "No." This, I thought, was a critical question; much of the success of the occupation could be gauged by the answer. If people want desperately to be *un*purged it surely means that, as of the moment, the great bulk of the Japanese favor the occupation. There are few cases of rightist purgees becoming conspicuously martyrized. Few people take patriotic pride in being purged, and few ever think that Japanese who play closely with the Americans are "collaborationists." Most citizens feel, in fact, that to be purged is a veritable mark of dishonor (if only because it means association with the military who lost the war ignominiously) and they hate to be stamped as militarists, even by Americans.

*

The dissolution of the *zaibatsu* (big holding companies and industrial combinations), though allied to the purges, was a totally different operation under a different law. Early in the occupation—before the purges—SCAP ordered the Japanese government to break up forthwith the great family monopolies. Fifty-seven men from eight families were designated (eleven of the fifty-seven were Mitsuis), their securities taken over for disposal, and their active participation in responsible industrial and commercial positions restricted. The *zaibatsu* themselves aside, eighty-three other large industrial combines and holding companies were broken up—thirty-two of these were completely liquidated.

The *zaibatsu* were an institution unique in the modern world; industrial concentration existed in Japan on a scale never known elsewhere. It was estimated that not less than 60 per cent of the *total* economic life of Japan was before the war in the hands of eight families; Mitsui and Mitsubishi between them controlled—to name one specific field—70 per cent of Japan's entire export trade. Mitsui had overpowering interests in banking, insurance, cotton, shipbuilding, coal, chemicals, cement, newspapers. An analogy might be if a *single* family group in the United States owned and controlled Standard Oil, United States Steel, several of the biggest New York banks, General Electric, Anaconda, the biggest insurance companies, the Loew theater chain, and the New York *Times*.

The American attitude was not merely that the *zaibatsu* had certainly contributed to Japanese militarism, but that the country could never be successfully democratized while such excessive concentrations of economic power existed. MacArthur's own explanation of his motive is that it was to "permit a wider distribution of income and of ownership of the means of production and trade."

We did not, as is sometimes charged, seek to destroy Japanese industry. It was never part of our conception that a Japanese who had made money should be punished. What we did want to work out was a policy of "deconcentration," so that the holding companies would no longer be an overlapping crazy quilt, smothering the entire economic life of the nation. SCAP felt that an insurance company should be an insurance company, not a cloak for a movie theater. One healthy result was that as the *zaibatsu* were excluded young blood came up in business; another was that, with the grip of the family system at least partially broken, incentive came to make business more efficient and profitable. We had to teach the Japanese *how* to compete.

Critics of SCAP are divided into two fields on this score. One thinks that we did not go far enough and that the *zaibatsu* should have been punished further; the other thinks on the contrary that the "New World boys" in SCAP went much too far. At any rate the *zaibatsu* have been completely broken up as functioning organisms. Perhaps, after SCAP goes, they may rise again; but there can be no doubt that they have lost practically all their power today.

Person of the Prime Minister

I have heard Mr. Yoshida, the prime minister and dominant Japanese personality in the political life of Japan, described as "an autocrat, a bureaucrat, and an aristocrat." He is in his early seventies, and, like almost all Japanese, looks younger than his years. If you ask who is the next most important Japanese politician, people are apt to be puzzled. It is a long drop from Mr. Yoshida to the next rank. Politics in Japan seldom give much room to a Number Two. Yet he is a political accident; he would in all probability have no important rank today had not SCAP purged the previous leader of the Liberal party.

We met Yoshida twice, once at tea, once at a small dinner party

155

at his house. He is tenacious, shrewd, somewhat inelastic but with a nice sense of humor, and obviously a man of great superiority and cultivation. His house, in the Meguro neighborhood, was once the foreign minister's official residence; it has an enchanting garden, and he showed us his favorite miniature trees. He was Japanese Ambassador to London before the war, and SCAP feels that he still shows traces of British influence. His euphemism for prewar Japanese militarism is "the Japanese anti-American and anti-British beginnings of sentiment."

Shigeru Yoshida was born in Tokyo in 1878; he went into the diplomatic service, and had a worthy career in posts all over the world—Mukden, Rome, Seoul, various Chinese cities, Paris, Stockholm, London. He retired from the London Embassy at his own request when war broke out in 1939, returned to Tokyo, and lived in complete retirement till 1945. He is one of the very few Japanese who, from beginning to end, and at great risk, refused absolutely during the whole course of the war to have anything to do with the Japanese militarists. This, of course, is one reason why SCAP favors him. He became president of the Liberal party (the "Liberal" party is the one most conservative) in 1946, and has been prime minister three times.

When Sir George Sansom, the illustrious British orientalist and authority on Japan, visited Tokyo in 1941, just before Pearl Harbor, he stayed in Yoshida's house. He asked him if this did not compromise him. Yoshida replied, "There is so much against me now that it doesn't matter. One more black mark will not hurt." As a matter of fact during the war, Tojo held him under detention for a brief interlude, but he never served an actual sentence.

The day after the Japanese surrender Yoshida left Tokyo for his villa in the country. On the road to Yokohama he was stopped by some early G.I. arrivals. He was convinced that he would be killed. The G.I.'s gave him cigarettes.

Mr. Yoshida rules, so they say in Tokyo, partly through an "inner circle." One member is the exceptionally brilliant Cambridge-educated Jiro Shirasu; another is Katsuo Okasaki, whom I met years ago when he was Japanese consul general in Shanghai, and who is now the cabinet secretary (he was a famous Olympic sprinter in his youth); a third is his pretty, devoted daughter, Mrs. Aso, who is married to a rich industrialist.

His relations with SCAP are close, and he has an almost fanatical reverence for MacArthur. He complained once that young GHQ officers were interfering with his appointments; the Supreme Commander's winning answer was, "But don't you understand—my officers are your *friends.* Their only motive is to help you to get *better* men!" Yoshida, despite his closeness to SCAP, is seldom thought of as an American puppet; on the contrary, many Japanese feel that he is prime minister largely because he is the only politician that has consistently dared to stand up to the Americans, to an extent. He "uses" MacArthur, just as MacArthur "uses" him. He can get things that *he* wants through a refractory Diet by saying that SCAP wants them too. On anything serious, the General can make him toe the line like any Japanese. Yoshida knew nothing whatever about the purge of June 6, 1950, outlawing a group of communists, until 9:35 that morning when a messenger arrived with the text of the directive.

I was permitted in Tokyo to look through the whole file of MacArthur's personal correspondence with Mr. Yoshida since the occupation. The letters told me much about Yoshida; they also told me much about the Supreme Commander. The range of his interests is to be expected; nevertheless it was astonishing. He sends out suggestions, questions, hints, to the Japanese government from week to week on the widest possible variety of subjects, from the Dodge plan to fisheries, from how much it costs the United States to help feed Japan to the land reform. Several times MacArthur sharply—even curtly—slaps Yoshida down. One occasion was in regard to nominees for the new Supreme Court; the wily Yoshida wanted these to be named before the constitution went into effect; the General insisted that they be named by the new Diet then coming into being. Another was about two men whom Yoshida wanted un-purged, so that they could join his cabinet; MacArthur's "No" is so firm as to be almost rude.

*

SCAP does not actually *control* the course of Japanese domestic politics. There still exists, I heard one American say, "a hidden Japanese government in Japan." The Japanese are extraordinarily long-minded, clever, durable, and just plain tough. Nowadays many Japanese are getting restive in some respects, and criticism of SCAP, even though technically illegal, is more outspoken and persistent than heretofore. Twice on important recent issues SCAP measures were actually beaten in the Diet, incredible as this may seem.

There have been three general elections to date. In April, 1946, Yoshida's Liberals won comfortably, though the Social Democrats (socialists) showed unexpected strength. A year later, in April, 1947, Yoshida was roundly beaten and the Social Democrats formed a left-wing coalition government. In January, 1949, Yoshida won again. By-elections held in 1950 show, however, that the pendulum has begun to swing away from him again.

The party structure is simple enough. To the extreme right are the Yoshida Liberals; to the extreme left the communists. The Social Democrats and a party known as "People's Democrats," which calls itself a New Deal party, stand in between. The upper house has a group called the "Green Breeze," mostly composed of former peers and wealthy reactionaries, who usually support the liberals. The House of Councilors contains 77 Liberals, 63 Social Democrats, 54 Green Breezers, 29 People's Democrats, 4 communists, and a scattering of independents. The House of Representatives has 286 Liberals, 67 People's Democrats, 46 Social Democrats, 29 com-munists, and twenty or thirty independent members mostly on the left. Discussion in the Diet can be spirited, and several outright brawls have taken place.

One first-class scandal has occurred under SCAP; it caused the downfall of the Ashida (socialist) cabinet in October, 1948. An official memorandum prepared by Government Section talks of "the veritable cesspool of official corruption, collusion, and depravity uncovered" by this episode. The prime minister, the deputy prime minister, the welfare minister, and the president of the economic stabilization board, as well as several other high officials, went to jail accused of "bribery, fraud, and malfeasance." A chemical company, the Showa Denko, which had borrowed billions of yen from the government, spent approximately 100 million yen to bribe "deserving" political leaders and officials, and then got found out.

Communists to Conclude

The communists have never been suppressed as a political party. They are, even today, quite legal. Yoshida wants to suppress and outlaw them bag and baggage; SCAP is reluctant to do so, for fear of driving them underground and because it does not want them to infilter into the socialist and other left parties. The communists had five seats in the House of Representatives in 1946, four in 1947, and thirty-five in 1949. This was obviously a sharp and important rise, and it worried people. After four years of MacArthur, the Communist party polled 2,984,583 votes, elected 774 party members to various posts throughout the country, and won not less than 9.6 per cent of the total vote. The electorate of MacArthur's Japan was, in other words, almost a full 10 per cent communist a year ago.

Again I quote an official SCAP document:

Early this summer [1949] the occurrence of a series of scattered but suspiciously related incidents threw the people into an alarming state of uneasiness. Coinciding with the initial stages of the government's personnel retrenchment program and the repatriation from Soviet-held areas of 90,000 thoroughly indoctrinated Japanese ex-soldiers, lawless mobs overpowered the local police in several communities of Fukushima-ken, began operating "people's trains" in Yokohama, released driverless tramcars near Tokyo which killed a number of people, indiscriminately wrecked trains and destroyed railroad property, and forcibly assumed control of a big factory in Hiroshima-ken. Rumors were rife of "the impending proletarian dictatorship" to be set up in Japan. Efforts of the Attorney General and the police forces to restore and maintain law and order were labelled "fascistic, dictatorial, feudalistic, unconstitutional, and undemocratic" by the vociferous left-wing segment of the press.

My wife and I met several Japanese communists; their general line was much that of communists anywhere. Most of them, we found, despised the servility of other Japanese. I asked one leader if he hated Americans during the war; his answer was, "I never saw one—there were just planes overhead. We hated Tojo and the Japanese militarists much more." I asked another if he would not concede that SCAP had done a good job in breaking up the *zaibatsu*, creating a land reform, and so on; he did so, but said that the reforms had not come out of the people themselves and did not go far enough. To another I put the question, "How can Japanese economy survive after American withdrawal?" His answers were that Japan would base its economy on trade with communist China, and that improved methods of agriculture could augment the rice crop. I asked another if he approved of the measure in the constitution disarming Japan in perpetuity; this question produced long hesitation, and finally an answer so ambiguous as to be without much meaning.

The titular leader of the Japanese Communist party, which numbers about 100,000 members, is Kyuichi Tokuda. He helped found it in 1922, and has been secretary general ever since; he spent seventeen years in prison, from 1928 to 1945. His background is that of an intellectual, not a worker; he was educated as a lawyer.

More interesting is the second in command, Sanzo Nosaka, who was also an original founder of the party. He is fifty-seven, looks thirty-five, and has an extremely alert mind and, something unusual among communists, a spirited sense of humor. In 1912, after graduation from Keio University, he helped found Japan's first labor union. He is widely traveled; he studied at the London School of Economics, and then in France, Germany, and Russia. Nosaka became the representative of Japan on the Third Internationale, or

Comintern, thus achieving as high rank as any communist can normally reach. He went to jail several times, lived underground, escaped to China, and passed most of the war at the headquarters of Mao Tse-tung in Yenan. For a time he had close relations with several agencies of the American government in China; he was an important personage in our political warfare against Japan. A striking thing happened to Nosaka after he returned to Tokyo during the occupation; Moscow purged him. (MacArthur purged him too, somewhat later.) He was accused of nationalism and criticized because he pursued a "constitutional" policy instead of advocating revolutionary violence. Nosaka recanted, but not slavishly; he is one of the few international communists ever to talk back to the Cominform, and get away with it. Moscow eventually unpurged him, and he resumed his duties. Since June, 1950, he has been in hiding. Warrant was issued for his arrest, but scap has not been able to lay hands on him.

Strange as the irony is, it is General MacArthur himself who gave legal existence to the Japanese Communist party. When the occupation began communism was, of course, illegal; all important communists were in jail or exile. The civil-liberties directive of October, 1945, ordered the Japanese government to remove all restriction on political freedoms, and all political prisoners were forthwith released. The Communist party was, in fact, the first party in Japan to emerge and be reorganized. It sought at once to make a Popular Front with the socialists and other left parties, and to infilter into labor. Labor grew in strength steeply (Japan is one of the few countries in the world where collective bargaining is guaranteed by the actual constitution) and the communists got control of at least two important unions, that of the railway workers and the "Communications Union" representing government telegraph workers. Political power grew too. The communist vote rose from 300,000 to almost 3,000,000 between 1947 and 1949.

Several factors help to explain this. The communists said that they alone had opposed the Japanese militarists who brought shame

161

and degradation to the nation. Disintegration of Japanese morale naturally assisted a subversive movement. Communist promises were something *new* for the poverty-stricken to seize upon. Communism promised reward to those nationalist Japanese who hated the occupation, and it offered hope (spurious hope, of course) to those who were disappointed by the miserable record of the Social Democrats. The advance to victory of Mao Tse-tung in China strongly impressed many in Japan. The economic retrenchment and rising unemployment that came with the Dodge plan stimulated grievances. Also the communists of course sought to gain ground by attacking SCAP. An "alien and degenerate colonial culture," as they put it, "was being imposed by force on the Japanese people by American imperialists." Above all, communism attracted many Japanese because it purported to satisfy several of the deepest and most elemental cravings in the national character—desire for faith, desire for discipline, and the hope of a good life for the next generation. Almost all Japanese care more about their sons than for themselves. And of all Asiatic countries Japan is the one that, in theory, would seem to be the most naturally vulnerable to communist penetration, because the Japanese people are so deeply attracted by both (a) fanaticism, and (b) organization.

On May 30, 1950, the Communist party held a rally in the Imperial Plaza in Tokyo. American soldiers and Japanese police mingled with the crowd, and somebody started a scuffle. The brawl spread, rocks were thrown, and five Americans received minor injuries. The business was over in five minutes, but this was the first time in the history of the occupation that any Japanese had attacked and injured G.I.'s. Eight communists were arrested promptly, and a trial took place which was, all things considered, a rush job. Sentences were severe. One Japanese got ten years at hard labor; the other seven got from seven years to five.

On June 6, 1950, following the excitement of this affair, MacArthur cracked down on the communist leadership. A directive ordered the removal and exclusion from public life of the twenty-four members of the Central Committee of the party, including Tokuda and Nosaka; among those proscribed were seven members of the Diet. This was the first time that MacArthur had ever purged the left. On June 7, the next day, he additionally ordered the exclusion from public service of seventeen editors of *Akahata*, the communist newspaper. Then, a few weeks later, orders went out for the actual arrest of those purged, and on June 26, the day after the outbreak of the Korean war, communist cells were raided by the police all over Japan and 229 communist newspapers and other publications suppressed. But, as of the moment of writing, the actual party has not yet been outlawed, and nonpurged communists still take part in sessions of the Diet.

*

Perhaps one may pause to mention here that, even if communism may be potentially dangerous to Japan, the Korean war proved that as of today the overwhelming majority of Japanese are loyal to the occupation. The country was all but denuded of American troops; yet not the faintest tremor or quiver of public emotion was directed against Americans. MacArthur himself* has described this in vivid language: "I can think of no finer tribute [to the Japanese] than their conduct during this difficult war in Korea. The question arose, 'Now that we must strip our occupation forces, will the Japanese sabotage the work of the past five years?' I did not deliberate five minutes on this, for I knew that the Japanese could be trusted implicitly." Then the Supreme Commander describes how in short order he was reduced to the cannibalized remnants of just *one* American division, say 5,000 troops, to occupy a country of 83,000,000 that only five years before had fought against the Americans one of the most savage wars in history. But nothing at all untoward took place, and most Japanese were even friendlier to Americans than before. It is a massive tribute to (a) Japanese character, and (b) his leadership.

* In an interview with Bob Considine in the New York *Journal-American*.

Chapter Nine

KOREA

MY WIFE and I returned to Tokyo from Kyoto early on Sunday morning, June 25, and almost immediately took off again for an expedition to Nikko, the exquisite mountain village ninety-one miles to the north. This trip had been planned long in advance. Our hosts were General and Mrs. Whitney, and MacArthur's private car was put at our disposal. (The Supreme Commander himself, so far as I know, has never once used this car, because he has never taken a trip by rail in Japan.) At the last moment General Whitney, seeing us off, told us that he could not come along, because MacArthur needed him in the office that Sunday. This, however, did not seem to be anything unusual; most senior members of SCAP are on Sunday call. At that hour, 8:20 A.M., I do not think that anybody at headquarters knew what had just happened in Korea.

Getting into the station and aboard the cars hitched onto the regular northbound train was a picturesque experience, because we used the special entrance reserved for the Emperor. A long, tattered, literally red carpet covered the underground passageway, and a covey of little Japanese officials in shabby uniforms bowed and scraped and squirmed as we climbed in. Two important members of the occupation were with us. Just before lunch at Nikko, and after we had visited a temple which is one of the most ornately spectacular sights in the world, one of these was called unexpectedly

164

to the telephone. He came back and whispered, "A big story has just broken. The South Koreans have attacked North Korea!"

I suppose it will always be a matter of mild interest to me that this news, so wildly inaccurate as to who the aggressor was, but which signalized the opening of the Asia War of 1950, came just after I had spent an hour in stocking feet inspecting stone monsters carved in 1636 in the tomb of the founder of the Tokugawa shogunate, gazing at snails coming out of the heads of representations of Lord Buddha, and admiring with incredulous eyes the gold and scarlet lacquer adorning a series of ancient timbered monuments, and just before we spent an amiable afternoon watching the Kegon water-falls in the summer mist, driving around the gray-green shores of Lake Chuzenji, and otherwise enjoying spectacles that were totally, ineffably remote from contemporary warfare and the harsh pressures of modern politics.

Korea had not been much of a preoccupation to most people in Japan; in a month, I heard the word "Korea" mentioned only twice. The fact that the first information reaching Tokyo, as relayed to our party, was of an attack by South Korea on North, instead of vice versa, is not particularly important. The message may have been garbled in transmission. Nobody knew anything much at head-quarters the first few hours, and probably people were taken in by the blatant, corrosive lies of the North Korean radio.

The fact, however, that Americans were sensationally ill-informed about Korea in general and that our intelligence services on the spot were caught flatfooted off base is important in the extreme. Details of this are so well known by this time as to be supererogatory. The chief of the American military mission to Korea was absent from Seoul when the attack occurred; so was his second in command. An experienced American newspaperman reported before the out-break that a United States official in South Korea had just sent for his family to join him from America, after a year's delay, because at last the country had settled down. A high American intelligence officer gave it as his opinion that week that South Korea was the "safest place in Asia," but that, if an outbreak did occur, the South Korean forces ("the best army in Asia") could wipe out the North Koreans with no difficulty. Yet, on the morning of June 25, the North Koreans launched an attack by no fewer than four divisions, assisted by three constabulary brigades; 70,000 men were committed, and about 70 tanks went into action simultaneously at four different points, while an ambitious amphibious landing was successful. Ask any military man what all this means. To assemble such a force, arm and equip it, and have it ready to wheel into precalculated action over a wide front with perfect synchronization, on the appointed date, must have taken at least a month; most military men would say that it could not have been done in under six weeks or longer. Yet the South Koreans and Americans in Korea, to say nothing of scap in Tokyo, were taken utterly by surprise. They were as blankly astonished as if the sun had suddenly gone out. The North Koreans achieved complete tactical and even strategic surprise. It was more disgraceful than Pearl Harbor. Our eyes were shut, and even our feet were sound asleep.

No doubt this will all be investigated in good time. One point worth mention is that the United Nations Commission on Korea reported to Lake Success (on September 14) that United States officers in Korea refused to accept at face value and in fact completely ignored well-documented warnings by South Korean intelligence of an impending attack a full six weeks before it occurred.

Even after the outbreak, up to noon or beyond on June 25, Japan time, the disposition in Tokyo was to treat the matter as a new border "incident," nothing more. John Foster Dulles, who had just visited Korea, urged MacArthur to take the matter more seriously than he seemed to be doing. A journalist in his party went up to the Supreme Commander just before boarding the plane, asked him the significance of the first news, and said that he, as a newspaperman, would like to stay in Japan if there was any possibility that the outbreak was serious and that the United States would be involved. MacArthur minimized the importance of the event and told him

166

not to bother to stay to cover it. (The preposterous story put out by the Russians later, that Mr. Dulles in Seoul "incited" the South Koreans to attack the North, is a lie so outrageous that it does not need rebuttal.)

By the time we, of our small party, returned from Nikko to Tokyo that Sunday night, things were furiously astir. Several officers met us at the station to tell us correctly and with much amplification what had happened. One report was that North Korea had actually declared war on South Korea. In any case there was no doubt whatever that North Korea was the aggressor. North Korean tanks had penetrated miles into Southern territory, below the 38th parallel, and North Korean aircraft had strafed the Kimpo airfield at Seoul, destroying several planes. The American attitude seemed to be a mixture of inarticulateness, confusion, and alarm. Would the Russians come in? What was the United States going to *do*? Then, driving to the Imperial, we passed the Dai-Ichi Building. It was still brightly lit, and hundreds of Japenese were patiently waiting on the streets for a glimpse of the Supreme Commander.

Most interesting to us were the comments of the Japanese. On Monday night, the twenty-sixth, it was still unknown in Tokyo whether or not the United States, or the United Nations, would take any really decisive action in support of the Republic of Korea. The suspense and tension were intolerable. That evening we dined with several Japanese—a dinner which began with the formal, antique tea ceremony, and which progressed, almost as if in arrested motion, with the stateliness of a ballet. But after dinner our hosts broke out with frightened, violent excitement; all the porcelainlike calm of the Japanese was shattered. They were seized with passionate alarm. Let me paraphrase: "If the United States does nothing, if it permits this affront to civilization to proceed unchecked, you will have lost all Asia. Your prestige will decline to nil. This is the Rhineland, this is *Anschluss*, this is Munich, all rolled into one. You *must* act. Do not be so gentlemanly. Otherwise all of us are lost, the Philippines are lost, Indonesia is lost, even Australia is lost, and Europe is lost too. . . . First China, now Korea, next it will be us. If Korea goes, even the Japanese who hate communism will be tempted to admire it. Japan itself will go communist unless you fight. Make a declaration that you will continue to protect *us* even if Korea should be lost. We need you for another twenty-five years. Make us a colony if you will! *Annex* us!"

Such talk of the Rhineland, *Anschluss*, and Munich came strangely from the men who made Pearl Harbor. Yet to hear sentiments like these from distinguished citizens of Tokyo was impressive. No people in the world could want a new world war less than the Japanese, who were all but blasted out of history by the last one.

The next night, June 27, we dined at the house of an American friend to meet a group of Japanese painters, musicians, literary men, and other artists. Lanterns were glowing over the lawn of the calm small garden, and we admired with rapt attention our host's collection of Chinese and Japanese antiquities. At about 9:20 a noise split the sky and we looked up. One low-flying plane tore the night sky apart and then another and still another. They came ripping and grunting over us five minutes apart. The airlift to relieve Seoul and get munitions to Korea had begun. The war was on. What kind of war would it turn out to be?

MacArthur and the Korean War

The United States had no legal commitment whatever to defend the Republic of Korea; we were under no treaty obligation at all. Our moral and ethical obligation was, however, indisputable, and this had been reinforced by an off-the-cuff remark by MacArthur to Dr. Rhee, when the Korean leader came to Tokyo for a brief visit in 1949. MacArthur's statement does not appear in the official records, so far as I know, but it was reported at the time. Seeing him off at the airport MacArthur patted the old man on the back and declared, in substance, "You can depend upon it that I will defend South Korea as I would defend the shores of my own native land."

MacArthur had, however, paid comparatively little attention

to Korea. He visited the country only once up to the outbreak of the war, and then only for one day, in August, 1948, to take part in the ceremonies inaugurating South Korean independence. His general impulse was to steer politely clear of a political situation that had become a mess, and to dissociate himself so far as possible from all the bungling that was going on. Nor did he have any political or military responsibility whatever for Korea after August 15, 1948. It is only fair to state this with emphasis inasmuch as several of his critics have sought to lay to his door some responsibility for our negligent intelligence. The General was not to blame. Korea was not part of his domain. On the other hand, as commander in chief of the Far East Command, he might well have given developments in Korea a more penetrating scrutiny than he did. A commander in chief in Great Britain might, let us say, have no formal responsibility for what might be going on in Ireland, but in an analogous situation he would be ill-advised if he ignored Irish affairs altogether. MacArthur, as a matter of fact, *talked* about Korea from time to time. At the Seoul ceremonies inaugurating the Korean Republic he proclaimed:

Yet in this hour, as the forces of righteousness advance, the triumph is dulled by one of the great tragedies of contemporary history—an artificial barrier has divided your land. *This barrier must and will be torn down.* Nothing shall prevent the ultimate unity of your people as free men of a free nation. Koreans come from too proud a stock to sacrifice their sacred cause by yielding to any alien philosophies of disruption.

As early as the year 1882 . . . it was proclaimed that there should be "perpetual peace and friendship between the United States and Korea." The American people have never deviated from this pledge and you may rely upon the invincible continuance of that friendship.

President Rhee, you and the distinguished group which has been chosen to assist you in the leadership of this infant republic will face issues of the most complex nature known to political experience. The manner in which those issues are resolved will determine in large measure not only the unity and wellbeing of your own people *but also the future stability of the continent of Asia.* I have faith in you . . . and pray that Almighty God may sustain you in your hallowed task.

A year later, in August, 1949, he wrote Dr. Rhee:

Under your wise and fearless leadership the past year has shown magnificent progress by the Korean people in the fabrication of their new Republic, and men of good will everywhere take heart in witnessing the erection upon so vital a sector of an edifice representative of human freedom.

Happily there appears to be a growing consciousness in the minds of men who cherish liberty of the insidious threat which any form of despotic outlawry holds for man's ability to walk erect upon the earth free and unafraid, and a growing tendency for men of all races and creeds to unite in defense against the common peril of a hypocrisy, which, while giving lip service to the democratic form, seeks through falsehood, stealth, and violence to destroy its substance.

The General's prose style has, we may note, not become less baroque as the years move on.

On June 27, 1950 (Washington time), came Mr. Truman's historic announcement committing us to the defense of Korea. The main paragraphs were:

In Korea the Government forces, which were armed to prevent border raids and to preserve internal security, were attacked by invading forces from North Korea. The Security Council of the United Nations called upon the invading troops to cease hostilities and to withdraw to the 38th parallel. This they have not done but on the contrary have pressed the attack. . . . In these circumstances I have ordered United States air and sea forces to give the Korean Government troops cover and support.

Later, on July 1, MacArthur was authorized "to use certain supporting ground units as well."

Also Mr. Truman said:

I have ordered the Seventh Fleet to prevent any attack on Formosa. As a corollary of this action I am calling upon the Chinese Government on Formosa to cease all air and sea operations against the mainland. The Seventh Fleet will see that this is done. The determination of the future status of Formosa must await the restoration of security in the Pacific, a peace settlement with Japan, or consideration by the United Nations.

When this text was published in Tokyo it pierced the atmosphere like an electric-shock treatment. At first it was thought that Mac-

Arthur himself was the chief influence in moving the President to his decision. Now we know that several influences converged on Mr. Truman, notably that of Secretary of State Dean Acheson, and that the President didn't need much influencing anyway. He did not like the idea of the United States and the United Nations being kicked around.

MacArthur got his instructions from the Joint Chiefs, just as any other general in the field should, in a long "conversation" held on the teletype just before the Truman announcement was released. He was, in the words of a witness, "completely surprised at the decision, but gratified because it reflected positive policy and action." His responsibilities would be grave, but he was delighted by the order to go ahead.

There were two schools of thought in Tokyo at the time, though few people doubted the prime necessity of our intervention. We *had* to go in, and everybody sober and perspicacious greeted with satisfaction the fact that the operation was performed in the name of the United Nations. But some wary observers were deeply worried about the eventual military outcome, particularly if the Soviet Union should send in Chinese or Manchurian troops. I heard it said as early as July 2, "If our forces triumph quickly and the Korean fighting remains localized, MacArthur will go down into history as one of the greatest men of all time—the man who for the first time stopped militant communism dead in its tracks. But if the war spreads and the Soviet Union comes in, or even China, he may find himself responsible in part—no matter how pure his motives—for precipitating the Third World War."

At this period not many people thought that the Chinese would enter the Korean war. One story was, in fact, to the effect that they deplored it—strange as this may seem now. For the North Korean aggression had, for the moment at least, cost Mao Tse-tung a prize he coveted above all—Formosa. This was because he could no longer move against Formosa, which previously had been within easy reach of his hand, without risking formal warfare with the United States. Looking at the sequence of events with hindsight, it seems clear that the North Koreans made two enormous miscalculations: (a) they had not dreamed that the United States would intervene, beyond the shipment of token material aid; (b) they expected to conquer the whole peninsula in a few weeks. To what extent their Russian masters were responsible for these miscalculations is unknown. If North Korea had won a complete victory quickly, then an attack by communist China on Formosa might well have followed; perhaps that was the timetable. But the United Nations intervention in South Korea scotched it.

Later (when I was in Hong Kong) another theory, the "trap" theory, developed. It was that, quite without regard to Formosa, intervention by China in Korea was altogether inevitable. The Kremlin, having lost the first round, and with no intention of committing its own troops, would throw in Mao's Chinese armies (and very good armies they are too)—"just feed us the Manchurians and Chinese," as I heard it put. Thus Korea would become a vast, bloody open drain into which American manpower and resources would have to be poured endlessly. Some observers went beyond this to say that Moscow deliberately started the Korean business as an attempt to provoke a full dress, wholesale conflict between the United States and the giant body of Mao's China, on the hypothesis that such a war might last thirty years, that China would in the end be unconquerable, that the United States would thus be sucked into permanent war in Asia, and that Stalin meantime would have his hands free to do whatever he wanted in Europe.

In any case the United States took full cognizance of the possible trap, and it was established on a high level that we would with scrupulous care try to avoid being inveigled into a war with China. "Fight China, and we lose Europe," became an administration watchword.

But to return to Korea. One tragic irony was that the United States had deliberately pared to a minimum the shipments of munitions to the *South* Koreans before the war, out of fear that the Rhee government was trigger-happy and might let loose an onslaught on the North. We did not altogether trust Dr. Rhee. Other factors played into this, of course. The United States defense program was going through an "economy" phase, and there were not enough arms to go around.

That South Korea would be difficult to defend was well known; one American officer called it "a strategical nightmare." Moreover our intelligence made the grave blunder of assuming that Korea was impossible terrain for tanks and that tanks would not be used much in the event of war. Because our emphasis was on defense, not attack, we built up a constabulary rather than an army. And, though we left $53,000,000 worth of military equipment in Korea when we pulled out, much of this was obsolete and ill-balanced. The South Koreans, to sum up, were underarmed. General Roberts, the head of the American military mission, has said that they had only "eight or ten miles of signal wire," and that the antiaircraft defense consisted of "two water pistols and a sling shot."

MacArthur took off on the first of his inspection trips to the Korean front on June 29. He did not know where his plane, the *Bataan*, would land, since Kimpo had been taken and the field at Suwan was unsafe. Moreover the weather was extremely bad. At Haneda airport, as the *Bataan* was getting ready to take off, Lt. Gen. Stratemeyer, chief of the Far East Air Force, strenuously tried to persuade him not to go. MacArthur said, "But you would go yourself, wouldn't you?" Stratemeyer answered, "Yes, but I don't count. You're a different matter." MacArthur's reply was, "We go." A photographer caught him entering the plane, head thrown back, chin erect, arm outstretched, finger pointing, with a gesture that, if it had been anybody but MacArthur, could easily lay the performer open to the charge of infantile posturing. We had a talk with Stratemeyer a few days later. If he ever needed to be sold on MacArthur, he was sold now. "He's the greatest leader, the greatest commander, and the greatest hero in American history," Stratemeyer said.

Background to the Hermit Kingdom

As is well known Korea was the cause of several notable wars before this one. The peninsula, about the size of Utah, hangs down out of Manchuria like a heavy tassel; its upper frontier is only 100 miles from Vladivostok, and in the south it is separated from Japan only by the 120-mile-wide Strait of Tsushima. Hence, as a kind of bridge between the Japanese islands and the mainland of Asia proper, its strategic importance and vulnerability had always been marked. Korean history is full of turmoil, civil strife, and the aggressions of hungry outside powers. Its own nationalism has alternated between periods of being dormant and fiercely renascent. But it has always been there. Koreans are like the Poles—or the Irish —a stubborn, emotional, strongly individualistic race perpetually tortured by invasion, the gloomy mark of the conqueror, and enforced partition. An unfortunate geography is the hardest of all masters.

Why was Korea important to the Kremlin? Because, obviously, a united Korea under Russian control would dominate strategically an unarmed Japan as well as much of the China coast.

Why had Korea been so important to the Japanese in their militarist days? Because, obviously, Korea was their indispensable mainland corridor to conquest in Manchuria, China, and the rest of Asia.

Korean history—or perhaps we should say mythology—goes way back. Some authorities put the foundation of the country in 2333 B.C.; some say 1122 B.C. Even the later date was 2,854 years before George Washington was born. An early Korean dynasty lasted till the second century before Christ, when the Chinese took most of the area, and the first recorded Japanese invasion occurred in A.D. 200, during the reign of a Japanese empress with the appropriate name Jingo. (Our use of the word "jingo" does not, however, derive etymologically from this estimable lady.) For a time Korea was divided into separate kingdoms; in A.D. 668 it became a Chinese province under its own administration. In 1392 a native dynasty was set up that lasted till 1910. The Japanese sought to conquer the country in 1592, under their stout warrior Hideyoshi; they were beaten back largely because Korean forces (aided by China) invented an early type of ironclad battleship, which destroyed the Japanese fleet. In 1627 came the Manchus; Korea remained nominally independent, but paid tribute to Peking. The nation became known as the "Hermit Kingdom," or the "Land of the Morning Calm."

The modern history of Korea begins in the 1870's, when an American admiral sought to pry open its stiff doors, much as Commodore Perry had done in Japan; after a fierce little fight the Americans withdrew. Then, in 1876, Japan did open Korea up, by forcing a treaty on her ruler of the time, a queen who was later murdered (by the Japanese) in circumstances almost as spectacular as those attending the murder of Queen Draga of Yugoslavia in a different quarter of the world some years later. The Korean king, to save face, was forced to say that his queen had been a prostitute. The United States reentered the Korean scene in 1883, and gradually the peninsula turned to the modern world. Came the Sino-Japanese War of 1894-1895. Japan attacked China in order to gain control of Korea. The Japanese won; Korea was taken away from China and given "independence" under Japanese tutelage. Now the Russians, having acquired the maritime provinces of Siberia, began to show adhesive interest in Korea. It was at this time, interestingly enough, that the first use came of a mechanism later to become world-famous—the 38th parallel. It was proposed in 1896 to divide Korea between Japan and Russia at this meridian, but the plan fell through.

Came the Russo-Japanese War of 1904-1905; again the issue at stake was Korea and again the Japanese won; Korea became a Japanese protectorate. President Theodore Roosevelt acceded to this step, or, to put it in other words, "connived at the Japanese seizure of Korea" by agreeing at the Portsmouth Peace Conference to give Japan a free hand in Korea as a price for calling off the Russian war. Another man later to become an American President—William Howard Taft, who was then TR's Secretary of War—also had grave responsibility for the destruction of Korean independence; he went to Tokyo and signed an agreement with the Japanese foreign minister Katsura whereby the U.S. "recognized Japan's right to Korea in return for Japanese disavowal of aggressive designs on the Philippines," which we had recently acquired from Spain. Deals have occurred in American foreign policy—before Yalta.

For five years Korea remained a Japanese protectorate, and then Japan ended this falseface and annexed the country outright in 1910, abolishing the Korean dynasty which had lasted 518 years.

No country has ever suffered greater humiliation and misery than did Korea under Japanese slavery between 1910 and 1945. (One is apt to forget or minimize nowadays how villainous Japanese state policy has been in the past, not to mention how villainous has been the conduct of innumerable individual Japanese.) Systematically, ruthlessly, the Japanese stamped out and ground under every manifestation of Korean nationalism. The Japanese governor general in Seoul had absolute power, subject only to the Emperor; only Japanese were permitted to hold important official jobs; all vestiges of representative government disappeared; the great bulk of the land was expropriated and worked by Japanese companies; the country was drained of its rice, on which it lived; use of the Korean language was forbidden. I remember traveling from the Manchurian frontier through Pyongyang, Seoul, Taejon, Taegu, and Pusan —such familiar names today!—before World War II. Korea was a prison, and a prison that the Japanese sucked completely dry. The only traces remaining of things Korean were the white peasant costumes—and white, in Korea, is the habiliment of mourning.

Yet a vigorous resistance and independence movement continued to exist; sporadic uprisings were put down by the Japanese with crude ferocity. In 1919, following the end of World War I, the Koreans thought innocently they might find succor from Woodrow Wilson at the Paris Peace Conference; but Japan had fought (a little) on the Allied side, and hence had to be rewarded; Wilson

176

could do nothing for the Koreans, and they remained the prey of the Japanese. It is a shameful story. Brokenhearted, the Koreans attempted to revolt; they were crushed like insects. But two different groups of staunch Korean exiles set up provisional "governments" in exile, one in Chungking headed by Kim Koo, one in the west under the leadership of Dr. Rhee. And many thousands of Koreans fought fiercely against the Japanese during the Japanese war against China (the well-known Sino-Japanese "incident") in the middle 1930's. These were mostly communists or guerrillas who became communists. The Kremlin had the prescience to "recognize" the Korean communist party way back in 1922. From these hard-bitten guerrillas—to jump to the present—came much of the fighting quality of the North Koreans in 1950.

Korea was at last reborn, so to speak, in Cairo in December, 1943, when Roosevelt, Churchill, and Chiang Kai-shek declared that in due course Korea should become free and independent. This declaration was reaffirmed at Potsdam in 1945, with subsequent Russian adherence. Little did anybody know what somber realities the future held.

The Tragic Parallel

Now we must treat briefly of this celebrated 38th parallel; all manner of inaccurate stories have been told about its origin. And, because the truth is not all that it should be ideally, a tendency exists nowadays to gloss over how it came to be drawn.

When Russia entered the war against Japan on August 8, 1945, Soviet troops were in a position to swoop into Korea at once and swallow up the great mass of Japanese stationed there. The nearest troops at the disposal of the United States were, however, in Okinawa, hundreds of miles away. The Russians had an army ready, whereas we had only one corps available, the XXIV. The Russians had merely to step across the frontier, and clean up; we had to gather and transmit men by ship and air. Therefore it was imperatively necessary to work out some mechanism by which the Soviet troops

177

would not simply flood down and take *all* of Korea. We had to stop them at some line of demarcation.

All this should have been pondered and worked out long before the Japanese surrender, but the suddenness with which the end of the war came caught us by surprise. It is absolutely not true, as is often said, that the 38th parallel was specifically drawn at Yalta or Potsdam. Things might have been better if it had been. But neither Roosevelt (at Yalta) nor Truman (at Potsdam) had anything whatever to do with the 38th parallel, reports to the contrary notwithstanding. Nor did MacArthur.

Actually the line was drawn in early August in Washington by a group of comparatively junior officers operating under the State-War-Navy Coordinating Committee. The decision to cut Korea in half was not a top-level policy decision, nor was anybody in high political authority consulted. Mainly, it was an Army job. Lewis Haskins, the executive secretary of the American Friends Service Committee, has related some of the circumstances:

Just before the surrender of Japan several one-star generals hurried into an office in the Pentagon with the statement, "We have got to divide Korea. Where can we divide it?"

A colonel with experience in the Far East protested to his superiors, "You can't do that. Korea is a social and economic unit. There is no place to divide it."

The generals insisted that it had to be done and the colonel replied that it could not be done. Their answer was, "We have got to divide Korea and it has to be done by four o'clock this afternoon."

As noted above, the Japanese and Russians had flirted with the idea of using the 38th parallel some fifty years before (also in 1903-1904 there was talk of establishing a neutral zone on the 39th parallel) and so, in a way, a precedent existed. Also such procedures were not uncommon. For instance the 16th parallel became a temporary line of demarcation between the British and Chinese zones of occupation in Indochina. Both the British and Chinese dutifully observed it, took the surrender of Japanese troops on either side, and withdrew as planned (the Chinese needed a bit of push-

178

ing before they got out); few people remember nowadays that this 16th parallel ever existed.

The American motive as to Korea was, it goes without saying, correct enough—to keep the advancing Russians from pushing down too far. And the parallel was meant to be a purely military mechanism—to ensure that Japanese north of the line would surrender to the Soviet Union, those south of the line to the United States. Nevertheless it was adopted as a result of a hurried decision, without proper study of political factors or consequences, and utterly without regard to the people of Korea itself or the nature of the peninsula. One American official has stated frankly, "The 38th parallel makes no political, topographical, geographic, economic, or military sense." It cut right through whole towns, and even, in one case, separated one wing of a factory from another.

So Korea became, almost at once, two Koreas. North Korea had roughly 48,000 square miles, and most of the industry of the country, its biggest mineral and timber deposits, and, above all, its water power whereby electricity for the whole peninsula was generated. South Korea, with approximately 37,000 square miles, was largely agricultural; it grew the rice on which the country fed. By the time war came in 1950, North Korea had a population of roughly 10,-000,000, South Korea roughly 20,0000,000. Few people realized that if Korea were united it would have 30,000,000 people, and would thus be the thirteenth biggest country in the world.

As time went on the United States several times proposed to the Russians abolition of the parallel. They refused, and made it an impassable, impenetrable barrier.

Arrival and the First Tussles

The Russians, under General Chistiakov, entered Korea on August 12, 1945, and proceeded to occupy the peninsula down to the parallel. They did not cross the parallel. The United States was unable to get troops in from Okinawa till September 8, almost a month later. Our commander might have been General Joseph W. ("Vinegar Joe") Stilwell, but according to one widely believed story, Generalissimo Chiang Kai-shek would not accept him. Had Stilwell been our leader in Korea, the whole story might have turned out profoundly for the better. Instead the American commander became Lt. Gen. John R. Hodge, a tough, bluff soldier who had a good gristly record as a combat general, but who knew nothing whatever of Korea and who was not—let us be gentle—what anybody would call a political genius.

Hodge, though his motives were of the best, made blunders almost at once. For instance it became known that, shortly after his arrival in Seoul, he said that "Koreans are the same breed of cats as the Japanese." He may have been misquoted, but the damage was done; it was almost as if somebody had said, "The Jews in Buchenwald and the Poles in Oswiecim are the same breed of cats as their Nazi jailors." Second, because he did not understand or trust the Koreans, he allowed the chief Japanese officers on the spot to remain in power and administer the occupation. This caused such an outcry that the order was promptly countermanded by MacArthur in Tokyo. But it made a shocking impression on the Koreans. Korea was, after all, a liberated country, not an enemy. It is revealing to look back to the dispatches of American correspondents who flew from Tokyo to Seoul at this time; most were horrified at the way things were shaping up. One episode was that half a dozen Koreans, of a large crowd assembling to welcome their American liberators, were shot down by the *Japanese* police, and the Americans did nothing to protect them.

Another blunder had disastrous repercussions; some people think today that if Hodge had acted differently, Korea would be united at this moment, and there would never have been a war in 1950. A group of Korean personalities organized secretly in the last days of the Japanese tenure, and set up the machinery for a "People's Republic" to govern the whole peninsula. Its leader was a reputable enough Korean, Dr. Woon Hyung Lyuh, and his so-called Republic probably represented as well as anything could at that time the aspirations of most Koreans. But Dr. Lyuh was a socialist, and the

Russians in the north were prepared to recognize his government. It is commonly said now, in extenuation of Hodge, that Lyuh's "Republic" was a communist conspiracy. Certainly it was left-wing and it contained communist members, but it was demonstrably not exclusively communist. But Hodge would have nothing to do with this early, short-lived Korean "Republic." When Dr. Lyuh waited upon him, in fact, Hodge called him, of all things, a *Japanese* agent, refused to recognize his authority or have anything to do with him, and all but threw him out of his office. So the first— and best—chance for building a united Korea was tossed away. Now, in defense of Hodge, one may say that he had every right to be suspicious of any Korean organization with communists in it. But in those days the Soviet Union was an ally; people's governments were being formed almost everywhere; Hodge would not have risked much if, under sharp control, Lyuh's "Republic" had been permitted to begin functioning. It had roots in every village, and the Russians made all too effective use of it later. The result *might* have been a communist Korea. On the other hand, if our political skill had equaled our military skill, *we* might have been able to guide a united Korea into a viable democratic state. In any case— the chance was lost.

Hodge had to take these early decisions without much support from home or even from MacArthur in Japan; he was like a blind man fumbling in a fog. MacArthur had over-all strategic responsibility, but he left Hodge to himself on matters of administration. One story is that for a period of nine months Hodge never got a single directive from the State Department, which at that time was in the hands of James F. Byrnes.

Course of Events During the Occupation

This is a hopelessly gnarled and ugly tale. Our Korean policy was a mess. The Russians took advantage of this, outsmarted us straight down the line, and made political capital out of our every blunder. This, it goes without saying, should not be taken as justifying what they did themselves; Soviet activity on its side of the parallel was brutal, imperialistic, totally intransigent, Machiavellian, and corrupt.

In South Korea General Hodge did his best to set up a functioning regime, and what came to be known as the Korean Interim Government emerged; half the members of the assembly were elected (more or less), half were appointed by the Americans. The Americans themselves were split into three different areas of authority, with jealousies and disagreements rife amongst all three. But this was as nothing compared to the confusion among the Koreans. There arose before Hodge's bewildered eyes no fewer than *seventy* different political parties (some authorities, expert in calculating the width of splinters, say that there were more than two hundred). In the words of one American commentator, not at all a left-winger, the Koreans around Hodge were "a motley assortment of expatriates, collaborators, Fascist reactionaries, professional assassins, and confused intellectuals." What became known as "government by interpreter" began; i.e., the American occupiers, practically none of whom knew Korean, were at the mercy of their translators.

Beyond this was something else. Hodge, a natural conservative, and Rhee, whose political support came largely from the landlords, assumed an extreme rightist position. Words like "leftist" and "rightist" have been so abused that they scarcely have meaning nowadays unless defined with reference to the connotation. But it can be safely said that in the eyes of Hodge and Rhee, particularly at the beginning, almost any Korean not an extreme rightist was a communist and potential traitor.

Thus arose a tragic situation comparable to that in China; we were fighting against communism in the name of democracy, but at the same time we handicapped ourselves by association with reactionaries who were almost as undemocratic as the communists.

Reference to these difficulties makes the observer appreciate more keenly the record of General MacArthur in Japan. If Korea had had an American administrator with half his wisdom and political insight and skill, the story might well have had a different ending.

Dr. Syngman Rhee is an extremely distinguished old gentleman. He is seventy-five. He has devoted his entire life to the cause of Korean independence, and was exiled from his native land for no fewer than thirty-three years, after a period of being jailed by the Japanese. His wife, a Viennese by the name of Francesca Donner, is hotly disliked by many; much of Rhee's fanaticism is supposed to derive from the stimulus of this lady. He was educated in the United States, and attended both Harvard and Princeton; at the latter he came strongly under Woodrow Wilson's influence, and his Ph.D. thesis was, interestingly enough, on the neutrality of small nations. He is the author of several books, among them one called *Japan Inside Out*. The first half of his life was fiercely dominated by his hatred of the Japanese; the second, by his hatred of the communists. He left Korea in 1912, and did not return till 1945. During all that time, he never ceased working in New York, in Paris, in Geneva, in Honolulu, for the cause of his country's rebirth and independence. He even went to Moscow on one occasion, but was sharply rebuffed by the Soviets.

Dr. Rhee and Hodge got along well at first, but later came to dislike each other. The fact that the two chief authorities in the new state quarreled venomously did not make the atmosphere easier.

Negotiations between the United States and Russia to work out a *modus vivendi* for Korea were grievously handicapped by the parallel. Soon most contact between North and South ceased. At the Moscow conference of foreign ministers in December, 1945, it was agreed that Korea should be a "trusteeship" for five years under the joint tutelage of the United States, Great Britain, the Soviet Union and China, and that, as a first step, the American and Russian commanders on the spot should work out details for an all-Korea provisional government. But nothing came of this. The Russians wanted representation heavily weighted in their favor, and the conservative South Koreans, rather than submit to strong leftist influence in a united Korea, worked for a republic of their own. Negotiations broke down in May, 1946, and a tedious, angry period followed in which the Russians continued to obstruct and nullify every avenue of solution. Finally the United States washed its hands of the dispute, in effect, and turned it over to the United Nations. In November, 1947, the U.N. set up a Korean Commission; this in turn was empowered to supervise a nationwide election in Korea. But the Soviet Union boycotted the election, and so it took place (on May 10, 1948) only in the American Zone. It was supervised by U.N. officials and was as fair as any election in a newly born Asiatic country is likely to be. The newly elected assembly convened promptly and promulgated the Republic of Korea in August, 1948; it carefully left open seats for North Koreans should they ever be willing to come down and participate. The new republic was recognized by the United States, and Dr. Rhee became its first president. Of course its authority only held good in the American Zone—up to the parallel. But the South Koreans *claimed* the whole country.

Things did not go smoothly in South Korea. Rioting, largely instigated by communists, took on an anti-American flavor; political confusion became worse confounded, as rival personalities struggled for position; guerrilla fighting began out in the hills and terrorist bands made depredations at large; the Korean authorities put down this and other leftist activity with such rigor and abuse of normal police power as to produce what has been called "a rightist reign of terror." Even the American position became untenable.

Let no one think, however, that North Korea was any paradise by comparison. It is true that the North Korean regime distributed something like 2,500,000 acres of land to 725,000 landless peasants, while Hodge-Rhee delayed putting a comprehensive land reform into effect, the most pressing and imperative need of the country as a whole. It is also true that whereas a sharecropper in South Korea (and 80 per cent of the people are miserably poor share-croppers) had to pay roughly 80 per cent of his crop in tax payments, the tax structure in North Korea was substantially reformed. Industry was nationalized in North Korea, the old monopolists dispossessed, and an eight-hour day instituted. *Nevertheless*—and this is the point to make—something like a million North Koreans slipped across the parallel into South Korea in a short period. North Korea might have been "reformed," but plenty of North Koreans did not like the "reform" they got. This is proof enough, it would seem, that a great many Koreans, whatever their location, preferred the United States to the Soviet Union, and that no matter how Dr. Rhee's regime may have been disliked by some, plenty of Koreans vastly preferred it to the outright police state of the communists. Practically no Koreans went from South to North. But the movement from North to South, despite harsh obstacles, was so substantial that a name new to political science came to be used for these *émigrés*—they were called "defectees."

Korea above the parallel was formally transformed into the "People's Republic of North Korea" on May 1, 1948; the Russians stole a march on the U.S. by setting up their republic a few days before our election took place, and several months before the independence of Dr. Rhee's republic was proclaimed. North Korea, like South, claims the whole peninsula. In basic pattern and design, North Korea is indistinguishable from any other Soviet satellite. The same dreary stigmata characterize it—a constitution that reads nicely on paper, a handpicked People's Assembly, "free" elections which produce a virtually unanimous vote, a well-drilled and equipped People's Army, complete dependence on the Soviet Union in foreign policy, a Five-Year Plan, and a crushing totalitarianism in every aspect of domestic life, enforced by the communist party operating through a United Front.

The leader of the North Koreans is, or was, an apparently remarkable young man named Kim Il Sung. He is of the same type (but younger and with more military experience) as the new puppet leaders of Bulgaria and Rumania. He was trained in China under Mao Tse-tung, and then in Moscow. One story is that he is an impostor, having taken the name of a previous Korean guerrilla who had gained renown fighting the Japanese. (The same kind of legend was told about Marshal Tito of Yugoslavia in the early days.) Kim Il Sung's basic strength comes out of a double root—the peasants who hated the tyranny of the old landlords, and the guerrilla fighters who hated the Japanese. Like all similar leaders, he draws on a combination of nationalist and socialist desires.

Until the last moment, Korean patriots sought to stave off the formal disruption of their country. Several South Korean leaders continued to work for unification until just before the 1948 elections, and the North Korea People's Committee (at that time the directing body in North Korea) issued an invitation for a round-table conference on unification at Pyongyang, the northern capital, that was actually attended by more than fifty prominent South Koreans. The conference called for a single government, the withdrawal of both American and Soviet troops, and the institution of democratic reforms throughout the whole country. General Hodge called this conference a communist plot, and said that the South Koreans who attended it were "blind men who had been baited by the reds."* In any case it came to nothing. But the South Korean delegation included nearly every man of eminence in the country except Dr. Rhee—even rightist leaders like Kim Koo, the heads of two of the chief political parties, and the chairman of the interim assembly. Quite possibly the invitation to Pyongyang was a communist ruse. But that so many South Koreans accepted it shows how deep is their instinct to be unified, no matter what.

*

We come now to the curious episode of the withdrawal from Korea of both American and Russian troops. Official accounts of this do not quite tell the whole story. Once again, the United States was outbluffed and outmaneuvered. In 1947 the Russians proposed the

* See *Korea Today*, by George M. McCune (Harvard University Press), the best modern text on Korea, p. 263.

withdrawal of troops of both nations; of course this would have stood to their advantage. They were close by, and, in the event of wanting at some future date to intervene in Korea, they could simply walk in from across the Manchurian border; American forces, on the other hand, would have to be moved to Korea by ship or air from a considerable distance. It was all to the Russian advantage to get out, if we would get out too. Meantime various pressures pushed the United States toward withdrawal. Many South Koreans, even though they liked America and needed American help, felt that the occupation had gone on long enough; the morale of our G.I.'s on the spot became lower and lower; officials in Washington wanted to save money by withdrawal; politically Korea was a headache. Strange to say, it was the much-maligned State Department which urged prudence, and thought that our army should not withdraw too precipitously. What happened then was that the Russians forced our hand. While we were haggling with the South Koreans, Moscow announced suddenly that all Russian troops would be withdrawn from Korea as of January 1, 1949, and this put us on a spot. If the Russians actually did withdraw, we would have no choice but to do likewise. But the decision was uncomfortable, because everybody knew that the reason the Soviets *were* taking the big gamble to withdraw was that they had trained and equipped the North Korean army so well that it was no longer necessary for their own troops to remain on hand. Somewhat lamely, the United States sought to pass responsibility to the U.N. Finally, we had no recourse but to follow the Russians and get out, and some six months after the Soviet withdrawal (on June 29, 1949, to be precise) we disbanded our military establishment in South Korea and left the country. So ended the American occupation.

(One should mention that a small American group of military advisers remained in Seoul to assist in training the South Korean army. The Russians similarly maintained a mission in North Korea. It was probably more than just a "mission.")

Dr. Rhee and his fledgling government did not have an easy

time thereafter. American economic aid was extended to Korea, but it was not enough. One recent revelation is that the prime minister's office spent three times its entire budget on intelligence alone, i.e., espionage.* The communists dove underground in the towns, and made sharp guerrilla warfare in the hills. Disturbances were put down with ferocity; anybody even faintly to the left or in the labor movement was suspect, and when war broke out in 1950 no fewer than fourteen *thousand* political prisoners were in the South Korean jails awaiting trial. But the very survival of the new republic was at stake; Dr. Rhee's police had to sustain the most vigorous kind of action against the communists, or go under. In March, 1950, the New York *Times* reported that fourteen members of the parliament had been arrested and sentenced to ten years in jail for "taking instructions from the underground Labor Party." Nor was the foreign policy of the South Korean government altogether edifying; from time to time Dr. Rhee made remarks that, to say the least, did not improve his reputation for pacifism. The New York *Herald Tribune* quoted him some months before the war as saying that his government "would not much longer tolerate a divided Korea," and that "South Korea was strong enough to take Pyongyang in a few days." He even said, "If we had our own way we would, I am sure, have started up already. But we had to wait. . . . The American government keeps telling us, 'No, no, no. You are not ready.' "

One member of the American ECA mission in Korea, by name Stanley Earl, resigned as labor adviser in 1950, saying that "the American mission in Korea should have been investigated by Congress in order to expose the weakness of American policy there," and that "the oppressed South Koreans would have rebelled against the Rhee government" had not the war broken out.

Authorities in Washington began to put pressure on Dr. Rhee. In January, 1950, the House of Representatives voted to abolish further aid to Korea; later this vote was reversed, after urgent intervention by the White House and the State Department, and

* McCune, *op. cit.,* p. 312.

when Mr. Acheson stated flatly that the Korean government "would fall within three months" if it did not get substantial ECA help. And it is an open secret (largely ignored nowadays, however) that in April the Department felt it necessary to warn Dr. Rhee sharply that further American assistance would not be forthcoming unless he put his house in order, balanced his budget, inaugurated democratic reforms, and held elections.

The elections were duly held on May 30, 1950. Dr. Rhee's party retained only 22 of 210 seats, and control of the assembly passed to a confused mishmash of middle and independent groups. The fact that this election took place at all, under Dr. Rhee's supervision, and that Rhee himself suffered a damaging defeat, has great significance. I have heard South Korea called "a nauseous little police state," and Dr. Rhee assailed as a "dictator." But no "nauseous little police state" allows free elections, and no "dictator" ever permits himself to be defeated at the polls. Rhee's popularity may have gone down, but it is unfair to denounce him, or his regime, for ills beyond his province. He was holding the line against the communists on an extremely delicate and exposed frontier. Maybe he did things wrong, but it was our fight that he was fighting.

Word About the War Itself

The history books will tell the story of the campaign; it is too early to write it now. The fighting went through five clearly demarcated phases up to the recapture of Seoul on September 27; (1) the early rout of the South Koreans, who lost two thirds of their equipment in the first week; (2) the arrival of American reinforcements, following the courageous decision of General MacArthur to commit them piecemeal; (3) the stubborn, hard-fighting withdrawal of Americans and South Koreans to the Pusan-Taegu beachhead; (4) the holding of this tiny beachhead against furious North Korean attack, while we built up reinforcements; (5) the brilliant amphibious landing at Inchon on September 15, which broke the back of North Korean resistance in South Korea, and cleared the way for the United Nations forces to the parallel.

The Inchon landing was from top to bottom a MacArthur concept. The Joint Chiefs were frightened by it, and General Collins and Admiral Sherman went all the way to Tokyo to talk to MacArthur before they were convinced that it was not too dangerous and risky. MacArthur was, as usual, brilliantly persuasive, and the landing went through without a hitch. His chief motive for Inchon was to try to end the war quickly. He had felt as far back as July that the Inchon operation provided the best hope for bringing victory before winter, and at all costs—the irony seems tragic now—he wanted to avoid a prolonged campaign.

Immediately after the capture of Seoul came a major policy dispute—whether or not the United Nations forces should penetrate into North Korea above the 38th parallel—and ferocious polemics between MacArthur and his critics in Washington, London, Paris, Lake Success, and elsewhere, have been proceeding ever since. The General, on the basis of his instructions from the U.N., took the line that his armies must of course proceed above the parallel, or else risk the same situation that existed at the beginning of the war—the enemy could mass unmolested and immune from attack in a privileged position, and so be able to hamper or frustrate our offensive.

His critics, like Mr. Nehru, thought the opposite—that our moral position would be better if we did not go into North Korea, and that it would be wise strategically to have a buffer area, so that the same paradox—an enemy army immune from interference—would not result on the Yalu River. MacArthur's viewpoint won. It is a grisly paradox that, following Chinese intervention and the ugly sweep south of the Chinese armies (which may conceivably be checked by the time this book is in print), observers are now expressing the pious hope that the Chinese and North Koreans, chasing us, will conveniently stop of their own accord at the parallel.

For a time, strictly military news from Korea was all but inundated by the fierce exchange of charges and countercharges between MacArthur and his various critics. Several times he issued communiqués or messages denying vigorously that he had overstepped military bounds, made his own policy, or refused to obey his superiors.

*

Why did the South Koreans do badly at the beginning? (1) They were taken by surprise, and were miserably short of arms. (2) Few able officers had been trained, particularly above the rank of major. (3) They had no adequate defense against tanks. (4) Morale factors. I have mentioned that vast numbers of North Koreans, hating communism, migrated to the south. True. But it is also true that many South Koreans, out of ignorance and for other reasons, were secret communist sympathizers and supporters of the Northern regime. They infiltrated behind the lines, slipped from uniform into peasant costume and vice versa, and were a savage nuisance.

In the early days of the war I heard one exasperated American colonel say angrily, "South Koreans and North Koreans are identical. You cannot tell one from another. Why, then, do North Koreans fight like tigers, and South Koreans run like sheep?" But he probably would not have said this later.

American troops too were criticized—for being undertrained, and for not having adequate tanks and armor. The MacArthur explanation of this is twofold. First, Japan is a country where every square inch of space is taken up; he could not have confiscated the large areas necessary for serious maneuvers without destroying some of the food crops on which Japan lives. Second, Japanese roads are so narrow and fragile and the bridges so light that full-scale training with tanks was impossible. All this being true there were many sober lessons to be learned from Korea even before the Chinese intervened. A minor Soviet satellite (of course aided substantially by Russian arms) came within an inch of inflicting on the United States what would have been the most ignominious defeat in our history.

A mystery that still perplexes us is why the Chinese did not enter the Korean arena openly *before* Seoul fell to the Americans and *before* we moved north of the parallel; also why, at the beginning, the Russians did not lend more active support to their Korean satrapy. As is well known now, even a small extension of pressure might have pushed us off the Pusan beachhead in early August. It was touch and go. If the Chinese had sent even a few troops down, we might well have been beaten into the sea, and if Pusan had been taken the American forces would have been destroyed. General Walker himself has said that no evacuation like that of Dunkirk would have been possible.

Late in November, after the American capture of Pyongyang and when it seemed that the war would end soon with a resounding U.N. victory, the Chinese did throw troops in. They started to fight, so it seemed, *after* North Korea had lost the war. It would be premature to give a full explanation of this now. The United States and the United Nations behaved with great restraint, in the hope that we would not be drawn into a major war with China proper. Such a war, as explained above, would exactly suit the diabolical Russian game. But why did the Chinese come in so late? They chose to wait until we had crossed the parallel, then drove us back. What were their motives? At least four, of varying consequence, might be listed. (1) To protect the Yalu river dams and hydroelectric plants, which serve most of Manchuria with electric power. (2) To prevent Dr. Rhee's agents from taking over administrative duties in North Korea, and to forestall indefinitely U.N. plans for rehabilitation of the peninsula. (3) To keep the whole pot boiling, ruin our prestige, transform Korea into a kind of Greece, feed us guerrillas, embarrass American foreign policy, cost us money, pin down large numbers of American troops in an exhausting winter campaign, and in short keep the ulcer permanently open. (4) Provoke a general war.

All this was, needless to say, a profound and brutal shock to MacArthur. A shower of statements trying to explain what had happened continued to pour out of him. He cried out that he was suddenly forced to face "an entirely new war," and that he confronted handicaps "without precedent in military history."

192

Chapter Ten

MACARTHUR, TRUMAN, AND FORMOSA

TRUMAN, the President at home; MacArthur, the proconsul in the field—some sort of argument, if not conflict, was inevitable between them. Civilian versus officer; Democrat versus Republican; politician versus soldier; commander in chief versus subordinate—all this played a role. Two more different types of men can scarcely be imagined, and the issue—who was boss—was classically fundamental. Moreover the fact that the General, while only too obviously a stronger, more colorful personality, was at the same time a loyal officer of indubitable patriotism added drama to the picture. Truman was Rome; MacArthur Caesar. But MacArthur, though striving to the utmost to press his point of view, did not cross any Rubicon.

Let us interrupt chronology to go back a bit. Formosa, or Taiwan as the Chinese call it, is the last refuge of the Chinese nationalists under Chiang Kai-shek. According to one school of military theorists, this remote island off the China coast became essential to American strategy in Asia when the Korean war broke out, as a link in the chain embracing Japan, Okinawa, Hong Kong and the Philippines. This link, in the hands of a communist enemy, would severely imperil United Nations communications in the region; Formosa was (and is) as strategically decisive in the area as, say, Gibraltar is in the western Mediterranean. Chiang Kai-shek, fleeing with the remnants of his mildewed army, kept the flag of the Kuomintang flying there. The Chinese communists, lacking only Formosa to make their conquest of China complete, prepared an amphibious invasion to take the island. As already mentioned, Mr. Truman on June 27, 1950 made a celebrated double reference to Formosa. First, he ordered the United States Seventh Fleet to "prevent any attack on Formosa" by the Chinese communists. Second, he requested the Chiang Kai-shek government to stop any military action against the mainland, out of fear that this might precipitate a wholesale conflict between the United States and China. Strategically the President and his advisers felt that we must keep Formosa out of communist grasp; on the other hand we did not wish to give moral and political support to the Kuomintang and certainly did not relish the idea of being sucked into a permanent world conflict because Chiang Kai-shek's men might start shooting.

Though Mr. Truman's statement was thus double-edged, it marked a sharp reversal of American policy. As recently as January 5 the President had formally announced, "The United States government will *not* provide military aid or advice to Chinese forces on Formosa."

Public opinion in the United States and elsewhere had long been hotly divided on Chinese issues, as everybody knows. One wing felt that Chiang Kai-shek was too completely discredited to be of any use whatever, that the sodden weakness and depravity of his regime had lost him all legitimate excuse for support, that it was obviously throwing good money after bad to give him further succor, and that in the end we would have to accept Chinese realities for what they were (as did the British) and, however reluctantly, recognize the Chinese communists whether we liked them or not. Views of the rival group were exactly opposite. Its spokesmen felt that, no matter how feeble Chiang was, or how corrupt his entourage, he merited our concrete support because (after a long period of giving way practically without resistance) he was prepared to fight the communists, our common enemy. They felt that, even if subleaders around Chiang were reactionaries of such extremity as to make even

Dr. Rhee seem like a glowing liberal, we would have to swallow this for the time being and do everything we could to strengthen his forces in Formosa. Nobody I ever met went so far as to think that we should declare war on communist China for the Generalissimo's own sake and carry him into Peking or Nanking on a red-white-and-blue tank—but many did feel that we had to defend him (and ourselves) in Formosa, pat him on the back, and treat him like a respected friend.

The Washington administration, by and large, took the first of these views. MacArthur, it soon became quite clear, took the second.

On July 31 MacArthur suddenly flew to Formosa, and spent a day and a half consulting with the Generalissimo. (It was the first time he had been out of Tokyo overnight since he arrived in Japan almost five years before.) Neither Mr. Truman nor MacArthur's chiefs in the Pentagon were informed beforehand of this step, according to the *first* news released. The General took the line that, as American commander in Japan and United Nations commander in Korea, he had not merely the right but the duty to inspect personally the Formosa sector, since he had the specific obligation to defend it. A competent officer could scarcely have done less. It was, however, not exactly tactful for him to do this before consulting Washington, if indeed he neglected to do so. Moreover the fanfare attending his arrival gave the impression that he sympathized vehemently with Kuomintang aims and policy, as he undoubtedly does. The visit was interpreted almost everywhere in the East—particularly by Chiang's own people—as meaning that the United States at long last had come around to welcoming the Generalissimo back into the fold and forgiving all. It seemed that we were reversing the processes of history. Chiang himself said, "The foundation for Sino-American military cooperation has been laid"—almost as if the United States was about to enter into a new Chinese civil war.

This was too much for Washington to take. After all it is the function of the President, not of any theater commander, to make foreign policy. Mr. Truman sent Averell Harriman out to Tokyo, it was

195

explained, "to brief General MacArthur on what American policy was" and to ask him "to improve his timing." Harriman made the trip out to Japan and back in five days. There followed much bleary face-saving. Harriman announced that the administration leaders had, after all, known of the MacArthur trip beforehand (but not exactly when he was going) and that it was "entirely natural" that the Supreme Commander should want to visit Formosa. The American attitude to Formosa, Harriman said, was unchanged—it was to neutralize the island and deny it to any hostile power but "not to condone or support the regime of Chiang Kai-shek." Then on August 10 MacArthur issued a statement in his most furious vein. He said with aggressive emphasis that his visit to Formosa was "limited entirely to military matters" and (letting down Chiang with a bump) that Chinese domestic affairs were altogether out of his own responsibility and province. "My visit," the General stated, "has been maliciously represented to the public by those who invariably, in the past, have propagandized a policy of defeatism and appeasement in the Pacific. . . . I hope the American people will not be misled by the insinuations, speculations, and bold misstatements . . . which tend, if they are not indeed designed, to promote disunity and destroy faith and confidence in the American nation and institutions and the American representatives at this time of great world peril."

This uproar had important repercussions abroad; in particular the British and Indians were alarmed. It was repeatedly pointed out that, whereas the United Nations had given sanction to the defense of Korea against communist invasion, Mr. Truman's pronouncement on Formosa was strictly an American matter, with which the United Nations had nothing whatever to do. In important organs of the London press came editorials under such titles as "The Menace of General MacArthur." In reply the Supreme Commander issued another indignant statement, this time directed against London, and protesting at the attempt of the British government "to arrogate to itself, under the guise of membership in the United Nations," the right to pass judgment on "the propriety of the mission of an American officer." One result was that, even at the time when British troops from Hong Kong were arriving in Korea to strengthen the hard-pressed Americans there, General MacArthur refused to receive the British Ambassador in Tokyo "for many weeks."

The next step occurred on August 25, when Ambassador Warren R. Austin announced that the United States would welcome a complete investigation by the U.N. of the Formosan problem. This was done partly to reassure opinion in Asia—particularly in India—by saying that we had no desire to stay indefinitely in Formosa, that we were not imperialists or conquerors, that we were not committed to the further support of Chiang Kai-shek, and that the presence of our fleet had one purpose only, resistance against aggression.

But on almost the same date came another explosion between Mr. Truman and MacArthur, and once more a lot of morbid fat was in the fire. The Supreme Commander had written a statement of some length on Formosa, as a message to the Veterans of Foreign Wars, who were about to hold their annual meeting in Chicago. The release date was August 28, and SCAP—somewhat oddly—had sent advance copies direct to several American news agencies, newspapers, and even magazines. There are two contrary stories as to whether MacArthur had also informed his superiors about this message. One is to the flat effect that "the Administration was *not* informed of General MacArthur's intention." The other is that SCAP had indeed sent the text to Washington, as well as to the press, and that it had kicked around in the Pentagon for ten days without being noticed. MacArthur did not specifically submit it to higher authority because, in the words of one of his advisers, "he saw no necessity for doing so." In any event an alert newspaperman got hold of it and called it to the attention of the White House. This was at midnight on August 25. The White House was outraged (because it is an inflexible rule that statements on high policy must be cleared with the President) and so was the State Department; one report is that Mr. Acheson threatened to resign. In any case Mr. Truman called a meeting of his chief military and civilian advisers for 9 A.M. on the twenty-sixth, gave them the gist of the MacArthur statement, and asked if any of them had ever heard of it. Nobody had. Truman thereupon instructed Louis Johnson, then the Secretary of Defense, to order MacArthur to eat his words, i.e., withdraw the message. This the General proceeded to do—though not with much grace. But it was too late, because one magazine had already gone to press with the full text, and by Monday morning everybody in the nation knew what he had said.

The MacArthur statement was, in itself, not as sensational as all the fuss made over it. It sketched the geographic position of Formosa in relation to the defense of the Pacific, saying, "Formosa in the hands of a hostile power could be compared to an unsinkable aircraft carrier and submarine tender ideally located to accomplish offensive strategy and at the same time checkmate defensive or counter-offensive operations by friendly forces based on Okinawa or the Philippines." The General did not specifically state that the United States should remain in Formosa for keeps, but this was strongly implied. He said, for instance, that World War II had made the entire Pacific Ocean a "vast moat to protect us so long as we hold it." Also, "Nothing could be more fallacious than the threadbare argument . . . that if we defend Formosa we alienate continental Asia. Those who speak thus do not understand the Orient. They do not grasp that it is the pattern of Oriental psychology to respect and follow aggressive, resolute, and dynamic leadership." This proposition by the Supreme Commander was, many people thought, debatable to say the least. It seemed to smack of the Asia of Curzon and Rudyard Kipling, not of the modern Asia gripped by profound revolutionary impulses and devoted passionately to native nationalism.

After Mr. Truman ordered the message to be withdrawn because it was badly timed and "dangerous sabre-rattling in a delicate international situation," a reporter went to the late Charles G. Ross, the

President's press secretary, and asked, "Will General MacArthur be relieved?" "The President regards the incident as closed," Mr. Ross replied. "Isn't it a fact," the reporter went on, "that General Mac-Arthur has disregarded instructions and policy a number of times since the outbreak of aggression in Korea?" "No comment," said Mr. Ross.*

Nobody, during all this, seemed to give much heed to what the Formosans themselves might be thinking. Yet it is their island, though they have had no voice in its rule since 1895. In Hong Kong I talked to an American official who had just flown in from Taipeh; probably he knew the situation there as well as anybody. He said that if the fate of Formosa were up to the islanders themselves, they would prefer the following regimes in the following order if they could not be independent: First, a trusteeship under the United Nations. Second, temporary occupation by the United States. Third, return to Japan. Fourth, continuation of the regime of Chiang Kai-shek. Fifth and last, the communists.

The Meeting at Wake

Apparently Mr. Harriman did not convey the views of the administration to the Supreme Commander with lasting force. Also Mr. Truman had for a long time wanted to meet in the flesh this man, MacArthur, about whose spirit he knew so much. One reason was simple curiosity; another was that an exchange of views would be profitable. At this period Chinese intervention was not anticipated; even so there was plenty to talk about from problems of Korean reconstruction to the whole picture of Far East strategy. The President wanted, among other things, safeguard that Mac-Arthur would not intervene in diplomatic affairs and embarrass the administration as he had done over Formosa. He did not want to have to rebuke the Supreme Commander again, and he thought that a few hours of conversation might clear the air.

Communications between heads of state and viceroys took a lot

* The New York *Times*, August 29, 1950.

of time in older days. It was not easy for Madrid to keep tabs on Cortes, or for London to tell its will to Warren Hastings; even in modern times things were not always smooth between Paris and Marshal Lyautey. Today the instantaneousness of communication solves many problems, but not all. Occasions exist when a good talk face to face, a good laugh, or even a good cry, can work wonders. Initiative for the meeting came from the President. He went to Mac-Arthur, not vice versa.

Some MacArthur advisers disliked the idea of this confrontation, and the General himself was somewhat reluctant to go. He had the Wonsan landing coming up, which might be very dangerous on account of Russian mines, and he wanted to superintend it in person. Anything except adhesive day-to-day prosecution of the war seemed an irrelevance, even if the irrelevance was the President of the United States.

The meeting took place on Wake Island, in the shabby, primitive quarters of the Civil Aeronautics Administration, on Sunday, October 15, 1950. The atmosphere was cordial. Truman and Mac-Arthur talked for an hour privately first, and then for two hours with their advisers, including General Whitney for MacArthur, and a small group of illustrious Washingtonians for Truman— Harriman, Bradley, Philip Jessup, and a few others.

A communiqué was drafted, which was initialed (as one reporter on the scene described it) by both men "as if they were heads of different governments." Later the General seemed to be restless and in a hurry to get away. "Once he took out a gold pocket watch, looked at it, rubbed a finger slowly over its crystal, and returned it to his pocket." It was a shock to almost everybody that the proceedings were so brief; Mr. Truman had planned to leave that evening, but he was able to get off at noon. MacArthur left five minutes later.

The President said as he departed, "I've never had a more satisfactory conference since I've been president." MacArthur refused to talk to reporters, with the words, "All comments will have to come from the publicity man of the President." Mr. Truman does not, of course, have a "publicity man"; doubtless the General was referring to Mr. Ross, the senior White House press secretary. But it is unlikely that he meant this as a slight; it is merely an example of his somewhat old-style way of expressing things.

Back in Washington Truman denied heatedly that any reference at all had been made to Formosa. That whole question, he told reporters firmly, had been settled five weeks before, when he first silenced MacArthur on Formosan policy, and consequently there had been nothing more of any kind to say. The General, in other words, was obeying orders. It was illuminating to read accounts of Wake in some newspapers, which behaved as if MacArthur had been subjected to some terrible affront. Perhaps they forgot that the President of the United States is also commander in chief.

MacArthur, having traveled more than 4,000 miles in thirty hours, got back to Tokyo ready to deliver what he hoped would be the *coup de grâce* of the Korean war. Little did he know that, far from being over, a new and shockingly dangerous phase of the war was about to begin, and that he would soon face the most inexplicable and humiliating defeat of his entire career.

Chapter Eleven

ASIA SOFT SPOTS AND U.S. POLICY

LET us proceed beyond MacArthur briefly to inspect some aspects of Asia from a new perspective. Where, aside from Korea, are other subterranean fires likely to burst into open flame? What are the softest of the soft spots, and what should the United States do about a situation that could bring irremediable tragedy to us all? Has World War III already begun in Asia? Can we save Asia from communism without a major war? If so, how?

Perhaps the first—and most obvious—generalization is that Asia, an enormously variegated continent, is not easy to generalize about. Consider how difficult it is for the ordinary American to understand fully and get along fully with the average Italian, Frenchman, Pole, or even Englishman, to whom he is tied by the stout rope of a common language and a joint political ancestry and culture. It is incomparably more difficult for him to get along with, comprehend, and have community with people so intricate and transcendentally foreign as, say, the Indonesians, the Nepalese, the Pakistanis, or even the citizens of Tokyo. To get the United States on the same wave length as Great Britain is a hard enough job. To get it on the same wave length as that of China is enormously more difficult.

Another point almost too rudimentary for mention is that most Asiatics do not understand and often do not share the American concept of democracy. Our democratic structure is based on the idea

202

of individual dignity, human freedom, and the Bill of Rights. Asia may, in time, become fully conscious of these factors, but as of the moment many Asiatics have other preoccupations much more pressing. Civil liberties are apt to be an issue somewhat remote to a farmer whose children are starving under his very eyes, and who owes forty years of taxes to the landowner a county away. The principle of free speech may be a matter of the utmost moment to a citizen of Pittsburgh or Minneapolis. It may not mean so much to the illiterate citizen of a derelict Indochinese village who has never, so to speak, had any speech at all.

Democracy is not always an epidemic phenomenon; Germany lived near democracy for centuries, and does not understand it yet. The point need not be labored that if Europeans of the highest literacy, political experience, and intellectual capacity find it extremely difficult to absorb even the primary tenets of democracy, the task is overwhelmingly more difficult for illiterate and poverty-smitten Asiatics.

The bulk of the people of Asia want two things above all: *First*, economic amelioration. *Second*, national freedom. After these come a host of other desiderata, such as education, land reform, political stability, public health, emancipation of women, various social loosenings, and so on, which should not be minimized. But the first two are those that count.

As to political nationalism, i.e., national freedom, that has been largely gained. India, Pakistan, Burma, Ceylon, the Philippines, Indonesia, and, on the other side of Asia, Israel, have all become free, independent republics since the end of World War II. This evolution, whereby no fewer than 533 million people became emancipated in seven nations, is one of the most remarkable events of all history. Only two countries in Asia have not yet gained independence—Malaya and Indochina. That is one reason why Indochina is potentially the most dangerous spot on the continent next to Korea.

Few people thought that the old colonial empires, which had

ruled most of Asia since the eighteenth century, would break up with such velocity. I asked Prime Minister Jawaharlal Nehru if, ten years ago when I first met him in Bombay, he even so much as dreamed that within a decade he would be the head of an independent sovereign India. "No," he smiled.

I mentioned this recently to a lady exceptionally well informed on foreign affairs, and she exclaimed, "Don't you see—what really happened was that *Japan* won the war!" This is not quite correct, but the remark contains a lively substratum of truth. Japan certainly did lose the war so far as Japan itself was concerned—lost it totally—but, paradoxically, one of the things that the Japanese said that they were fighting for, "Asia for the Asiatics," the freedom of the Asian peoples from the old imperialist domination, came remarkably close to being achieved. Japan lost, but the convulsion was so universally disruptive that the rest of Asia won.

The Japanese, being good mimics, and being on the surface the most westernized of Asiatic peoples, promptly learned—before World War II—how to imitate the imperialist West; hence their occupation of Inner Mongolia, Manchuria, and China, and their febrile campaigns in Burma, Malaya, the Philippines, and what were then called the Dutch East Indies. I remember writing years ago, "The Japanese are marching fast, and it may be that in many regions the rule of the white man has gone never to return."

In most of the reborn Asia countries, India conspicuously excepted, the present leaders collaborated with Japan during the war. This point, often forgotten, should be rigidly kept in mind. It is a clue to much. The local nationalists hated the whites so much that they were willing to work with Tokyo. Or, to put it another way, they played with the Japanese not because they necessarily liked them but to gain nationalist advantage. The Japanese had to use such leaders, because Japan's own policy was built on the slogan of "liberated" Asia. Then the nationalist leaders, if possible, doublecrossed them, and were delighted to be rescued from brutal Japanese oppression by us, the western allies. Yet they wanted so desperately, so stubbornly, to be free that they fought us too, even though we theoretically represented the forces of liberation, if we opposed their irresistible claim to national independence.

As to economics the Asiatics still have formidable difficulties to overcome. The poverty of Asia is proverbial; this does not make it any the less real. Nobody can understand the permanent realities of Asia who has not seen an Indian beggar paw through offal for bits of grain to eat, or Chinese babies with their faces pitted by sores and their bellies transparent from starvation, or, for that matter, the way of life of someone very rich for Asia—a Japanese farmer, say, who has all of $200 per year to live on.

The basis of life in most of Asia is the land; predominantly the 1,200,000,000 Asiatics live—if you can call it living—out of the fruits of the soil. But the soil is frightfully impoverished; agricultural methods and techniques are primitive beyond belief; there is a desperate lack of fertilizer in most areas; above all vast numbers of farmers do not possess their own land, but are tenants at the mercy of the owner. But it is difficult in the extreme to make a successful land reform in any country, those of Asia not least. First, a land reform is as a rule bitterly opposed by the ruling class, and hence by governments dominated by the privileged. Second, a comprehensive land reform demands considerable technical and administrative equipment, as well as capital, which most of Asia sadly lacks.

As the old Asia began to deliquesce under the burden of dissatisfaction and poverty the communists gained rapid advantage. The continent was gripped by a convulsion partly of disintegration, partly of rebirth. As Moscow put it to the suppressed millions duped into listening, "capitalism" was the villain on both counts; the western powers kept Asia from freedom by their imperialist policy, while the local ruling class enforced economic slavery by exploitation. The Russians cogently played on the nationalist theme, always encouraging the Asiatics to revolt against the West (they would have revolted anyway, Moscow or no Moscow), while at the same time encouraging the unrest that might be provoked out of economic distress and lack of opportunity. Thousands upon thousands of Asiatics became communists, partly because of ignorance, but also out of hatred of the West, hatred of the landlords, and for the simple reason that they thought communism promised them a new way out.

The word "communism" does not, by itself, arouse as much instinctive antipathy in the average Asiatic as it does in the average European or American. Our own propaganda might be more successful in Asia if we did not use the word "communism" quite so much, as a blanket label for everything evil, and instead talked of "Russia" or "Russianism," which has a more menacing connotation and which many Asiatics already have good reason to abhor.

So much for background. If we look at the present situation in the China area and southeast Asia (excluding Japan and Korea) this is what we find:

China. Area 3,858,900 square miles; population 463,000,000. China counts so much, not merely because of its immense heft and bulk and because it is, of course, the only outright communist state so far established in Asia, but because of its profound and pervasive influence—historical, political, cultural—on other Asiatics. Mao Tse-tung and his communist armies completed the military occupation of the China mainland last year (I say military "occupation" rather than "conquest" because Chiang Kai-shek's forces largely surrendered and melted away instead of fighting—the people would not support them), and the People's Republic of China has been functioning since September 21, 1949.

How stable is Mao's regime? Most competent observers would say that it is fairly firm for the foreseeable future. True, guerrilla resistance still continues in many quarters, and economic and administrative problems of the most staggering magnitude afflict Mao's men. They will not be easy of solution. But for the first time in thirty years there is no civil war in China; for the first time since the mid-1930's the railways are running over the entire nation. The new regime managed to stabilize the currency, after years of catastrophic inflation; it has even gone far to abolish "squeeze" (graft) in tax collections. Taxes are, of course, murderously high; the middle class is being squeezed out; much of the peasantry still grumbles; and we do not even need to go into what the Chinese people will have to pay in human values for what economic improvement they may get. But if we restrict ourselves to the single question, "Is the regime tolerably stable?" the answer—as of the moment of writing—is bound to be a fairly emphatic "Yes."

This correspondent confesses that he was flabbergasted in Hong Kong, for instance, to find the degree of support vouchsafed for Mao in British and Chinese circles normally classed as conservative. I met Englishmen who hated the Labor government in London more vehemently than they hated Mao. I met Chinese—rich Chinese at that—who said they would much rather have Mao Tse-tung in Shanghai than Chiang Kai-shek. Probably this is because (a) the British want to restore their age-long trade with China no matter what kind of government it has; (b) Chinese bankers and businessmen think that for a time at least they *can* do business with the communists, even on disadvantageous terms, whereas under the Kuomintang things were so chaotic that most business was impossible.

Is Chiang Kai-shek himself finished? Most people would say "Yes," so far as the possibility of reconquest of the China mainland is concerned. He has many admirable qualities, and his Formosan army could be of great value to us, but it will not be easy to resuscitate the Kuomintang, if only because it was so corrupt. I heard one experienced American put it this way, "Chiang's gang did not serve the interests of the Chinese people. They served themselves. The whole future of this part of the world depends on whether or not communist China succeeds. But whether it does or not, the alternative cannot be the Kuomintang. Mao may or may not collapse, but Chiang cannot be his successor, even with American help, because all that he stands for is hopelessly worn out."

Another question invariably asked is whether Mao Tse-tung is an outright Russian puppet or a kind of partner. Opinion on this differs sharply; Mao's exact status is one of the most obscure—and important—puzzles in the world. The chief argument put forward to "prove" that he is not a complete tool or marionette, and that he has considerable free will of his own, is that, when he went to Moscow, two months of tough, taut negotiation were necessary before signature of a Sino-Russian treaty in February, 1950. The Kremlin does not often spend two months negotiating with a puppet. (Of course, even if he is a partner and not a slave, Mao may out-Kremlin the Kremlin in zeal.)

As to American attitudes it is fascinating to look back and recall that many of those who staunchly defend Chiang Kai-shek and the Formosa regime nowadays were the selfsame folk who, in the period before World War II, strenuously appeased Japan. Their motive remains the same—to help save China, Asia, and the world from communism. But whether they are going about this the right way is dubious. We are apt to forget that the pro-Chiang people today were those who encouraged Japanese aggression *against* Chiang in the 1930's. Japan was the "spearhead" against communism in those days; Formosa is supposed to be the spearhead against communism now. Of course Japan ("the great stabilizing force of Asia") was inordinately more powerful than Formosa can ever be. But the attempt of the Japanese, supported by Americans who wanted to give them a free hand in Asia, to frustrate the immense revolutionary march of China to freedom and unity was a ghastly failure. Actually the Japanese war in China was a major factor in stimulating communist growth there. Japan destroyed itself, and, an ugly irony, helped bring communism to China too. The lesson for us, to put it mildly, is that nobody should assault China without careful calculation of what the risks will be.

This brings up another point—the hatred that most Chinese still bear for the Japanese. "China's attitude toward Japan," it has been written, "is precisely that of France toward Germany . . . China's alliance with Russia is not based on mutual love but on a common fear of a resurrected Japan." Part of the contemporary Chinese antipathy to the United States derives out of this, since the Japanese are now regarded by communist Chinese as *our* tools and "imperialist" puppets.

Indochina. Area 280,849 square miles, population roughly 25,000,000. Indochina, we have already noted, is one of the two countries in Asia not yet free, and a savage civil war is being fought there. On one side are the rebels of the Viet-Minh movement, largely communist, under their powerful leader Ho Chi Minh, whose "government" has been recognized by Mao Tse-tung; on the other are the French and their puppets in Viet-Nam, which has partial autonomy within what is called the French Union, under the "shadow emperor" (or "playboy emperor") Bao Dai. This young man has a doubtful past, a doubtful present—mostly spent in fashionable resorts in France—and an even more doubtful future. But even Bao Dai, who is generally thought of—perhaps unfairly—as the epitome of things reactionary, has the sweet smell of nationalism in his nostrils. Once he worked closely with Ho as his "Supreme Political Adviser," though this fact is conveniently ignored nowadays. Recently Bao Dai told a distinguished European statesman, "Just wait till we finish off the civil war. *Then* we'll throw out the French!"

But it is not going to be easy to finish off Ho Chi Minh. This veteran agitator with a long and variegated revolutionary past is a dangerously able character, and he is supported by a substantial part of the population. Ho was a communist for many years, high in the international hierarchy; nowadays he denies that he is a party member. But there is no doubt that his Viet-Minh force is communist inspired and led. The Chinese communists help train his troops across the border, and give him counsel and assistance, although to date they have made no formal intervention. His armies are numerous and well-trained, and have won consistent victories over the French.

During the war *both* the French and some Indochinese nationalists collaborated with the Japanese—odd as this may seem. Even more oddly, American agents worked with Ho's underground. When Japanese power crashed, Ho Chi Minh set up the original Democratic Republic of Viet-Nam. The history of Indochina has derived ever since from the fact that the French overthrew this new republic, and attempted to resume their prewar role. With Ho are most of the Indochinese who (a) hate the French, (b) hate economic despotism, (c) hate the past.

The French have been forced to maintain in Indochina for almost five years at least 150,000 troops (half their total army), and this has naturally been an exhausting drain on French economy; moreover the formidable fact that France has to fight a quasi-permanent war in Asia serves to weaken it militarily and politically in Europe, where the United States would like it to be as strong as possible.

The French are having abstruse difficulty not merely in beating down Ho's rebellion, but in keeping control of their own marionettes. Day by day, Indochinese nationalist sentiment grows stronger, and resentment at further French control more piercing. The Bao Dai regime has found it almost impossible to raise troops, maintain an effective administration, or otherwise function as a viable government. Late in October, 1950, the Viet-Nam prime minister, Tran Van Huu, though he has been regarded as an outright French puppet and is in fact a French citizen, announced that his government would demand *complete* independence from France as soon as practicable.

The United States is, according to the terms of Mr. Truman's statement of June 27, formally committed to the defense of the French position in Indochina. No single item in American foreign policy toward Asia, except that involving Chiang Kai-shek and Formosa, has provoked so much criticism as this. Sooner or later, if history has any meaning at all, France will be bound to withdraw from Indochina, as the British withdrew from India, as the Americans withdrew from the Philippines, as even the stubborn Dutch withdrew from Indonesia. So—critics ask—why should we bind ourselves to a policy leading toward reaction and sterility? The answer lies in the realm of strategy, both political and military. We are supporting the French not because we necessarily like the French or a puppet like Bao Dai, but to keep communism from grabbing off an immensely vital strategic area.

Malaya. Area 50,580 square miles; population 4,908,000. The British are still holding on here, for a variety of reasons. (1) They do not want to give up Singapore. (2) Malayan production of rubber and tin is vital to British dollar balances. (3) Malayan nationalism— the Malayans are a docile people—has not been strong enough to force the issue.

Nevertheless guerrilla activity is so widespread that since June, 1948, a state close to civil war has existed. The British have had to divert crack troops from Hong Kong to help keep order, and a big garrison is constantly on the alert. Assassinations in remote plantation areas; ambuscades along the railways; organized banditry by communist-led guerrillas who strike at night, and are hidden by day by a friendly peasantry—these are conspicuous. About 400 "incidents" a month occur, and the cost to the British is £25,000 per day or more.

There is a large Chinese community in Malaya, the Straits Settlements, and Singapore, and of the Chinese (even the prosperous Chinese) many are communist. It is the Chinese, rather than the Malayans, who are revolutionists and nationalists. The situation in Malaya has not, however, deteriorated to the point where there is much danger of an actual *coup d'état* by the Malayan Communist party, nor is there immediate possibility of communist invasion from outside.

The Philippines. Area 114,830 square miles; population 19,964,000. The position is nasty here, and getting nastier. There is little possibility of organized overthrow of the government, but the communist-led "Huks" (short for Hukbalahaps) have made mince-meat of internal security in some areas of the islands. The Philippine army and constabulary have done their best, but the elusive Huks, though not very numerous, are hard to lay hands on, and harder still to liquidate.

It is impossible to contend with guerrilla activity successfully without the supreme weapon of information. A guerrilla war is 90 per cent intelligence, 10 per cent combat. So long as parts of the countryside are, by and large, sympathetic to the Huks rather than to the government, the authorities are almost helpless in attempting to wipe out guerrilla bands permanently, because they are so well hidden by friendly villagers. They melt invisibly into the dilapidated countryside.

Most Huks are not outright or official communists, if only because few Filipino peasants have any real conception of what communism is; they are simply rebellious desperadoes who hate the government. The way to handle the Huk rebellion is to get the countryside as a whole on the government's side. But this is difficult, because the government has been inefficient, riven by financial difficulty, beset by landlordism, and monstrously corrupt.

Siam (Thailand). Area 198,000 square miles; population 17,676,000. Siam, alone among the countries of southeastern Asia, was independent before the war, largely because the great powers were too busy elsewhere to interfere with its sovereignty. Also it was convenient to have Siam, or Thailand as it is called officially these days, as a kind of buffer.

Siam is a political curiosity of picturesque interest; the best description I heard of it came from a friend in Bangkok, "This country just isn't *true!*" It is the only state in the whole area that is underpopulated, not overpopulated; it grows enough rice to feed itself and has an exportable surplus of food; it has a balanced budget and a favorable trade balance. Also it is the country where the pedicabs are lit up at night like juke boxes, where the priests wear orange robes the color of a Mae West life jacket, where boxers fight with their feet, and where the King is an expert devotee of jazz.

The prime minister, a leathery and astute old gentleman named Phibun Songgram, was not merely a Japanese collaborator during the war, but was actually the man who brought Siam into the war against the United States after Pearl Harbor. Now, however, we support him vigorously, if with a watchful eye, because his own policies have veered in our direction—we need him, but he *has* to have us—and because he is probably the only man with sufficient acumen and prestige to hold the kingdom together.

Most Siamese, like Malayans, are not much interested in politics. They have their own independence and (though the rank and file of the population is certainly poor by our standards) enough rice to eat as a rule. The country is not in much danger of direct Soviet aggression, if only because other areas outrank it in Russian priorities. But the country holds some 3,000,000 Chinese, and, since many of these are communists, there is always the possibility of internal disturbance. The Communist party numbers 50,000 in all. Moreover, if Indochina or Burma should fall into the Soviet lap, Siam would almost certainly follow suit.

The Siamese were among the first people to offer a contingent of troops to the United Nations forces in Korea, and the United States has established close military contacts in Bangkok.

Indonesia. Area 735,268 square miles; population 76,500,000. This great new republic, one of the largest, richest, and strategically most important nations in the world, is in process of agglutination and consolidation. Its temper, like that of India, is to avoid participation in the cold war between Washington and the Kremlin; its government is strongly anticommunist—in fact it put down a communist rebellion in 1948—and at the same time is somewhat hostile to the democratic West.

Indonesia is in little immediate danger of falling to communist aggression, unless a third world war should destroy the whole structure of contemporary Asia. Russia is too far away, and the local communists have been thoroughly slapped back. Plenty of nationalist and other unrest still exists in Indonesia—for instance outer islands like the Moluccas have risen militarily against the central government— but steadily the political situation has become more stable.

The chief problem of the country is national integration with concomitant financial troubles. Indonesia is being transformed from a federal to a unitary state. The government is moderately left-wing, which means that it has to promise the people a lot, and cannot always deliver what it promises. Its three chief leaders, Achmed Soekarno, Soetan Sjahrir, and Mohammed Hatta, all youthful, are men of the utmost consequence. What all three believe in above all is *merdeka*—freedom.

America should do its utmost to smooth over Indonesian suspicions, make this far-flung new republic friendly to the West, heal the bitter wounds left by Dutch intransigence, and take full advantage of the miraculous fact that Indonesia, like India, is a democratically governed state. Here we can give full support to legitimate Asian nationalism without having to play with extreme rightists on the local scene.

Burma. Area 261,000 square miles; population 16,800,000. This country is probably the softest spot in Asia, and the easiest way to describe its situation is to say frankly that it is a mess. Ever since national independence was established on January 4, 1948, Burma has been in turmoil. There have been at least four civil wars in two years. The prime minister at present, who has been a virtual prisoner in his capital, is an ardent nationalist, Buddhist, and socialist (also a poet and playwright) named Thakin Nu; he is friendlier now to the United States than heretofore. He faces armed insurrection on two sides—from marauding communist bands of several varieties (Burma has "Red Flag" and "White Flag" communists) and from a minority group known as the Karens, who want autonomy. A third hostile force, that of the dissident leftist "People's Volunteer Organization," has been beaten down, and lately the Burmese situation has improved. But the country is extremely vulnerable, not merely to trouble from within, but to aggression from without. It has a long common frontier with China, where

Chinese communist troops are posted in strength. If Mao Tse-tung should ever decide, with or without orders from the Kremlin, to invade Burma the country could hardly be saved except by vigorous and concerted action by the United Nations, and even that might not be enough. And Burma is a rice bowl for which communism yearns.

India. Area 1,221,000 square miles; population 342,000,000. To try to compress the Indian situation in a paragraph or two is impossible; one feels like a mouse nibbling at an elephant. India is, next to China itself, the most important of all these countries, not merely because of its size—its population is more than twice that of the United States—but because it represents what might be called "a third force," a vast area that seeks to be neutral as between America and Russia, and that casts its weight on the side of negotiation, amity, and the hope of peace.

As of the moment anyway, India is in little danger of overt aggression from the outside, and it keeps its domestic communists under tight rein. The Indian Communist party is not big numerically, but it has made much nuisance with sporadic violence, strikes, and political agitation. Recently the powerful minister of home affairs, Sardar Vallabhbhai Patel (who is second only to Nehru in Indian consequence) stated, "Whatever shifts may have taken place in the tactics of the communist party, there has been absolutely no change in their fundamental strategy of seizing power through violent revolt. The Government of India is determined to give no quarter to any such attempt, and will use all the resources at its disposal to put it down."

Nehru himself is by all odds the most important Asiatic in Asia. This fastidious intellectual, who spent an aggregate of fourteen years in British jails, has inherited the mantle of Gandhi; sometimes his politics, like those of the late Jan Masaryk, are so high-minded as to seem almost naïve. Nehru is an exceedingly complex character, an aristocrat of the most ancient lineage who became a socialist, a nationalist with a thorough understanding of western attitudes (he went to Harrow and Cambridge), and an individualist who became a great mass leader.

Mr. Nehru has been severely criticized in the United States—and by many Americans in India—because of his early attempts to settle the Korean war, his vigorous hope for the admission of China to the United Nations, and his general policy of mediation. He is often called "anti-American"; a more accurate description would be that he is pro-Asian. He is an Asiatic himself; he lives in Asia; on the immense arc of his frontiers are millions of Asiatics; he cannot possibly neglect or minimize the magnetic force of the Soviet Union (a great Asiatic power) on his territories; he cannot possibly afford to alienate or antagonize Red China without good reason. Nehru's attitude toward Asia is much like that of the United States toward Latin America or the Caribbean. It is his own back yard.

This is a factor still often underestimated in the United States, and it should be pasted in the hat of every American involved with Asia policy. *Asians believe in Asia for the Asiatics.*

The domestic problems facing Nehru are numerous and heavy, like food supply, political integration, and the quarrel with Pakistan over Kashmir. At the moment he is confronted with more pungent opposition from the extreme right than from the left; the Hindu fundamentalists cause him more trouble than the Kremlin. Independence from Great Britain did not bring the Indian nationalists Utopia over night. They have the colossal, unprecedented job of trying to make Utopia work. Nehru's ambition, it could be said, is to create a secular left-liberal state, with democracy both triumphant and efficient. No man could have a stiffer job.

I have mentioned the fact that Americans, by and large, do not understand Asia; the obverse is equally true—most Asiatics do not understand America. Perhaps this is partly because of our customary stress on things material. Asia is, heaven knows, poor enough; but Asia wants more from the United States than fertilizer, washing machines, and tin cans full of milk or movies. The instinct of many Asiatics is toward spiritual values as well as mere material assistance.

It was a severe shock to me in New Delhi and elsewhere to discover how cordially Americans have come to be disliked. The Indians get along nicely with the British now, and call *us* the new "colonists"; many fear our "imperialism" more acutely than Russian communism, which—for some reason I could not fathom—they think is remote. I heard one Indian of eminence, in reference to the Korean war, talk disparagingly of what he called the American *"incursion"* into Asia. In the early days of the fighting I came across one editorial in a left-wing paper, "Two reasons motivate MacArthur. One is the sagging morale of the American playboy soldiers in Korea. The other is that Wall Street wants MacArthur to appease the feelings of the American public." Such guff and nonsense has to be seen to be believed.

Nehru himself has often explained his own common-denominator attitude. He is worried by Russian truculence, Russian aggressiveness, and Russian totalitarianism, but he is on record as having said that—provided no general war occurs—communism will in the end fail in Asia, because it is fundamentally directed *against* the new national freedom that most of Asia has achieved. But he knows full well how dangerous communism can be, because it so often appears "in the guise of a liberation movement," and "the ideal of social justice embodied in communism attracts many people."

Recent events in Tibet were an unpleasant shock to Nehru and the Indian government, coming as they did directly after the Chinese intervention in Korea. Nehru had worked hard to keep China neutral, and fear that the Chinese might be provoked was one reason why he opposed the advance of MacArthur's troops above the 38th parallel. He had been worried about Tibet (he told us in New Delhi in August) for some months, but he did not think that the Chinese communists would go so far as to do what they did in late October—march crudely across the Tibetan highland and attempt to overthrow the Tibetan government by force. It was a severe eye opener.

Tibet, "the roof of the world," has been terra incognita for most of its history; nominally it was part of China, but for generations it had virtual autonomy under strong British and Indian influence. Nehru thought that the whole issue of Tibet's obscure status could be settled peaceably, and in fact a Tibetan delegation was en route to Peiping to begin negotiations when the communists suddenly let loose their troops. The Chinese consider Tibet to be a "domestic" problem. Their note to the Indian government employed a familiar device; they asserted that India had been "affected by foreign influences hostile to China." Nehru denied this indignantly, and gave China clear warning that it was endangering peace. All this may turn out to be a valuable lesson to the Indians. It has been wisely written that "the communists themselves may force India into the anticommunist camp."

*

American policy in Asia should be to be on the side of the Asian *peoples*. We should support middle-of-the-road democratic nationalism, as in Indonesia, India, Pakistan, and elsewhere, if only for the selfish reason that we badly need the friendship of these countries. India's largely untapped wealth and geographical position make it an indispensable ally, whether we like everything that goes on in Indian politics or not; the same thing is true of Indonesia. World War III is in the wings. Civilization is having to adjust itself to a period in which war and peace are inextricably intermingled. And if the world is to be divided perpetually into two hostile and mutually exclusive spheres, it behooves us to be sympathetically friendly to great neutral states that can tip the balance either way.

As to Indochina the present position is much more difficult; American policy should be just and generous, but also it must be practical. We may deplore the record and conduct of Bao Dai, and we may fervently wish that the French would clear out of Asia bag and baggage. But to withdraw support from them at this juncture would probably mean turning over Indochina to our communist enemies, which cannot be done.

218

It is easy enough to say, "We will never get anywhere in our effort to democratize Asia if we support the extreme right against the left," and it is certainly true that when we throw support to extreme rightists it hurts our cause with the rank and file of Asiatics elsewhere, since most of Asia is on the left. But we cannot afford to play directly into leftist hands if this means that they will then be taken over by the communists. Russia and China are on the march; our first duty is to defend ourselves against ruthless and premeditated communist aggression.

On the other hand American policy in Asia is doomed to grisly failure if we fail to keep in mind certain permanent and ineradicable realities, such as that the old colonial system is as dead as the Ptolemies or yesterday's mutton, that most of the continent is in the throes of a prodigious progressive revolution, and that the future belongs to those who will assist millions upon millions of peasants to better their state, and make a decent living out of the land.

*

Return to Korea for a final paragraph. Full-scale entrance of the Chinese communists into the fighting took Washington utterly by surprise; it took MacArthur utterly by surprise. SCAP had virtually announced that the war was over. In fact the prevailing mood at MacArthur's headquarters at the end of October was worry over something totally different—that the military victory so satisfactorily "won" in Korea might be frittered away or diluted by the politicians.

The General himself thought seriously, in the third week of October, that the American and United Nations' troops in Korea would be back in Tokyo safe and sound by Thanksgiving. Recent events have, as we all know, proved him tragically wrong. Then, an optimist and an idealist as always, he gave it as his view—when the United Nations began their ill-fated advance to the Manchurian border—that the war would be over by Christmas. Again his hopes were dashed down. Meantime, after an interlude of turbulent international confusion, negotiations began with the Chinese communists at Lake Success. It is not beyond the realm of possibility that—in spite of everything—Chinese intervention will be short-lived; some sort of settlement *may* be reached. On the other hand the Americans *may* be faced with a continuing debacle. The war may spread. It is Russia that counts, not just China. Russia, having gained its original objective of getting us inextricably involved in Asia's warfare, could make another coup. As this book goes to press any prophecy at all is as risky as predicting next week's weather. In any case the future of Korea dovetails into that of Asia as a whole, because almost all the problems we may have to face elsewhere exist in Korea in microcosm. So it would seem to be wise to digest well the lessons Korea should have taught us. One of these is that we will lose the struggle against communism in Asia in the long run if we cannot, with all our magnificent strength, wealth, and democratic power, do more for Asia than the Russians do.

Chapter Twelve

THE TREATY AND THE FUTURE

WE RETURN now to Japan and the spine and substance of this report —the pro and con of MacArthur's five years of occupation. First a word about the impending treaty. Technically the United States is still in a state of war with Japan, and vice versa. Japan surrendered unconditionally to the General's forces, but no peace treaty has been signed. The Korean war has, of course, complicated the treaty issue, which was complex enough before. Since June 25, 1950, although our "enemy," Japan has been our major armed base for military operations on the Asia mainland that may, or may not, be prolonged for a substantial period. No one can question our temporary right to utilize the Japanese islands for this purpose, but the situation is uncomfortable, and must be brought to legal resolution before too long.

There is something positively Alice-in-Wonderlandish about the fact that MacArthur, from headquarters in Japan (an "enemy" state), and with full Japanese cooperation, directs a war against the satellite of a power, the Soviet Union, that still has the right (even if it does not exercise it) to sit in Tokyo side by side with the Americans on an Allied Council. It is not unusual historically for an enemy to become an ally, or an ally to become an enemy. But it is unusual for a former ally (Russia) to support a satellite (North Korea) which is being fought from another country (Japan) by still another country (the United States) in the name of the United Nations (of which it is a member) while at the same time it insists on its prerogative to sit in on treaty negotiations with Japan (its enemy) that will bring "peace" between Japan and its other enemy, the United States.

MacArthur wants a peace treaty with Japan for ample reasons:

1. Probably, if the Korean war is over, he would consider his mission in the Far East concluded by a treaty. He is, after all, past seventy, and a successful treaty will be an altogether fitting climax to his career. He has several times said he would "see the job through *to* the treaty."

2. The Korean war and Chinese complications make it doubly necessary for the United States to take the political and diplomatic lead in a step making for permanent peace and security in Asia.

3. MacArthur is shrewd enough to know that scap cannot continue to rule Japan indefinitely. In fact he is on record as having stated, some years ago, that the ideal period for occupation would be three years, and that under no circumstances should it last longer than five. The point of diminishing returns has, indeed, already been reached. If we stay much longer Japanese nationalism is bound to become resentful, and the subterranean communists will gain ground; we (and the Japanese too) will be subject to the risk of losing more than we have gained. The only way to make a man trustworthy, Henry Stimson once said, is to trust him. We took over in Japan in order to do a job, and have done it; now it is up to the Japanese to carry on. To prolong an occupation beyond a reasonable period is fatal, because the occupying power must either (a) give, give, give more than it can afford, or (b) become a tyrant.

4. On moral as well as practical grounds MacArthur feels that it is high time for us to go. We did not enter Japan to assume sovereignty; it is our plain ethical duty to get out as soon as possible.

What, then, have been the obstacles to a treaty? Why has no treaty ever been negotiated, much less signed?

This question can be answered in a single sentence. There is no peace treaty because nobody has been able to work out a formula which will enable the United States to withdraw while at the same time maintaining Japanese security, which means security for Japan in the first instance, but also security of us, the United States, in the Far East.

In two different areas, one the realm of American domestic policy, the other that of relations vis-à-vis Russia, the issue has been argued, fought out, and deadlocked.

A. By and large two contrary schools of American thought existed. The Joint Chiefs, taking the military view, held that a treaty was premature; Mr. Truman and the State Department, while fully aware of the risks involved, favored a quick treaty. General MacArthur leaned more closely to the State Department than to the Joint Chiefs; the Department was astounded to find him a willing bedfellow. The chief reason why former Secretary of Defense Johnson and General Bradley went to Tokyo in June was to win the Supreme Commander to their side. They did not do so, but a compromise was reached. This could not be put into effect, however, because of the Korean war.

It was a severe blow to most of the high personnel of scap to concede that some measure of militarization in Japan would have to be permitted. They based their whole moral case on the assumption that, if we withdrew, the Japanese would then have to live up to their part of the bargain, i.e., remain demilitarized. Sometime before Korea I heard one of MacArthur's generals say, "But it is preposterous to think that Japan should ever be permitted to rearm! It will jeopardize all that we have worked for; it will destroy the ethical basis of our regime. How can a country be democratized under militarism? Remember how prone the Japanese are to militarist excess. Besides the Japanese cannot possibly afford to create an army. It would cost them eighty million dollars the first few months."

The issue was, in addition, a heavy personal trial for MacArthur in that, of all the things he is proudest of, the famous provision (Article Nine) in the Japanese constitution outlawing war and

223

forbidding Japan ever to have a military establishment was the foremost. But this would have to be scrapped if Japan rearmed, which might be interpreted as a repudiation of the spirit of the whole constitution.

But there are pressing, inflexible military realities to face. Japan is utterly defenseless, a complete vacuum devoid of power; Korea has been wantonly assaulted; the Chinese communists are on the march; what guarantee exists that Japan will not be attacked if we withdraw? Moreover from the point of view of the Joint Chiefs, Japan is the "perfect" base for American military and air power in the event of future trouble. We felt no hesitation about keeping Okinawa and the Ryukyus. To hold them, and let Japan go, would be like holding on to forty cents and chucking away a fortune.

But all sorts of questions remained knotty. Could we leave American troops in Japan, and yet assert truthfully that Japan had full sovereignty? Could we legitimately set up permanent bases in Japan without risking the development of strong anti-American sentiment in Japan? Would, in any case, a handful of troops and a few bases be enough? Did not possession by Russia of the atomic bomb mean that our military protection of Japan would have to be "total"? Moreover how were we to defend the Japanese from a possible communist uprising from within, if we alienated a large segment of Japanese opinion by maintaining a military foothold? Most important of all, could we continue to trust the Japanese if we rearmed them? Once rearmed and sovereign, might not they, an intensely realistic people, attempt to make their own policy and play us off against the Soviet Union? What, in fact, would prevent them from becoming an actual Soviet ally some fine day, particularly if a left-wing government came to power in Tokyo? Wasn't it a dangerous gamble to assume that a rearmed Japan would remain permanently on the American side? Finally, how were we to placate people like the Filipinos and Australians, who (with good reason) viewed the rearmament of Japan with a cold and hostile eye?

B. Despite all these dilemmas a treaty with Japan would have been signed long ago except for persistent Soviet obstruction. The Russians, of course, prefer to keep the whole issue fluid, the better to fish in its periphery. They will certainly never agree to our leaving a garrison in Japan or setting up American bases there, and yet, as members of the Far Eastern Commission, they have (in theory) just as much right to an opinion about the future of Japan as we have. No full treaty with Japan is legally possible without Russian consent.

The Soviet attitude has been adamant since 1947, despite several attempts at compromise. Hence the United States began consideration recently of the idea of making a *separate* peace with Japan. Russia would simply be left out, and the Soviets could like it or lump it. But this might involve grave dangers for all concerned.

Japanese opinion was sharply divided too. The Yoshida liberals, at one wing, want an American guarantee and a treaty. The communists at the other want us to get out completely—no troops or bases, and no separate treaty. Other parties stand in between; they want protection, certainly, but they do not want any United States garrison to remain in Japan indefinitely. All Japanese want security against aggression, but they dislike intensely the presence of foreign troops on their soil; they want as broad a peace treaty as possible, with both full independence *and* protection. This may sound like wanting to eat your cake and have it too. In fact it is. But Japanese are experts in this maneuver.

Distilled to its simplest terms, the American problem thus became one of finding a solution that at one and the same time would (a) restore Japanese sovereignty; (b) maintain, if possible, the disarmament provisions of the Japanese constitution; (c) protect Japan from the possibility of internal disturbance; (d) give it international security without continuing the occupation; (e) keep the Russian foot outside the door; (f) preserve Japanese friendship for America. A tall order! And we had to find such a formula quickly, because the situation in Japan was running away from us. We had the tiger by the tail.

A preliminary decision appears to have been taken by Mr. Truman, the Joint Chiefs, and the State Department in September, 1950. The gist is to begin negotiations for a peace treaty at once, with or without Soviet participation, to permit Japanese rearmament on a modest scale, and to suggest stationing a limited number of American troops in Japan without any infringement of Japanese sovereignty, more or less in the way that we still retain troops in Great Britain. Also feelers have been put out for a proposal whereby the United Nations, not the United States, would guarantee Japanese security, with the United States as a kind of executive agent or trustee on the spot.

In any case there will be no final decision until MacArthur is closely consulted. Only MacArthur should have the right to terminate his own Japan.

Catechism in Conclusion

Perhaps the simplest way to add MacArthur up is to try to answer some questions everybody who visits Tokyo is apt to ask.

Do the Japanese really *like and admire MacArthur as much as they say they do?*

Yes.

Can you prove it?

No, but practically all evidence points to the affirmative. Some of this has already been presented, and all manner of further weight of detail is available. For instance I was enchanted to hear that some Japanese think that MacArthur himself is partly Japanese; the story (of course crazy) is that his great-grandmother was a Japanese woman born in Kyoto. It is just like the Japanese to cook up such a legend. Another item is that many Japanese confidently expect Arthur MacArthur, the General's son, to marry a Japanese princess when he grows up. I even heard that some people in Tokyo credit him with having a daughter (nonexistent), so that she too may marry into the royal circles.

Does this Japanese admiration and reverence for MacArthur embrace his underlings?

Decidedly not.

May not the wily Japanese be pulling our leg about all this kind of thing?

To an extent, yes.

How can Japanese friendliness to their American conquerors possibly be genuine? At bottom, don't they hate our guts? Can they be sincere?

To be friendly to us is good sense. The Japanese are by and large a profoundly pragmatic people, and their friendship for us is "sincere" in that it serves their national self-interest and future policy. Besides Americans are, on the whole, not unpopular, though the Japanese think many of us are naïve. They like us better than the British, the Russians, or the Chinese. On the other hand much underlying hatred for the United States is probably hidden. Perhaps it would be near the truth to say that most Japanese like most Americans as individuals, but not in the mass.

Has Japanese militarism been permanently eradicated?

Of course not.

Have the Japanese learned their proper lessons from their defeat?

Probably not, in the sense that, having been smacked down for being bad boys, they will now be good. The issue is much too complex for that. Japanese have very little sense of sin, which it happens is not substantially recognized in the Japanese religions.

Do they repent Pearl Harbor?

Only to the extent that it caused their eventual humiliation and defeat.

Do they know that they were beaten?

Oh, yes.

But what is the chief impression the defeat has given them?

Not to be defeated again if there is another war.

Have they learned anything politically?

A great deal. The Japanese thought genuinely before World War II that they had the best army, the best navy, the best air force, the best industry, and the best civilian morale in the world. Yet they were ignominiously crushed and beaten. Why? An almost childlike

227

curiosity about this has beset them ever since. They had vastly exaggerated their own merit and of course many factors, like the atom bomb, contributed to their defeat. But one of the weapons the Americans had, and that they didn't have, was apparently this inexplicable western concept known as democracy; therefore they became fiercely interested in democracy. They have sought ever since to find out how and why it produced strength, and whether or not its precepts and procedures could be applied beneficially to Japan.

Why, in the name of all that is peculiar and mysterious, have they remained so docile?

Easy. It is good sense to be docile.

Has the American occupation been too soft?

On the whole, no. (But some of the British think so, also the Australians, Filipinos, and New Zealanders.)

Do the Japanese despise us for having been soft?

No. They think we are being astute.

Will they rejoice when we leave the country? Will there be a great carnival of jubilation when we pull out?

They will rejoice if, upon departing, we leave them security. No country likes to be occupied indefinitely, and most Japanese will be delighted when we go provided we do not go prematurely. Yet combined with this will be much genuine regret, if only because Japan has found the United States, in the person of MacArthur, such a beneficent taskmaster. And a great many Japanese, even if they do not know this now, will miss us profoundly after we are gone.

What are some other Japanese views about democracy?

One Japanese told me, "I admire democracy, I think it is by far the best type of government to be had in the world, and I can even say that I *love* democracy. But it is an extremely difficult form of government and nobody can learn it overnight. Also it is an extremely expensive form of government. What I hope with all my heart is that we Japanese can manage to afford it. But this will entail great effort and great sacrifice."

Is there any danger of a neo-Fascist reaction, of a coup promoted by people like the prewar Japanese oligarchs and militarists?

Probably not—at least for many years. We should keep in mind that most Japanese, perhaps as an excuse for their own failings, blame the catastrophe of the war and humiliating defeat on their military leaders. The frightful experience Japan went through is laid at the doors of the militarist junta, and it has not been forgiven. On the other hand I recall the answer to this question given me by a wise and distinguished Japanese; he paused a long moment, and then said, "I wish I could answer in the negative to that remark, but honestly I cannot."

How do they feel about being disarmed?

Provided they have security they will be delighted to be disarmed, because this means that they will not have to support a military establishment. I even heard one Japanese say, "Thank God for the disarmament provision in the Constitution! It means that taxation will be light and we will promptly become the richest nation in the world!"

Has MacArthur done a good job?

Of course.

How?

Almost any intelligent dictator can do a good job for a while, given the right material. Simply inspect the record.

Has he done the job he thinks he has done?

Not quite.

Is he sincere in his belief that Japan will become successfully democratized?

Absolutely. He thinks it is democratized already.

Is it?

No. But stupendous progress has been made.

Will it stick?

That is the most important question of all. *Some* of it will stick. It is unlikely that any Japanese government will ever dare to take away from at least three groups the reforms that have been given them—women, labor, and the peasants—and these comprise a substantial share of the Japanese electorate. There may be backsliding in many fields—women may go back to their kimonos, and so on. The chief factor that will serve to make some of it, at least, stick is that the Japanese people themselves have a vested interest in their own reform; it is decidedly to their national self-interest to remain reformed. Moreover the democratization of Japan, so far as it has proceeded to date, has undoubtedly made things substantially better for the average man, the middle citizen.

Beyond doubt the Americans have awakened something in Japan. For instance when the new school bill was being debated in the Diet, members got six *million* letters (an almost unbelievable number, but the figure is correct) from individual Japanese stating their belief that the educational reforms should not be tampered with or pared down. SCAP got an additional two million letters. Such a concrete, voluminous outpouring of public emotion would, of course, have been inconceivable in prewar times. Few ordinary Japanese, before the occupation, would have dared write any kind of letter to a member of the Diet. In the old days, they listened, trembled and obeyed.

A seed has been planted, and something is bound to grow, though we cannot know exactly what. Certainly Japan will never turn the clock back to what it was. The whole past is out—forever. Perhaps, an uncomfortable thought, the Japanese will proceed to a period of turbulence and unrest growing directly out of our reforms, though this is not at all what we intended. The communists may attempt to take advantage of the reforms, using them as loopholes.

Then SCAP *has in a sense made a revolution?*

Of course. It has not only made one, but it has made the only real revolution Japan has ever had. The Meiji Restoration was a kind of "managerial swap"; it was a reformation, a managed change, whereby power was shifted *within* the ruling class. But now the opportunity for exerting power—at least in theory—has been put in the hands of the whole citizenry, the people as a whole. The great question is what they will do with it.

What are some reasons for doubting the permanence of what we have done?

It came too fast, and some was administered like medicine. Democracy is a tonic, a nostrum, of unpredictable potency; perhaps the dose we gave was too massive for people like the Japanese. We behaved—to change the metaphor—almost as if we were putting air conditioners into an old house. In a peculiar way MacArthur, the idealist, operated on too high a level, not too low. If democracy does not endure in Japan, it will be largely because it is impossible for any oriental people to assimilate so much so quickly. It was asking too much. To make democracy work, people have to understand it, and this takes time, effort, and resolution. No people can simply "give" democracy to another people, much less impose it, until the other people are fully educated to its proliferating implications. It must be a process of growth—human as well as political. Finally the success of democracy is, as a rule, dependent on economic well-being, particularly the well-being of the middle class. But in Japan scarcely any middle class exists, and after the United States goes there may not be much of well-being.

But on the whole the SCAP *record is good, not bad?*

Absolutely.

The concrete merits of the occupation to date far outweigh possible defects?

Yes, beyond a doubt.

What, finally, is the basis of MacArthur's own zealous hope?

He believes with absolute conviction, on the highest plane, that, once a people have tasted freedom, they will never permit it to be removed.

INDEX

234

235

MacArthur, Gen. Douglas—*Cont.*
and Korean war, 168-73, 219-20
military career, 33-34
Chief of Staff, 35-37
World War I, 34-35
World War II, 38-44
office routine, 49*ff.*, 52-56
optimism, 1-3, 25
and peace treaty, 221-26
personal life, 44-48
philosophy and belief, 75-79, 231
political ambitions, 57-64
press relations, 51, 64-71
refusal to return to U.S., 5-6
and Roosevelt, 9-11
and Russia, 17-22
Wake Island meeting with Truman, 199-201
and Yoshida, 157-58
See also Japan; Korea; SCAP: Tokyo
MacArthur, Douglas, II (nephew), 45
MacArthur, Jean (second wife), 2-3, 7, 40-41, 45-46, 49, 75, 114
MacArthur, Louise (first wife), 44-45
MacArthur, Mary (mother), 32-33, 45
McCarthy, Joseph R., 62
McCormick, Robert R., 60
McCune, George M., 186*n*., 188
McEvoy, Dennis, 26
Madagascar, 12
Mainichi, Osaka, 99, 135-36
Malaya, 203, 204
political situation, 211
Manchuria, 34, 171, 172, 174, 187, 204, 219
Manila, P.I., 7, 9, 18, 20, 26, 27, 33, 37-38, 40, 44-45, 48, 71, 73
Mao Tse-tung, 161, 162, 171-72, 185, 206-8, 209, 215
Marianas Islands, 14
Marquat, Maj. Gen. W. F., 40, 71, 72, 73-74, 121, 144
Marriage Consultation Office, 134
Marshall, George C., 15
Masakozi, 100
Masaryk, Jan, 215
Matsudaira, Mr., 113
Matsui, Akira, 113-14
Mears, Helen, 70
Meiji Restoration, 230

Meiji shrine, 101
Merdeka, 214
Mikasa, Prince, 119
Miller, Dr. A. L., 58-60
Milwaukee, Wis., 32, 33
Mimatsu Cabaret, 86
Mindoro, P.I., 40
Minh, Ho Chi, 209-10
Missionary Ridge, Battle of, 32
Missouri, U.S.S., 1, 18
Mitani, Mr., 113
Mitsubishi family, 154
Mitsui family, 84, 154
Molucca Islands, 214
Mongolia, Inner, 204
Morocco, 12
Moscow Conference, 19-21, 183
Mukden Incident, 102
Murrow, Edward R., 67

Nagako, Empress, 7, 113-14, 118-19
Nagasaki, Jap., 103
National Guard, U.S., 34-35
Natural Resources Section, SCAP, 121, 145
Navy, U.S., 9-11, 43-44, 72, 102
Nebraska, 63
Nehru, Jawaharlal, 190, 204, 215-18
Neighborhood Associations, 130
Netherlands, 12
New Deal, 9, 11, 12, 78, 121, 142-43, 145
New Delhi, India, 217
New Grand Hotel, Yokohama, 2
New Guinea, 42
New York, N.Y., 5, 45
New Zealand, 20, 228
Newsweek magazine, 67, 78
Nikko, Jap., 8, 164
Nimitz, Adm. Chester W., 10, 18, 42
North Korea People's Committee, 186
Northwest Airlines, 6
Nosaka, Sanzo, 160-61, 163
Nu, Thakin, 214
Nugent, Col. D. R., 121, 146, 147
Nutrition, Japan, 139-40

Office of Strategic Services (OSS), 43
Office of War Information (OWI), 43
Okasaki, Katsuo, 157

239